W. Neuwirth · Glas 1905–1925 / Glass 1905–1925 · I

Waltraud Neuwirth

GLAS 1905–1925 · GLASS 1905–1925

VOM JUGENDSTIL ZUM ART DECO
FROM ART NOUVEAU TO ART DECO

Band I · Volume I

Selbstverlag Dr. Waltraud Neuwirth · Wien

1985

Schutzumschlag: Deckelvase von Josef Emanuel Margold, Ausführung Carl Schappel, Haida
Dust jacket: Lidded vase by Josef Emanuel Margold, manufacturer Carl Schappel, Haida

Katalog zur Ausstellung
„Glas 1905–1925. Vom Jugendstil zum Art Déco" im Österreichischen Museum für angewandte Kunst, Wien (26. 10. 1985 – 26. 1. 1986)
Exhibition Catalogue to
„Glass 1905–1925. From Art Nouveau to Art Déco" in the Austrian Museum of Applied Art, Vienna (26th October 1985 – 26th January 1986)

Dieser Katalog wurde vom Bundesministerium für Wissenschaft und Forschung mit einem Druckkostenzuschuß gefördert

This catalogue has been printed with a grant from the Austrian Ministry of Sciences and Research

Fotonachweis / Photographic acknowledgements:

Dr. Waltraud Neuwirth (alle Fotos und Reproduktionen wurden mit Olympus-Camera OM 2 N aufgenommen; für alle Farbaufnahmen wurde der Fuji-Film RF 50 verwendet / all photographs and reproductions have been taken with Olympus camera OM 2 N; Fuji RF 50 has been used for all colour photographs)

ISBN 3-900282-10-2 Selbstverlag Dr. Waltraud Neuwirth, Wien

Übersetzung ins Englische / English translation: Andrew Smith, Wien

Entwurf von Schutzumschlag und Einband / Dust jacket and cover designed by: Prof. akad. Restaurator Mag. Oberrat Ludwig Neustifter, Wien
Schwarzweißlithographien / Black-and-white lithographs: Offset-Reproanstalt Manfred Steiner, Wien
Farblithographien / Colour lithographs: Dolezal Offsetreproduktionen, Wien
Satz / Typesetting: Ueberreuter, Wien
Druck / Printed by: Dellerfuhs Offsetdruck, Wien
Bindearbeit / Binding: Oberösterreichischer Landesverlag, Linz

INHALT

CONTENTS

254

VORWORT

Die vorliegende Publikation ist der erste Teil eines zweibändig geplanten Kataloges, der den Gesamtbestand aller Gläser aus der Zeit von 1905 bis 1925 umfassen wird, die sich im Österreichischen Museum für angewandte Kunst befinden.
Dabei handelt es sich fast ausschließlich um Gläser aus der österreichisch-ungarischen Monarchie bzw. – nach dem Ersten Weltkrieg – aus Österreich und der Tschechoslovakei.
Bemerkenswerte Objekte aus dem Steiermärkischen Landesmuseum Joanneum (Abteilung für Kunstgewerbe) bilden eine wertvolle Bereicherung der Ausstellung. Privatleihgaben wurden nur in Ausnahmefällen aufgenommen.
Die obere und untere Zeitgrenze (1905 und 1925) wurde bewußt gewählt; wird doch die Glasproduktion jener zwei Jahrzehnte noch viel zu wenig beachtet und ist – da noch mit keinem einprägsamen Stilbegriff bedacht – namenlos, allenfalls entweder dem Jugendstil oder dem Art Déco beigegeben. Viele Publikationen über Jugendstil schließen die Jahre bis zum Ausbruch des Ersten Weltkrieges ein (so auch mein „Glas des Jugendstils, Wien", 1973 erschienen); die Jahre von 1914 bis 1918 werden fälschlicherweise, aber nicht selten, als ein kriegsbedingtes Vakuum angesehen, und das Art Déco läßt man bestenfalls mit den Zwanziger Jahren beginnen, wiewohl aufmerksame Forscher vereinzelt auf wesentlich früher auftretende Phänomene eines Art Déco-Stils verweisen. Auf diesen Fragenkomplex ging ich bereits in meiner Publikation „Wiener Werkstätte – Avantgarde, Art Déco, Industrial Design" (Wien 1984) ein.
Ein berechtigtes Unbehagen gegenüber Vereinfachungstendenzen lassen für die Zukunft eine vorurteilslose Einschätzung jener Jahrzehnte erhoffen, die vor jener Pariser Ausstellung von 1925 liegen, welche dem Art Déco seinen Namen gab.
Die Glassammlung des Österreichischen Museums für angewandte Kunst, wie jede Sammlung in ihren einzelnen Schwerpunktenverschieden gewichtet, ist dies besonders in der Zeit von 1905–1925, da der Aspekt des Internationalen fast völlig fehlt. Dies ist heute nur scheinbar ein Manko, denn vermutlich gibt es derzeit weltweit keine zweite derart umfassende Sammlung dieser spezifischen Art. Seit dem Jahr 1979, in dem ich die Leitung der Sammlung von Glas und Keramik übernehmen durfte, war ich bestrebt, diesen einmaligen Bestand abzurunden, und dies gelang im Zuge einer Sammlungspolitik, die Ankäufe, Widmungen und Dauerleihgaben einschloß, um das gesteckte Ziel zu erreichen.
Da die Besonderheit des vorgefundenen Bestandes in seiner gesicherten Provenienz lag, mußten auch die Neuerwerbungen diesen strengen Ansprüchen genügen. Waren durch zeitgenössische Ankäufe die wichtigsten Daten (Erwerbsjahr, Verkäufer, Glasfabrik, Entwerfer etc.) zwar nicht immer ganz vollständig, aber doch im wesentlichen vorhanden, so war für Neuerwerbungen die Provenienz einwandfrei zu belegen.
Nach der weitreichenden Sammeltätigkeit des Museums um die Jahrhundertwende ist in den Jahren von 1905 bis 1910 eine auffallende Zurückhaltung beim Ankauf von zeitgenössischem Glas festzustellen. Wie viele Gläser der vorangegangenen zwanzig Jahre das Österreichische Museum im Jahr 1925 besaß, wird in gewisser Weise immer eine Dunkelziffer bleiben, da die Nachinventarisierungen späterer Zeit beweisen, daß man etliche Objekte ursprünglich nicht einmal in die Inventare aufnahm. Nachprüfbare Eintragungen ergeben, daß von den seinerzeit nachweislich vorhandenen Objekten relativ wenige fehlen (Kriegsverluste etc.). Wenn möglich, wurden Abbildungen solcher Stücke ebenfalls in den Katalog aufgenommen.
Dieser ist wegen der Fülle des Materials zweigeteilt: der erste Band umfaßt Glas mit Schliff, der zweite wird dem übrigen Bereich gewidmet sein (Glas mit Beize, Ätzung,

Schnitt, Malerei etc.). Da keine noch so detaillierte Beschreibung das Bild ersetzen kann, erhält die Abbildung entsprechendes Gewicht, begleitet von den wichtigsten Daten. Der Dokumentation (Reproduktion von Entwürfen, zeitgenössischen Abbildungen bzw. Fotos) wurde im vorgegebenen Rahmen Rechnung getragen. Die Materialgliederung nach technischen Kriterien (Glas mit Schliff, Malerei, etc.) ermöglichte Einsichten in Zusammenhänge, die bisher in dieser Form noch kaum erkennbar waren. Ein weiterer Band, der einer ausführlichen Behandlung der Glastechniken sowie eingehender Dokumentation zeitgenössischer Quellen gewidmet sein könnte, ist in Aussicht genommen.

An dieser Stelle ist es mir ein besonderes Anliegen, Herrn Prof.akad. Rest. Mag. Ludwig Neustifter, dem Geschäftsführenden Leiter des Österreichischen Museums für angewandte Kunst, dafür zu danken, daß er sich für die Realisierung des Projekts und der Ausstellung „Glas 1905–1925" im Museum in kenntnisreicher und uneigennütziger Weise einsetzte sowie den Ausbau der Sammlung in jeder erdenklichen Art förderte.

Frau Dr. Inge Woisetschläger (Steiermärkisches Landesmuseum Joanneum, Graz, Abteilung für Kunstgewerbe) danke ich für ihre Bereitschaft, Leihgaben zur Ausstellung zu entsenden und damit bisher unbekannte Meisterwerke der Glaskunst jener Zeit der Öffentlichkeit zugänglich zu machen. Mein Dank gilt in gleicher Weise den Privatleihgebern.

Für die Erlaubnis, das umfangreiche und wertvolle Firmenarchiv zu benützen, danke ich den Herren Harry und Peter Rath von der Firma J. & L. Lobmeyr, Wien.

Herrn Andrew Smith bin ich für seine sorgfältige Übersetzung ins Englische zu großem Dank verpflichtet.

Wissenschaftliche Arbeit ist für den Forschenden immer eine Bereicherung. Sie wurde für mich weit mehr: zur Freude an der Schönheit des Werkstoffs, an der Kunst der Entwerfer, an der Vollkommenheit der Ausführung – zum ästhetischen Genuß.

Wien, im August 1985 — Waltraud Neuwirth

FOREWORD

The present publication is the first part of a planned two-volume catalogue which will contain all the glass dating from the period between 1905 and 1925 in the Austrian Museum of Applied Art. Nearly all this glass is from the Austro-Hungarian Monarchy or – after the First World War – from Austria and Czechoslovakia. Remarkable objects from the Joanneum Museum in Graz form a valuable addition to the exhibition. Private loans have only been included in exceptional cases.

The dates 1905 and 1925 have been chosen quite deliberately; the glass production of these two decades has received far too little attention and – as no definite stylistic designation has yet been given to it – is still without a name, being at best lumped together with art nouveau or art deco. Many publications on art nouveau include the years up to the outbreak of the First World War (even my "Glas des Jugendstils, Wien", published in 1973). The years between 1914 and 1918 are wrongly, but not infrequently, regarded as

a vacuum caused by the war. Art deco is usually thought to begin in the twenties at the earliest, although individual attentive researchers have also remarked on considerably earlier phenomena of an art deco style. I have already dealt with this problem in my book "Wiener Werkstätte – Avantgarde, Art Déco, Industrial Design" (Vienna 1984).
A justified uneasiness about this tendency to oversimplify may mean that in future the decades prior to the Paris Exhibition of 1925 that gave art deco its name will receive unbiased treatment.
The glass collection of the Austrian Museum of Applied Art is like any collection in that varying importance is attached to its individual strong points. This applies particularly to the period between 1905-1925, as the international perspective is almost entirely missing. Today this is only an apparent shortcoming, for there is probably no other such comprehensive collection of this specific nature. Since the year 1979, when I assumed responsibility for the collection of glass and ceramics, I have endeavoured to round off this unique inventory, and have been successful in attaining my declared objective by adopting a collecting policy which included purchases, dedications and permanent loans. In view of the fact that the exceptional character of the existing collection lay in its reliably established origins, the new acquisitions also had to meet these strict conditions. Although as far as contemporary purchases are concerned the most important information (year of acquisition, seller, glass works, designer, etc.) is not always quite complete, most of it is available, and the origin of the new acquisitions therefore had to be established beyond doubt.
After the considerable collecting by the museum around the turn of the century, there was a noticeable reluctance to purchase contemporary glass in the years between 1905 and 1910. Just how much glass from the previous twenty years the Austrian museum owned in the year 1925 will always remain to a certain extent a vague figure, as subsequent inventories at later dates have shown that many exhibits were originally not even entered in the inventory. Verifiable entries show that relatively few of the objects which we know existed at the time are now missing (war losses, etc.). Wherever possible, pictures of such pieces have also been included.
The catalogue is divided into two parts in view of the quantity of material. The first volume deals with cut glass, the second with the remaining types (stained, etched, engraved and painted glass, etc.). In view of the fact that no description, however detailed, can ever replace a picture, corresponding importance has been attached to the illustrations, which are accompanied by the most important information. The documentation (reproductions from designs, contemporary illustrations and photographs) has been taken into consideration as far as space allows. Classifying the material by technical criteria (cut, painted glass, etc.) gives us an insight into relationships such as could previously hardly be perceived in this form. A further volume is planned which will deal in detail with glass-making techniques and an exhaustive documentation of contemporary sources.
At this juncture I should particularly like to thank Prof. Ludwig Neustifter, the head of the Austrian Museum of Applied Art, for the knowledgeable and unselfish manner in which he supported the realisation of this project and the exhibition "Glass 1905-1925" at the museum and promoted the extension of the collection in every conceivable manner.
I should also like to thank Dr. Inge Woisetschläger, of the Joanneum Museum in Graz, Styria, for her readiness to make loans to the exhibition, thus enabling the public for the first time to see previously unknown masterpieces of the glassmaker's art of this period.
My thanks are also due to those who made loans from private collections.
I am grateful to Harry and Peter Rath of Messrs. J. & L. Lobmeyr, Vienna, for permission to use the company's extensive and valuable archives.

89

215

Finally, I should like to express my gratitude to Andrew Smith for his painstaking English translation of this work.
A scientific project is always an enriching experience for the research worker. This project meant a lot more to me: it afforded me pleasure in the beauty of the material, in the art of the designer, in the perfection of the execution – it provided aesthetic enjoyment.

Vienna, August 1985 Waltraud Neuwirth

EINFÜHRUNG

Die Vielfalt der Glasproduktion von 1905 bis 1925 aus dem Bereich der österreichisch-ungarischen Monarchie bzw. deren Nachfolgestaaten scheint nahezu unerschöpflich zu sein. Nicht zuletzt deshalb dürfte sie sich auch weiterhin einem einheitlichen Stilbegriff entziehen: vom dünnwandig geblasenen, undekorierten Hohlglas zum massiven Kristallglas mit Tiefschliff, vom klar abgesetzten Ziersaum mehrfacher Überfänge zu vielfarbigen Oberflächen mit Teilätzungen, vom flächendeckenden Edelschwarz zur dünnlinigen Federzeichnung, von opaker Malerei zum leuchtenden Schmelz des Transemail, vom aushöhlenden Schliff zu zartem Figurenschnitt reichen die unzähligen Spielarten von Form, Technik und Dekor, hier nur andeutungsweise aufgezählt. Dem Farbspiel im wechselnden Licht, das viele Gläser ständig zu verändern scheint, kann die einmalige Betrachtung ebenso wenig gerecht werden wie die einzelne Abbildung. Leuchtet im Auflicht das Gold, so weicht es im Durchlicht der Eigenfarbe der Glasmasse; stellt sich beim dunklen Farbglas im Auflicht die Form rein dar, so glüht das Kunckel-Rot im Spitzlicht und im farbigen Schatten des Durchlichts.
Der kostbaren Vase als Einzelstück steht das geschliffene Tafelservice gegenüber; in der Garnitur dominiert das zentrale Glas über die Trabanten: Bowlegarnituren, Likörservice, Bierservice etc.
Verschiedene Herstellungstechniken – Überfang, Beizung, Malerei – transformieren gleiche Grundformen in Variationen, die bis auf dieselbe Ausgangsform des Rohglases kaum Gemeinsames zu haben scheinen.
Stilistische Vereinfachungen sollen hier nicht stattfinden. Dennoch sei hingewiesen auf Reminiszenzen des Jugendstils in den Unterfanggläsern mit „gestrichenem“ Dekor (dem „Melusin-Gias“ von Loetz), dem reinen Art Déco im Farb-Zickzack einer Opakmalerei (Kriegsglas von Josef Hoffmann), dem ornamentalen Horror Vacui aus Schwarz-Gold in einer phantastischen, orientalisch anmutenden Ornamentik (Federzeichnungen von Karl Massanetz). Im Gegensatz dazu steht die „Form ohne Ornament“, das undekorierte Glas im glatten Schliff (J. & L. Lobmeyr).

KRITERIEN DER KATALOGISIERUNG

Die regionalen Grenzen waren durch die spezifische Eigenart der Sammlung vorgegeben, die zeitlichen durch die Jahre 1905 und 1925 gesetzt. Eine weitere Differenzierung durch eine alphabetische Ordnung nach Glasfabriken oder entwerfenden Künstlern war kaum ratsam; die Reihung nach Fabriken hätte eine nicht realisierbare Trennung in Rohglaserzeuger und Raffineure erfordert, und für viele Gläser sind keine Entwerfer überliefert. Von einem beachtlichen Teil der Sammlung kennt man Glasverleger, aber nicht Glaserzeuger. So blieben die Kriterien der Herstellungs- und Veredlungstechnik als probate Mittel zur Gliederung, die innerhalb der einzelnen Blöcke eine gewissen Chronologie mit sich bringt.

QUELLEN

Die verwendeten zeitgenössischen Quellen waren in ihrer Art sehr unterschiedlich: einmal die manchmal korrektur- und meist ergänzungsbedürftigen Inventareintragungen, dann Entwürfe und Werkzeichnungen (besonders der Firmen J. & L. Lobmeyr, Wien, E. Bakalowits, Wien, sowie der Wiener Werkstätte), zeitgenössische Fachzeitschriften (Studio, Deutsche Kunst und Dekoration, Dekorative Kunst, Kunst und Kunsthandwerk etc.) und Kataloge (vor allem die bedauerlicherweise nicht bebilderten Ausstellungska-

taloge des Österreichischen Museums für Kunst und Industrie), im besonderen zeitgenössische Fotos damals ausgestellter Gegenstände, sowie einige wenige erhaltene Firmenkataloge. Da das Museum eine beachtliche Anzahl der Schappelschen Borussia-Gläser besitzt, wurde der Spezialkatalog dieser Gattung Glas in die vorliegende Publikation vollständig eingearbeitet.
Das Archiv des Österreichischen Museums für angewandte Kunst erwies sich vor allem im Hinblick auf die große Ausstellung österreichischen Kunst- und Exportglases im Jahre 1915 als besonders ergiebig.

DATIERUNGS- UND ZUSCHREIBUNGSFRAGEN

Das in den Inventaren (W.I. = Wanderausstellungsinventar, GI = Glasinventar) festgehaltene Datum darf bei Anlegen strenger Maßstäbe bestenfalls als Inventarisierungsdatum, nicht immer als Datum des Erwerbs angesehen werden. Die Gläser selbst können, wie zeitgenössischen Abbildungen oder anderen Quellen zu entnehmen war, manchmal Jahre vorher entstanden oder aber auch unmittelbar nach ihrer Entstehung erworben worden sein.
Die Provenienzangaben in den Inventaren beziehen sich manchmal auf den Raffineur, dann wieder auf die Fabrik, häufig auf die genannten Glasverleger Bakalowits und Lobmeyr.
Die Ausstellung österreichischen Kunst- und Exportglases, als Wanderausstellung (Wien, Brünn, Reichenberg, Stockholm, Berlin, Hamburg) realisiert, führte auch zum Verkauf und – im schlimmsten Fall – zum Bruch eines Glases. Es ist nachweisbar, daß dann dasselbe Glasmodell nachbestellt wurde, sodaß nur exakte Vermerke in den Inventaren darauf hinweisen, daß das ursprünglich inventarisierte Stück ersetzt wurde und nicht mit dem heute vorhandenen identisch ist. Mit diesen Nachlieferungen hatten die böhmischen Glasfirmen in jener kritischen Zeit ihre Schwierigkeiten, und es kam vor, daß die Raffineure das benötigte Rohglas nicht mehr beschaffen konnten, was vor allem bei unkomplett gewordenen Ensembles schmerzlich spürbar wurde.
Im allgemeinen ist jedoch das inventarisierte Glas mit dem heute vorhandenen identisch, sodaß durch das Inventarisierungsdatum ein verläßlicher terminus ante quem für ein ganz bestimmtes Glas gegeben ist. Das erscheint deshalb besonders wichtig, als manche erfolgreiche Glasmodelle über längere Zeit erzeugt wurden (durch die erhaltenen Archivalien aus dem Bereich der Wiener Werkstätte nachweisbar).

KRISTALLGLAS

(Kat. Nrn. 1-162, S. 34-181)

Bekannte Künstler wie Kolo Moser, Emil Hoppe, Otto Prutscher und Josef Hoffmann entwarfen Gläser, deren Wandung verschiedenartig facettiert geschliffen war.
Erstmals 1906 abgebildet (Kat. Nr. 1), ist das Glasservice von Kolo Moser vom Entwurf her vermutlich einige Jahre früher zu datieren. In einem Band der Firma Bakalowits mit Werkskizzen (Inv. ÖMAK, B.I. 32066 c) sind die Formen des Tafelservices von 1902 in drei Ausführungsvarianten festgehalten (optisch, Pentagramm, Schuppen), wobei die letztgenannte Variante dem Glastypus mit sechseckigen Facetten (Kat. Nr. 2) entsprechen könnte.
Vom Tafelservice Nr. 130 der Firma Bakalowits von 1906 konnte der Großteil der Formen in den letzten Jahren erworben werden; Widmungen und Leihgaben komplettieren das Service in der Ausstellung (Kat. Nr. 7-33). Der Entwerfer Emil Hoppe schuf mit diesem Service und seinem horizontal sowie vertikal gegliederten Facettenschliff sicher eines

66

der schönsten Ensembles, das auch in einer Variante mit Golddekor (Kat. Nr. 6) ausgeführt wurde. Im reizvollen Kontrast zum farblosen Kristallglas die grüne Kuppe der Moselweingläser (Kat. 33).
Eine Serie von Kelchgläsern mit Schliff von Kuppa, Stiel und Fuß entwarf Otto Prutscher (Kat. Nr. 36-41). Die verschiedenartig gestalteten Silhouetten der Kuppa ermöglichen ebenso eine Variabilität innerhalb der Serie wie die gelb leuchtenden Ovale dreier Gläser (Kat. Nr. 36, 39, 40).
Die meisten der eben genannten Gläser dürften von der Firma Meyr's Neffe in Adolf bei Winterberg ausgeführt worden sein, wiewohl dies nicht immer nachzuweisen ist. Dies gilt auch für die 1909 datierte Jardinière (Kat. Nr. 43-45).
Eines der 1910 von Josef Hoffmann entworfenen Kelchgläser weist eine in dreieckigen Flächen facettierte Kuppa auf (Kat. Nr. 50, 51); die anderen Gläser dieser Serie variieren die Formen von Kuppa, Stiel und Fuß durch Diamantschliff, Abtreppungen des Fußes, geschliffene Motive in halber Höhe des Stiels u.a. (Kat. Nr. 48-54). Blumengläser ergänzen diese Gruppe (Kat. Nr. 55), die im Entwurf noch weitere Formtypen aufwies (Kat. Nr. 56-59), von denen jedoch nicht alle realisiert wurden. Ein Glas wurde als unausführbar (Kat. Nr. 50 links), einige mit 0 bezeichnet, bei manchen anderen wurde der Originalentwurf Hoffmanns abgeändert.
Zu einer Blumengarnitur waren zwei verschieden große Jardinièren mit Platten zusammengefaßt (Kat. Nr. 64-66), deren reicher Schliff zwar dem Entwurf (Kat. 64) entspricht, während dessen Form durch Weglassen des facettierten Fußes abgeändert wurde.
Eine Gruppe von Gläsern, die teilweise von Josef Hoffmann (Kat. Nr. 67-69) stammt, teilweise noch keinem bestimmten Entwerfer zugeschrieben werden kann (Kat. Nr. 72), ist durch tiefe Schälschliffe des Fußes charakterisiert.

153

Massivglas, das nahezu hochreliefartige Schliffe erlaubt, wurde ebenfalls für Gläser jener Zeit verwendet (Kat. Nr. 73-75).
Der Vertikalschliff einer Toilettegarnitur (Kat. Nr. 78-81), als Firmenentwurf von J. & L. Lobmeyr überliefert, besticht durch Einfachheit, verbunden mit größtmöglicher optischer Wirkung.
Deckeldosen religiöser (Kat. Nrn. 82, 83) und profaner Verwendung (Kat. Nrn. 84-87) bringen uns mit Oscar Strnad einen weiteren prominenten Entwerfernamen (Kat. Nrn. 86, 87), die nordböhmische Fachschule Haida ist mit kunstvoll geschliffenen Gläsern (Kat. Nrn. 88-91) aus der Zeit um 1910 vertreten, wobei der Deckelpokal (Kat. Nr. 91) in seiner effektvollen, aber dennoch einfachen Horizontal- und Vertikalteilung und dem nach oben verjüngten, abgetreppten Deckel zu den eindrucksvollsten Schöpfungen zählt und in der Art des Schliffs dem noch schlichteren Farbglas (Kat. Nr. 164) verwandt ist.
Die vor 1914 entworfenen Kristallgläser des Ateliers Artěl, Prag, gehören sowohl in der Formgebung als auch im Schliffdekor zum besten dieser Zeit. Die Bowlegarnitur von Jan Kotěra, um 1904 erstmals auf der Weltausstellung St. Louis präsentiert, zeigt noch einen überbordenden Reichtum an Oberflächenschliffen, der in der späteren Ausführung (Kat. Nr. 92) eine weitgehende Reduktion erfährt, wodurch die Klarheit der Form unterstrichen wird. Auch die Wandungen von Deckeldosen (Kat. Nrn. 93, 94) sind flächig geschliffen, während tiefe Einkerbungen die siebenfach geschwungene Form einer Vase (Kat. Nr. 95) kennzeichnen und der Rand eines Aufsatzes (Kat. Nr. 96) in großzügigem Zickzack gestaltet ist. Champagner- und Weingläser (Kat. Nrn. 97-99) mit geschliffenen Stielen und dünn eingeschliffenen, umlaufenden Linien sind aus Kristallglas gearbeitet, die Kuppa der Moselweingläser aus grünem Glas (Kat. Nr. 99). Die Likörservice von Artěl kombinieren geschliffenes Glas (Kat. Nr. 100) manchmal auch mit optisch geblasenem (Kat. Nrn. 101, 102).
Ein weiteres Likörservice (Kat. Nrn. 103, 104) stammt von Otto Prutscher, der als Glasentwerfer noch viel zu wenig beachtet wird. Von ihm wurde eine ganze Reihe weiterer Gläser (Kat. Nrn. 106-110, 112, Vasen, Aufsätze, Deckelpokale) geschaffen, die Carl Schappel in Haida ausführte.
Eine zeitgenössische Abbildung identifiziert Carl Thomas, der uns im zweiten Band des Bestandkataloges noch begegnen wird, als Entwerfer eines Deckelpokals (Kat. Nr. 111). Ist dieser Künstler als Glasentwerfer noch weitgehend unbekannt, so muß Josef Emanuel Margold in dieser Eigenschaft nicht mehr vorgestellt werden. Seinem Deckelgefäß in der Wiener Sammlung (Kat. Nr. 114) kann dank einer Leihgabe aus Graz eine achtseitige, geschliffene Deckeldose gegenübergestellt werden (Kat. Nr. 115), beide mit den Klebeetiketten mit dem Firmennamen von Schappel und dem Entwerfernamen sowie der Werknummer versehen.
Anonym hingegen sind bisher zwei Glasschöpfungen geblieben, die dessenungeachtet den höchsten Ansprüchen an Formgebung und Schliff gerecht werden: eine Kassette (Kat. Nr. 116) und ein Flakon (Kat. Nr. 117), erstere von der Firma Meyr's Neffe, Adolf, ausgeführt, letzteres von Lobmeyr an des Museum verkauft. Drei Leuchter mit Facettenschliff (Kat. Nrn. 118-120), einer zusätzlich mit Kantenschliff (Kat. Nr. 118) stammen ebenfalls von Meyr's Neffe, ebenso die ungewöhnliche Kombination Leuchter/Deckeldose (Kat. Nr. 121).
Über die Firma Lobmeyr für das Museum erworben, ist die Schreibtischgarnitur von Oswald Dittrich (Kat. Nr. 122) heute leider nicht mehr in der Sammlung erhalten.
Eine Deckeldose (Kat. Nr. 123) und eine Deckelvase (Kat. Nr. 151), beide nach Entwurf der Fachschule Haida von Oertel, Haida, ausgeführt, unterstreichen die Bedeutung der Fachschulen für die regionale Industrie. Von den später zu nennenden Überfanggläsern

sind viele nach Entwürfen der Fachschulen von den Glasfabriken realisiert worden.
Eine Sturzflasche mit Becher von Meyr's Neffe stellt ein vollständig erhaltenes kleines Ensemble dar (Kat. Nr. 124); meist fehlt der Becher.
Das nordböhmische Kristallglas ist weiters durch Beispiele aus den Fabriken von Gerner/Haida (Kat. Nrn. 125, 126, 143, 147), Meyr's Neffe/Adolf (Kat. Nrn. 127-132, 135-140, 142, 144-146, 149, 150, 152), Rasch/Ulrichsthal (Kat. Nr. 133), Mühlhaus/Haida (Kat. Nr. 134), Meltzer/Langenau (Kat. Nr. 148) vertreten, während die Vase (Kat. Nr. 141) vermutlich auch bei Meyr's Neffe entstanden ist.
Zählt die Vase (Kat. Nr. 142) zu den mit vielfältigen Schliffen gestalteten Gläsern, so sind einige Gläser (Kat. Nr. 145, 146) gesteindelt und sparsam mit Transparentfarben versehen, während die Kantenschliffe einigen Vasen (Kat. Nrn. 147, 148) besonderen Reiz verleihen.
Schwere Diamant-, Rauten- und Facettenschliffe kennzeichnen dickwandige Gläser, wie den Deckelpokal (Kat. Nr. 151), Vasen (Kat. Nr. 152, 153) und Jardinièren (Kat. Nr. 154). In diesem Zusammenhang begegnen weitere Fabriksnamen, wie Zahn/Haida (Kat. Nr. 153, 159-161) oder Harrach/Neuwelt (Kat. Nr. 154, 158). Vor allem Meltzer/Langenau, Meyr's Neffe/Adolf, Harrach/Neuwelt, und Zahn/Haida, widmeten sich dem „Kristallstil", der im Bleikristall voll zur Wirkung kam (Kat. Nrn. 156-161).
Eine Sonderleistung geschliffenen Glases stellt die Glasplastik (Kat. Nr. 162) dar, deren Schöpfer im Inventar als O. E. Wagner angegeben wird.

FARBGLAS

(Kat. Nrn. 163-180, S. 182-197)

Das in der Masse gefärbte Glas ist in Rot, Violett und Grün dominant. Das Vollrubin-Glas der Fachschule Haida (Kat. Nr. 164) vereint die Leuchtkraft der Farbe mit edler Formgebung und vollkommenem Schliff. Als „Kunckel-Glas" bezeichnete die Firma Goldberg/Haida eine Spezialität, die das dunkel leuchtende Rot der Glasmasse meist mit vertikalem Flächenschliff verbindet (Kat. Nr. 163, 167-169). Mühlhaus/Haida dürfte Gläser dieser Art bereits einige Jahre früher erzeugt haben (Kat. Nrn. 165-166).
Den eher traditionellen Formen der Haidaer Fabriken stehen die nach Entwürfen Josef Hoffmanns gestalteten Gläser aus violetten bis blauvioletten Farbnuancen gegenüber (Kat. Nrn. 172-174, 176), während der Aufsatz (Kat. Nr. 175) bisher weder einem bestimmten Entwerfer noch einer Glasfabrik zuzuordnen war.
Von Hoffmann stammt auch der Entwurf zu einem Flakon, dessen dunkles Grün nur gegen eine sehr starke Lichtquelle sichtbar wird (Kat. Nr. 177, 178), während die beiden Grünabstufungen der Vasen von Meyr's Neffe (Kat. Nr. 179, 180) in einer mittleren und hellen Farbnuance im Durchlicht voll zur Geltung kommen.

ÜBERFANGGLAS

(Kat. Nrn. 181-356, S. 199-334)

Beim mehrschichtigen Glas lassen sich einige Hauptgruppen unterscheiden: Kristallglas mit einem farbigen Über- oder Unterfang, Kristallglas mit mehreren farbigen Über- oder Unterfängen sowie Kristallglas mit Überfang in Weiß und Schwarz.
Manche dieser Gläser wurden überhaupt nicht oder nur geringfügig veredelt. Häufiger war die weitere Bearbeitung durch Schliff oder Ätzung (auf die letztere Gruppe wird im zweiten Band eingegangen).

332

174

EINFACHER ÜBERFANG

(Kat. Nrn. 181-242, S. 199-259)

Bei der künstlerischen Gestaltung des einmal überfangenen Glases scheint der Wiener Entwurf eine bedeutende Rolle gespielt zu haben: einmal in den berühmt gewordenen Kelchgläsern von Otto Prutscher, die bereits auf der Wiener Kunstschau 1908 zu sehen waren (Kat. Nr. 183) und von denen das Landesmuseum Joanneum Graz eines besitzt (Kat. Nr. 185). Sie wurden ebenso von Meyr's Neffe/Adolf ausgeführt wie eine weitere Variation (Kat. Nr. 186), deren Dekor durch Silbergelb und aufgeschmolzene grüne Emailpunkte bereichert wird.

Das blau überfangene, geschliffene Glas dominiert nicht nur bei dem 1909 datierten Entwurf Josef Hoffmanns (Kat. Nr. 187), sondern auch bei jenen Gläsern aus dem Bereich der Wiener Werkstätte, die zum größten Teil von Otto Prutscher stammten und deren Veredlung manchmals als „Linienschliff“ bezeichnet wurde (Kat. Nrn. 188-196). Als ausführende Firma dürfte auch hier wieder vor allem Meyr's Neffe/Adolf in Frage kommen.
Verwandt scheint dieser Schliffart die Technik einer Jardinière von Artěl/Prag, da auch hier der Überfang in verschieden breiten vertikalen Streifen stehenblieb (Kat. Nr. 197).
Ausgeschliffene Kreisflächen und Ovale dominieren hingegen die Entwürfe von Margold (Kat. Nrn. 198, 199) und die Gläser der Firma Mühlhaus/Haida (Kat. Nrn. 200-202, 204), die zum Deckelpokal der Haidaer Fachschule frappante Ähnlichkeit in der Strukturierung aufweisen (Kat. Nr. 203).
Über den Glasverleger Bakalowits kamen vier Gläser mit fast schwarzem Überfang (Kat. Nrn. 205-210) in das Museum; nicht in der Farbe, aber in den Motiven des Schliffs ist das Flakon (Kat. Nr. 211) vergleichbar, das ebenfalls über Bakalowits in die Sammlung gelangte.
Als Urheber von einfach überfangenen Gläsern mit gewellter Wandung und den sich daraus ergebenden Formen des vertikalen Schliffs wird einerseits die Wiener Werkstätte, andererseits die Fachschule Haida angegeben. Ausgeführt wurden viele dieser Gläser von Meltzer/Langenau (Kat. Nr. 212-215, 217); Pazaurek nennt in seiner 1925 erschienenen Publikation für drei dort abgebildete Gläser (Kat. Nr. 218) die Fachschule Haida als Entwerfer und Meltzer/Langenau als ausführende Firma. Eine Vase, die das Museum von Meltzer (Kat. Nr. 219) erwarb, ist in der zeitgenössischen Literatur (Kat. Nr. 216) der Fachschule Haida zugeordnet.
Bereits beim Kristallglas ist uns die Form der siebenfach gebauchten Vase mit vertikalem Schliff begegnet (Kat. Nr. 95); dieselbe Form mit blauem Überfang ist ihr hier gegenübergestellt (Kat. Nr. 222). Von anderer Form, aber gleichem Prinzip des Schliffs präsentiert sich die Vase (Kat. 223) von Artěl, während der Schliff von Schalen (Kat. Nr. 220, 221) tiefe Dreieckmotive im Überfangglas entstehen läßt. Langgezogene rote Dreiecksflächen bleiben auch beim Schliff des Bierservices von Artěl (Kat. Nr. 224) stehen; die Entwürfe Rosipals für Artěl hingegen sind charakterisiert durch ein rautenförmiges Motiv, das nach Glasform und -größe variiert und wiederholt wird (Kat. Nr. 225-231).
Ein besonders exquisites Glas stellt eine kunstvoll geschliffene Vase der Fachschule Haida dar (Kat. Nr. 232). Schliffgläser mit einfachem Überfang wurden häufig von Oertel/Haida nach fremden Entwürfen ausgeführt: entweder nach Entwurf der Fachschule Haida (Schale, Kat. Nr. 235; Aufsatz, 237) oder für die Wiener Werkstätte (Kat. Nrn. 241, 242). Einfache Überfanggläser mit Schliff hatte auch Leopold Forstner in seinen Stockerauer Edelglaswerken im Programm (Kat. Nrn. 233-234).
Einen violetten Überfang wie beim Aufsatz (Kat. Nr. 237) weist auch ein Flakon der Firma Goldberg (Kat. Nr. 238) auf; die grün überfangene Deckeldose (Kat. Nr. 240) wurde ebenfalls von Goldberg ausgeführt.

MEHRFACHER FARBIGER ÜBERFANG BZW. UNTERFANG

(Kat. Nrn. 243-262, S. 261-282)

Als Sonderform der mehrschichtigen Gläser ist eine Vase mit rotem Unterfang, Kristallkern und weißem Überfang, aus dem blattartige Motive geschliffen wurden (Kat. Nr. 243), anzusehen.
Eine typische Farbkombination mit doppeltem Überfang und Ziersaumschliff ist das Rot-Schwarz über dem Kernkristall, wie eine Vase (Kat. Nr. 246) nach Entwurf der Fachschule Haida in der Ausführung von Oertel/Haida zeigt. Die ebenfalls rot-schwarz über-

fangene Deckelvase von Jelínek für Harrach/Neuwelt (Kat. Nr. 247) besticht durch die Motivik des Schliffs. Derselbe Künstler schuf eine blau-grün überfangene Vase (Kat. Nr. 248).
Das Blau-Schwarz über dem Kernkristall wurde für eine Deckeldose (Kat. Nr. 250) und mehrere Vasen (Kat. Nr. 252, 257, 258, 261) verwendet. Farbig ungewöhnlich sind die gelb-schwarzen Überfänge einer Vase (Kat. Nr. 253), eher selten findet man weiß und blau überfangene Vasen (Kat. Nr. 254) mit vertikaler Gliederung. Der technisch sehr aufwendige dreifache Überfang (weiß, blau, schwarz) ist durch zwei Gläser in der Sammlung des Österreichischen Museums repräsentiert (Kat. Nrn. 255, 256). Die meisten der eben genannten Überfanggläser wurden nach Entwurf der Fachschule Haida durch Oertel/Haida ausgeführt.

ÜBERFANG IN WEISS UND SCHWARZ

(Kat. Nrn. 263-356, S. 283-334)

Auch für die doppelten Überfanggläser (weiß und schwarz) spielte die Fachschule Haida eine wichtige Rolle. Einige von der Fachschule selbst realisierte Gläser sind einerseits aus der zeitgenössischen Literatur (Kat. Nrn. 263-266) bekannt, andererseits im Original erhalten (Kat. Nr. 267). Größere Serien nach Fachschulentwurf wurden von Oertel/Haida (Kat. Nr. 271, 272) hergestellt. In diesem Zusammenhang muß darauf hingewiesen werden, daß ein bestimmter Glastypus zwar öfter ausgeführt werden konnte, sich dabei jedoch Unterschiede in der Detailbehandlung ergaben, wie z.B. beim Knauf der Deckelvase (Kat. Nrn. 271, 272). Eine weitere Variante desselben Prototyps zeigt einen schwarzen, ungeschliffenen Deckelknauf.
Dem Schwarzweiß wandten sich aber auch andere Fabriken zu: Harrach/Neuwelt (Kat. Nr. 270, Entwurf Jelínek), Goldberg/Haida (Kat. Nr. 273), Tschernich/Haida (Kat. Nr. 274, 275). Unter den Gläsern mit mehrfachem Überfang, die Margold für Schappel entwarf (Kat. Nrn. 276-279), befanden sich auch Schwarzweiß-Varianten (Kat. Nr. 278).
Die umfangreichste Gruppe von Schwarzweiß-Gläsern stellen jedoch die sogenannten Borussia-Gläser der Firma Schappel dar (Kat. Nrn. 281-356), die hier nahezu vollständig abgebildet werden können, da sich neben zahlreichen Originalen auch ein Katalog der Firma Schappel erhalten hat.

202

INTRODUCTION

The variety of glass produced in the period 1905 to 1925 in the area of the Austro-Hungarian Monarchy and the countries which succeeded it seems virtually inexhaustible. For this reason, if for no other, it will probably continue to have no uniform stylistic designation. The innumerable variations of shape, technique and decoration range from thin-walled, undecorated blown glass to solid, deep-cut crystal glass, from distinctive decorative seams with several overlays to multi-coloured etched surfaces, from continuous jet black to delicate line drawings, from opaque painting to brilliant vitrified enamels, from under-cutting to delicate figure engraving. The effect of colour in varying light which appears to make many glass vessels change continuously can no more be captured at one glance than it can in a single illustration. Though gold shines in reflected light, in transmitted light it gives way to the inherent colour of the glass itself; though reflected light emphasises the shape of dark coloured glass, red glass glows in focused light and in the coloured shadow of transmitted light.
Exquisite vases as individual pieces contrast with cut glass table services. In sets the central glass vessel dominates the smaller pieces: punch sets, liqueur services, beer services, etc.

197

Various manufacturing processes such as casing, staining and painting transform identical basic shapes into variations which appear to have hardly anything in common apart from the original shape of the glass.
Stylistic simplifications will not be used here. Nevertheless, there are traces of art nouveau in encased overlay glasses with "painted" decoration (the "Melusin Glass" by Loetz), of pure art deco in the colourful zigzag of opaque painting (war glass by Josef Hoffmann), of the ornamental "horror vacui" of black-gold in fantastic, slightly oriental ornamentation (line drawings by Karl Massanetz). These contrast with "shape without ornament", undecorated smooth cut glass (J. & L. Lobmeyr).

CRITERIA FOR CATALOGUING

The geographical limits were defined by the specific nature of the collection, the temporal limits by the years 1905 and 1925.
Further differentiation by an alphabetical listing of glass works or designing artists hardly seemed advisable. Classification by factories would have necessitated an impossible differentiation between producers of basic glassware and decorators, and the designers of many glass vessels have still to be discovered. We know the names of those who commissioned large parts of the collection, but not the names of the manufacturers. Thus the criteria of manufacturing and refining processes remain an established method of classification, within which a certain chronological order can be determined for individual blocks.

SOURCES

The contemporary sources used were of many different types: on the one hand, inventory entries, sometimes incorrect and usually incomplete, on the other designs and working drawings (particularly from J. & L. Lobmeyr, Vienna, E. Bakalowits, Vienna and the Wiener Werkstätte), contemporary magazines (Studio, Deutsche Kunst und Dekoration, Dekorative Kunst, Kunst und Kunsthandwerk, etc.) and catalogues (particularly the exhibition catalogues of the Austrian Museum of Art and Industry, unfortunately unillustrated), contemporary photographs of items exhibited, and some of the few surviving company catalogues. In view of the fact that the museum has a considerable number of Borussia glass vessels by Schappel, a special catalogue for this type of glass has been fully incorporated in the present publication.
The archives of the Austrian Museum of Applied Art proved particularly informative, especially with regard to the large exhibition of Austrian art and export glass held in the year 1915.

PROBLEMS OF ESTABLISHING DATES AND ORIGINS

Strictly speaking, the dates recorded in the inventories (W.I. = travelling exhibition inventory, GI = glass inventory) should be regarded as inventory dates only, and not always as dates of acquisition. As contemporary illustrations or other sources show, the glass objects themselves were occasionally made years before, or may in other cases have been acquired immediately after manufacture.
The origin of items in the inventories is sometimes given as the decorator, in other instances the factory, and often the above-mentioned commissioners of much of the glass, Messrs. Bakalowits and Lobmeyr.
The exhibition of Austrian art and export glass, which took the form of a travelling exhi-

bition (Vienna, Brünn, Reichenberg, Stockholm, Berlin, Hamburg), often resulted in the sale, and – if the worst came to the worst – even in the breakage of glassware. There is evidence that one and the same glass model was then reordered, with the result that only exact notes in the inventories indicate that the piece originally inventoried was replaced and is not identical with the piece in existence today. The Bohemian glassmakers had their share of difficulties with these repeat orders during this critical period, and it could happen that decorators were unable to obtain the glassware they required, a circumstance that was particularly unfortunate in the case of incomplete sets.
Generally speaking, however, the inventoried glass is the same as that existing today, and the inventory date can therefore be regarded as a reliable terminus ante quem for certain glass items. This seems to be of special importance in view of the fact that many successful glass models were manufactured over an extended period of time (as proved by the surviving archives of the Wiener Werkstätte).

CRYSTAL GLASS

(Cat. nos. 1-162, pp. 34-181)

Well known artists like Kolo Moser, Emil Hoppe, Otto Prutscher and Josef Hoffmann designed glassware, the walls of which were cut to form different kinds of facets.
The glass service by Kolo Moser (cat. no. 1) was first illustrated in 1906, though the design suggests that it probably originated several years earlier. A volume of working drawings of the Bakalowits company (ÖMAK, Inv. 32066 c) shows three variations on the shapes of a table service of 1902 ("optisch", "Pentagramm", "Schuppen"); the third variation may be the same as the glass type with hexagonal facets (cat. no. 2).
Most of the shapes of table service no. 130 commissioned by the Bakalowits company in 1906 have been acquired in recent years; dedications and loans have completed the service in the exhibition (cat. nos. 7-33). In this service, with its horizontal and vertical divisions, designer Emil Hoppe created a whole of exceptional beauty which was also produced in a version with gold decoration (cat. no. 6). The green bowl of the Moselle wine glasses (cat. no. 33) contrasts delightfully with the colourless crystal glass.
A series of glass goblets with cut bowls, stems and feet was designed by Otto Prutscher (cat. nos. 36-41). The differently shaped silhouettes of the bowls allowed a degree of variation in the series, as did the glowing yellow ovals of three glasses (cat. nos. 36, 39, 40).
Most of the above-mentioned glasses were probably manufactured by Meyr's Neffe, Adolf near Winterberg, although this cannot always be verified. The same applies to a jardinière dated 1909 (cat. nos. 43-45).
One of the glass goblets designed by Josef Hoffmann in 1910 has a bowl with triangular facets (cat. nos. 50-51); the shapes of the bowls, stems and bases of the other glasses in this series were varied by diamond cutting, steps in the base, cut motifs half-way up the stem, etc. (cat. nos. 48-54). This group is completed by flower vases (cat. no. 55), the designs of which exhibit further variety of shape (cat. nos. 56-59), though not all of them were actually executed. One glass was described as unproducible (cat. no. 50, left), several marked with 0, and Hoffmann's original designs for many others were altered.
A flower set consisted of two different sized jardinières with plates (cat. nos. 64-66); the rich cutting corresponds to the design (cat. no. 64), though the shape was changed by leaving out the faceted base. A group of glasses, some of which stem from Josef Hoffmann (cat. nos. 67-69), while others have yet to be attributed to specific designers (cat. no. 72), is characterised by the deep cuts in the base.

324

294

Thick glass, which permits almost high-relief cutting, was also used for glass of this period (cat. nos. 73-75). The vertical cutting of a toilet set (cat. nos. 78-81) that survives in the form of a design by J. & L. Lobmeyr has a striking simplicity combined with maximum optical effect. Bowls for religious (cat. nos. 82-83) and secular use (cat. nos. 84-87) are associated with the name of another prominent designer: Oscar Strnad (cat. nos. 86-87). The Haida school of glassmaking in northern Bohemia is represented by artistically cut glass (cat. nos. 88-91) from about 1910, and the covered goblet (cat. no. 91), with its simple, but effective horizontal and vertical divisions and tapering stepped cover is one of the most impressive such creations. The type of cutting is similar to that used for more austere coloured glass (cat. no. 164).
The glasses designed by the Artěl atelier in Prague prior to 1914 are some of the best of their time, with regard to both shape and engraving. The punch set by Jan Kotěra, first presented at the World Exhibition in St. Louis in 1904, has an excessive wealth of cut surfaces, which were considerably reduced in a later version (cat. no. 92), thus underlining the clear-cut shape of the vessels. The walls of the covered jars (cat. nos. 93-94) are also cut into facets, while deep grooves characterise the seven curves of a vase (cat. no. 95), while the rim of a centrepiece (cat. no. 96) takes the form of a wide zigzag. Champagne and wine glasses (cat. nos. 97-99) with cut stems and finely cut continuous lines are worked in crystal glass, and the bowls of the moselle wine glasses (cat. no. 9) are of green glass. The liqueur services by Artěl sometimes combine cut glass (cat. no. 100) with optical glass (cat. nos. 101-102).
Yet another liqueur service (cat. nos. 103-104) stems from Otto Prutscher, who has hitherto received far too little consideration as a glass designer. He also created a whole range of other glassware (cat. nos. 106-110, 112, vases, centrepieces, covered goblets) that was manufactured in Haida by Carl Schappel.
A contemporary illustration identifies Carl Thomas, whom we shall be coming across again in the second volume of the catalogue, as the designer of a covered goblet (cat. no. 111). Although this artist is largely unknown as a designer of glass, Josef Emanuel Margold needs no introduction in this capacity. Thanks to a loan from Graz, his covered vessel in the Vienna collection (cat. no. 114) can be compared with an octagonal cut glass jar (cat. no. 115). Both items bear adhesive labels with the Schappel company name, the designer's name and serial number.
On the other hand, two still anonymous creations in glass meet the highest standards of design and glass-cutting: a casket (cat. no. 16) and a bottle (cat. no. 117), the former made by Meyr's Neffe, Adolf, the latter sold to the museum by Lobmeyr. Three cut-glass candlesticks (cat. nos. 118-120), one of them also with cut edges (cat. no. 118), also stem from Meyr's Neffe, Adolf, as does the unusual combination of candlestick/jar (cat. no. 121).
The writing table set by Oswald Dittrich (cat. no. 122) was acquired for the museum through the Lobmeyr company, but is unfortunately no longer in the collection.
A box (cat. no. 123) and a covered vase (cat. no. 151), both to designs by Haida school of glassmaking, were manufactured by the Oertel company of Haida. These two items underline the importance of trade schools to regional industry. Many of the cased glasses mentioned below were manufactured by glass factories to designs by schools of glassmaking.
A bottle and beaker by Meyr's Neffe (cat. no. 124) represent a complete set from which the beaker is usually missing. Further examples of north Bohemian crystal glass are found among the glassware produced by the factories of Gerner/Haida (cat. nos. 125, 126, 143, 147), Meyr's Neffe/Adolf (cat. nos. 127-132, 135- 140, 142, 144-146, 149, 150, 152), Rasch/Ulrichsthal (cat. no. 133), Mühlhaus/Haida (cat. no. 134) and Meltzer/Lange-

nau (cat. no. 148), while the vase (cat. no. 141) was probably also manufactured by Meyr's Neffe/Adolf.
While a vase (cat. no. 142) is one of the glass vessels with a variety of different cuts, other glasses are embellished with strawberry diamonds with the sparing use of transparent colours, while the cut edges of many vases (cat. nos. 147-148) make them particularly delightful.
Thick-walled vessels such as the covered goblet (cat. no. 151), vases (cat. nos. 152-153) and jardinières (cat. no. 154) are characterised by austere diamond, lozenge and bevel cuts. In this context, we come across other factory names, such as Zahn/Haida (cat. nos. 153, 159-161), and Harrach/Neuwelt (cat. nos. 154, 158). But it was Meltzer/Langenau, Meyr's Neffe/Adolf, Harrach/Neuwelt and Zahn/Haida who were the chief exponents of the "crystal style", which is most effective in lead crystal (cat. nos. 156-161).
The glass sculpture (cat. no. 162), whose creator is specified in the inventory as O. E. Wagner, represents a supreme achievement in cut glass.

COLOURED GLASS

(cat. nos. 163-180, pp. 182-197)

Glass stained with a colouring material throughout its substance was manufactured mostly in red, violet and green. The ruby glass of Haida school of glassmaking (cat. no. 164) combines brilliance of colour with attractive form and perfect cutting.
The Goldberg company of Haida used the term "Kunckel" glass to describe a special product usually combining the dark glowing red of the glass with vertical faceting (cat. nos. 163, 167-169). Mühlhaus/Haida probably manufactured this type of glass several years earlier (cat. nos. 165-166). The rather traditional shapes of the Haida factories contrast with glassware in shades of violet to indigo made to designs by Josef Hoffmann (cat. nos. 172-174, 176), while the centrepiece (cat. no. 175) has not yet been attributed to a particular designer or glass factory.
Another design stemming from Hoffmann was that of a bottle whose dark green colour is visible only against a very bright source of light (cat. nos. 177-178), whereas the medium and pale shades of green in the vases by Meyr's Neffe (cat. nos. 179-180) can be seen to good effect in trasmitted light.

CASED GLASS

(cat. nos. 181-356, pp. 199-334)

There are several main groups of multi-layered glass: crystal glass with one coloured casing, crystal glass with several coloured casings and crystal glass with casings in white and black. Some of these glasses were not decorated at all, or only slightly. More frequently they were processed by cutting or etching (the latter category will be discussed in the second volume).

SIMPLE CASINGS

(cat. nos. 181-242, pp. 199-259)

Viennese design appears to have played an important role in the artistic decoration of single-cased glass. For instance, there are the famous glass goblets by Otto Prutscher, which were exhibited at the Vienna art show of 1908 (cat. no. 183), an example of which

174

is owned by the Joanneum Museum in Graz (cat. no. 185). They were manufactured by Meyr's Neffe/Adolf, and in another variation the decoration was enriched by silver-yellow and green enamel spots of molten glass (cat. no. 186).
Blue-cased, cut glass is predominant not only in a design by Josef Hoffmann dated 1909 (cat. no. 187), but also in glass commissioned by the Wiener Werkstätte, most of which stemmed from Otto Prutscher with a decoration sometimes referred to as "linear cutting" (cat. nos. 188-196). Once again, these were probably manufactured mainly by Meyr's Neffe/Adolf. The technique used for a jardinière by Artěl/Prague would appear to be related, as here, too, vertical strips of casing of various widths have been left (cat. no. 197).
On the other hand, cut-out circles and ovals dominate the designs by Margold (cat. nos. 198-199) and the glass of the Mühlhaus company/Haida (cat. nos. 200-202, 204), the

structure of which is strikingly similar to that of the covered goblet from Haida (cat. no. 203).
Four glasses with almost black casings (cat. nos. 205-210) reached the museum through the Bakalowits company (cat. nos. 205-210). The cut motifs of a bottle (cat. no. 211) that also came to the collection through Bakalowits are similar, though a different colour is used.
Both the Wiener Werkstätte and Haida school of glassmaking are specified as the originators of single-cased glasses with corrugated walls and the resulting shapes achieved by vertical cutting. Many of these glasses were manufactured by Meltzer/Langenau (cat. nos. 212-215, 217); in his book published in 1925 Pazaurek notes Haida school of glassmaking as the designer and Meltzer/Langenau as the manufacturer of the three glasses illustrated in it (cat. no. 218). A vase which the museum acquired from Meltzer (cat. no. 219) is attributed to Haida school of glassmaking in contemporary literature (cat. no. 216).
We have already encountered the shape of the vertically cut vase with seven bulges in the section on crystal glass (cat. no. 95); this is compared here with the same shape with a blue casing (cat. no. 222). Another shape, but the same principle of cutting is found in a vase by Artěl (cat. no. 223), while the cutting of dishes (cat. nos. 220-221) brings out deep triangular motifs in the cased glass. Long red triangular surfaces are also left in the cutting of a beer service by Artěl (cat. no. 224), while Rosipal's designs for Artěl are characterised by a lozenge-shaped motif which is varied and repeated depending on the size and shape of the glass (cat. nos. 225-231).
A particularly exquisite piece of glass is an artistically cut vase by Haida school of glassmaking (cat. no. 232). Cut glass with a simple casing was frequently manufactured by Oertel/Haida for other designers: either to designs by Haida school of glassmaking (dish, cat. no. 235; centrepiece, cat. no. 237) or for the Wiener Werkstätte (cat. nos. 241-242). Single-cased cut glass was also included in the range of Leopold Forstner's "Edelglaswerke" in Stockerau (cat. nos. 233-234).
A bottle by the Goldberg company (cat. no. 238) has a similar violet casing to the centrepiece (cat. no. 237). A green cased box (cat. no. 240) was also manufactured by Goldberg.

MULTICOLOURED CASINGS

(cat. nos. 243-262, pp. 261-282)

A vase with a red basis, covered by a crystal and a white casing in which leaf-like motifs have been cut (cat. no. 243) represents a special type of multi-layered glass. A typical colour combination with a double casing and decorative cut seam is red-black on a crystal basis, such as used for a vase (cat. no. 246) manufactured by Oertel/Haida to a design by Haida school of glassmaking. Another red-black cased covered vase by Jelínek for Harrach/Neuwelt (cat. no. 247) features a charming cut motif. The same artist created a blue-green cased vase (cat. no. 248).
A blue-black casing over a crystal basis was used for a jar (cat. no. 250) and several vases (cat. nos. 252, 257, 258, 261). Unusual colours are encountered in the yellow-black casings of a vase (cat. no. 253), and it is not often that one finds white and blue cased vases (cat. no. 254) with vertical decoration. Two glasses in the collection of the Austrian museum (cat. nos. 255, 256) have a technically very complicated triple casing (white, blue, black). Most of the cased glassware mentioned above was produced by Oertel/Haida to designs by Haida school of glassmaking.

CASING IN WHITE AND BLACK

(cat. nos. 263-356, pp. 283-334)

Haida school of glassmaking also played an important role in double cased glass (white and black). We know of several glasses executed by the school of glassmaking from contemporary literature (cat. nos. 263-266), and some originals still survive (cat. no. 267). Large series were produced by Oertel/Haida to school of glassmaking designs (cat. nos. 271-272). In this context it should be pointed out that although a certain type of glass may have been produced frequently, there were differences in details, such as the knob of a covered vase (cat. nos. 271-272). Another version of the same model has a lid with a black, uncut knob.
Other factories also produced black-white casings: Harrach/Neuwelt (cat. no. 270, design Jelínek), Goldberg/Haida (cat. no. 273), Tschernich/Haida (cat. nos. 274-275). The multi-layered glasses which Margold designed for Schappel (cat. nos. 276-279) also included black-white versions (cat. no. 278).
However, the largest group of black-white glass is the so-called Borussia glass by the Schappel company (cat. nos. 281- 356). Almost the entire range is illustrated here, as many originals have survived, as well as a catalogue of the Schappel company.

AUSGEWÄHLTE BIBLIOGRAPHIE · SELECTED BIBLIOGRAPHY

DK = Deutsche Kunst und Dekoration

DKD = Dekorative Kunst

Kat. Schappel, Borussia = Katalog der Firma Carl Schappel, Haida, Borussia-Glas, o.J. (1914) / Catalogue of the Carl Schappel company, Haida, Borussia Glass, undated (1914)

Kat. Schappel, Kunstgläser = Katalog der Firma Carl Schappel, Haida, Kunstgläser, o.J. (um 1914/15) / Catalogue of the Carl Schappel company, Haida, artistic glass, undated (around 1914/15)

KKH = Kunst und Kunsthandwerk

Neuwirth 1973 = Waltraud Neuwirth, Das Glas des Jugendstils, Wien, München-Wien 1973

Pazaurek 1925 = Gustav E. Pazaurek, Kunstgläser der Gegenwart, Leipzig 1925

WWMB = Kalkulationsbuch der Wiener Werkstätte, WW-Archiv, ÖMAK / Calculation book, WW archives in the ÖMAK

KATALOG · CATALOGUE

ABKÜRZUNGEN · ABBREVIATIONS

Inv. = Inventar / Inventory
Joanneum, AKGW = Steiermärkisches Landesmuseum Joanneum, Abteilung für Kunstgewerbe / Joanneum, Provincial Museum of Styria, Department of Applied Art

AUSSTELLUNGEN

ÖMAK = Österreichisches Museum für angewandte Kunst, Wien
ÖMAK 1967 = Wiener Werkstätte, ÖMAK 1967
ÖMAK 1973 = Das Glas des Jugendstils, ÖMAK 1973
ÖMKI = Österreichisches Museum für Kunst und Industrie, Wien
ÖMKI 1909/10 (1910/11, 1911/12, 1912/13) = Ausstellung österreichischer Kunstgewerbe, ÖMKI 1909-1910
ÖMKI 1912 = Frühjahrsausstellung österreichischer Kunstgewerbe, ÖMKI 1912
ÖMKI 1915 = Ausstellung des österreichischen Kunst- und Exportglases, ÖMKI 1915
Berlin 1916 = Ausstellung des österreichischen Kunst-und Exportglases, Berlin 1916
Brünn 1915 = Kunstglas-Ausstellung, Brünn 1915
Köln 1914 = Werkbundausstellung, Köln 1914
Reichenberg 1915 = Kunstglas-Ausstellung, Reichenberg 1915
Stockholm 1916 = Ausstellung österreichischen Kunst- und Exportglases, Stockholm 1916

EXHIBITIONS

ÖMAK = Austrian Museum of Applied Art, Vienna
ÖMAK 1967 = Wiener Werkstätte, ÖMAK 1967
ÖMAK 1973 = Art nouveau glass, ÖMAK 1973
ÖMKI = Austrian Museum of Art and Industry, Vienna
ÖMKI 1909/10 (1910/11, 1911/12, 1912/13) = Exhibition of Austrian arts and crafts, ÖMKI 1909-1910 etc.
ÖMKI 1912 = Spring exhibition of Austrian arts and crafts, ÖMKI 1912
ÖMKI 1915 = Exhibition of Austrian art and export glass, ÖMKI 1915
Berlin 1916 = Exhibition of Austrian art and export glass, Berlin 1916
Brünn 1915 = Exhibition of artistic glass, Brünn 1915
Köln 1914 = Werkbundausstellung, Cologne 1914
Reichenberg 1915 = Exhibition of artistic glass, Reichenberg 1915
Stockholm 1916 = Exhibition of Austrian art and export glass, Stockholm 1916

MASSE IN ZENTIMETERN	DIMENSIONS IN CENTIMETRES
H = Höhe	H = height
D = Durchmesser	D = diameter
Do = Durchmesser oben	Dt = diameter at top
Du = Durchmesser unten	Db = diameter at bottom
Dg = größter Durchmesser	Dm = max. diameter
L = Länge	L = length
B = Breite	B = breadth
T = Tiefe	T = depth

1

1
TEILE EINES
TRINKSERVICES
Entwurf: Kolo Moser
Glas mit Facettenschliff
Reproduktion aus:
Studio 1906 (Special
Summer Number, The Art-
Revival in Austria),
unpag., Abb. D 45

1
PARTS OF A
DRINKING SERVICE
Design: Kolo Moser
Bevel-cut glass
Reproduced from:
Studio 1906 (Special
Summer Number, The Art-
Revival in Austria),
unpaged, Fig. D 45

3
TABLE SERVICE NO. 130
Design: Emil Hoppe
Cut crystal glass
Reproduced from:
Catalogue no. 3 of
Messrs. Bakalowits, Vienna

4
PARTS OF TABLE SERVICE
NO. 130
Cut crystal glass
Design: Emil Hoppe
Commissioned by:
Bakalowits, Vienna
Reproduced from:
Studio Year Book 1907,
p. 221

5
TABLE SERVICE NO. 130
Price details
Reproduced from:
Catalogue no. 3 of
Messrs. Bakalowits, Vienna

6
PARTS OF TABLE
SERVICE NO. 130
Cut crystal glass,
gold decoration
Design: Emil Hoppe
Commissioned by:
Bakalowits, Vienna
Exhibition(s):
Kunstschau 1908, Vienna
ÖMKI 1909/10, no. 2089 a
(photograph ÖMAK,
VS Inv. 175 A)
Lit.: KKH XIII/1910,
p. 5 (carafe)
Reproduced from:
DK XVI/1908, p. 542

2
SECHS GLÄSER
Glas mit Facettenschliff
Entwurf: Kolo Moser
Verleger: Bakalowits, Wien
Maße: H 14,9-15
Do 7,4, Du 6,1-6,2
Inv.: ÖMAK, Gl 3449/1-6
(erworben 1984)

2
SIX GLASSES
Bevel-cut glass
Design: Kolo Moser
Commissioned by:
Bakalowits, Vienna
H 14.9-15, Dt 7.4,
Db 6.1-6.2
Inv.: ÖMAK, Gl 3449/1-6
(acquired 1984)

2

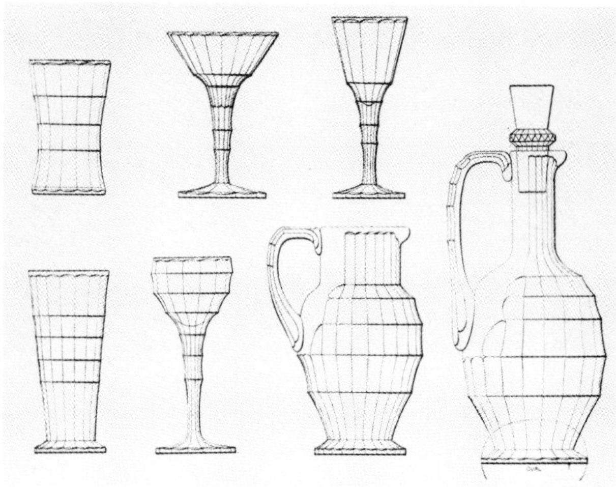

3

3
TAFELSERVICE NO. 130
Entwurf: Emil Hoppe
Kristallglas, geschliffen
Reproduktion aus:
Katalog Nr. 3 der
Firma Bakalowits, Wien

4
TEILE DES
TAFELSERVICES NR. 130
Kristallglas, geschliffen
Entwurf: Emil Hoppe
Verleger: Bakalowits, Wien
Reproduktion aus:
Studio Year Book 1907,
S. 221

DESIGNED BY E. HOPPE, ARCHITECT

DESIGNED BY E. HOPPE, ARCHITECT

4

5
TAFELSERVICE NR. 130
Preisangaben
Reproduktion aus:
Katalog Nr. 3 der
Firma Bakalowits, Wien

6
TEILE DES
TAFELSERVICES NR. 130
Kristallglas, geschliffen,
Golddekor
Entwurf: Emil Hoppe
Verleger: Bakalowits, Wien
Ausst.: Kunstschau 1908
ÖMKI 1909/10, Nr. 2089 a
(Foto ÖMAK, VS Inv. 175 A)
Lit.: KKH XIII/1910,
S. 5 (Karaffe)
Reproduktion aus:
DK XVI/1908, S. 542

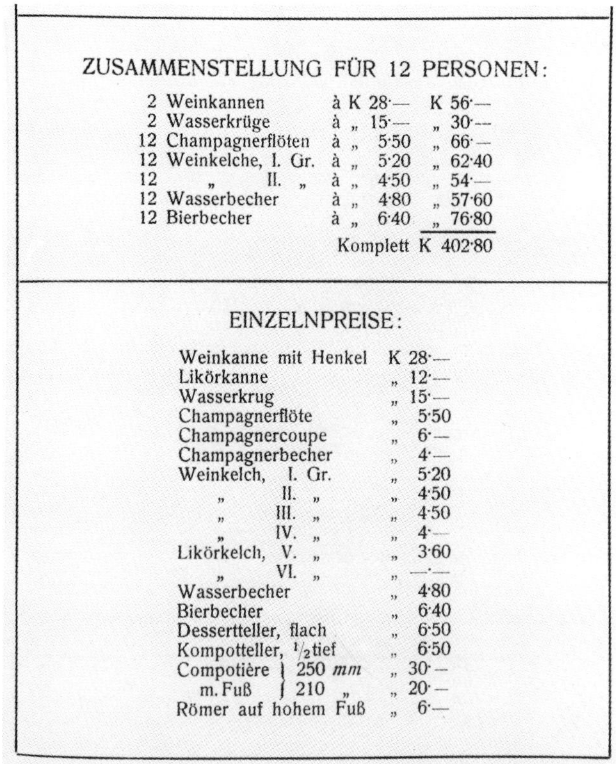

ZUSAMMENSTELLUNG FÜR 12 PERSONEN:

2	Weinkannen	à K 28·—	K 56·—
2	Wasserkrüge	à „ 15·—	„ 30·—
12	Champagnerflöten	à „ 5·50	„ 66·—
12	Weinkelche, I. Gr.	à „ 5·20	„ 62·40
12	„ II. „	à „ 4·50	„ 54·—
12	Wasserbecher	à „ 4·80	„ 57·60
12	Bierbecher	à „ 6·40	„ 76·80
		Komplett	K 402·80

EINZELNPREISE:

Weinkanne mit Henkel	K 28·—
Likörkanne	„ 12·—
Wasserkrug	„ 15·—
Champagnerflöte	„ 5·50
Champagnercoupe	„ 6·—
Champagnerbecher	„ 4·—
Weinkelch, I. Gr.	„ 5·20
„ II. „	„ 4·50
„ III. „	„ 4·50
„ IV. „	„ 4·—
Likörkelch, V. „	„ 3·60
„ VI. „	„ —·—
Wasserbecher	„ 4·80
Bierbecher	„ 6·40
Dessertteller, flach	„ 6·50
Kompotteller, $^1/_2$tief	„ 6·50
Compotière m. Fuß 250 *mm*	„ 30·—
Compotière m. Fuß 210 „	„ 20·—
Römer auf hohem Fuß	„ 6·—

5

6

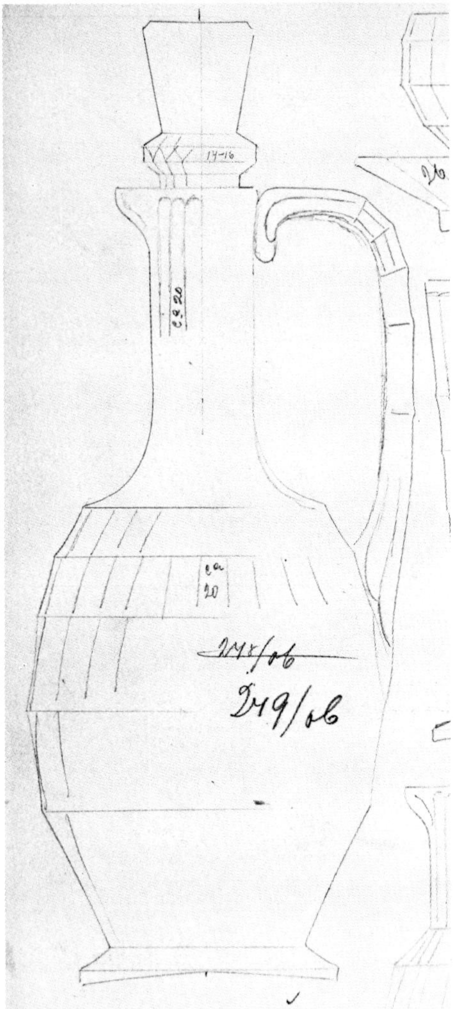

7

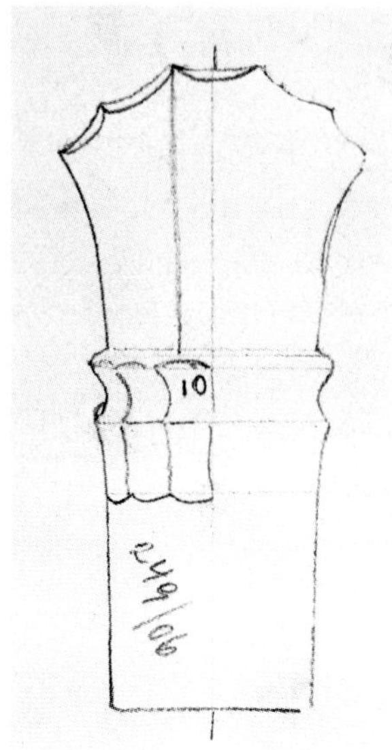

8

8
STÖPSEL
zur Karaffe Nr. 249/06
H 8,9
Inv.: ÖMAK, B.I. 32066 c

8
STOPPER
for carafe no. 249/06
H 8.9
Inv.: ÖMAK, B.I. 32066 c

7
KARAFFE
aus dem Tafelservice
Nr. 130 von Bakalowits
Werkskizze Nr. 249/06
Entwurf: Emil Hoppe
H 33,5 (ohne Stöpsel 27,7)
Inv.: ÖMAK, B.I. 32066 c

7
CARAFE
from the table service
no. 130 by Bakalowits
Working sketch no. 249/06
Design: Emil Hoppe
H 33.5
(without stopper: 27.7)
Inv.: ÖMAK, B.I. 32066 c

9
KARAFFE
aus dem Tafelservice
Nr. 130 von Bakalowits
Entwurf: Emil Hoppe
Werknummer 249/06
Kristallglas mit
Facettenschliff (20 Ecken)
H mit Stöpsel: 33,2
(ohne: 27,5)
Leihgabe
(Wiener Privatbesitz)

9
CARAFE
from the table service
no. 130 by Bakalowits
Design: Emil Hoppe
Serial number 249/06
Bevel-cut crystal
glass (20 sides)
H with stopper: 33.2
(without stopper: 27.5)
On loan (private
collection in Vienna)

9

10

10
GLASBECHER
Werknummer unbekannt
Glas mit Facettenschliff
Konische Form, 16 Ecken
H 9,9, Do 5,8, Du 3,9
Inv.:
ÖMAK, Gl 3473/1, 2
(Widmung Neuner & Henzl,
Wien, 1984)

10
BEAKER
Serial number unknown
Bevel-cut glass
Conical shape, 16 sides
H 9.9, Dt 5.8, Db 3.9
Inv.: ÖMAK, Gl 3473/1, 2
(donated by
Neuner & Henzl,
Vienna 1984)

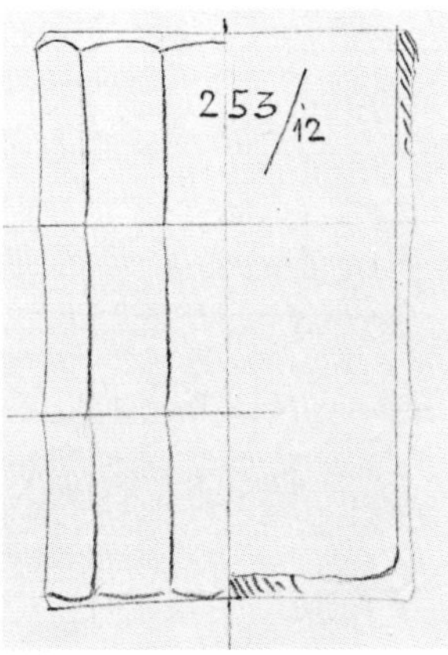

11

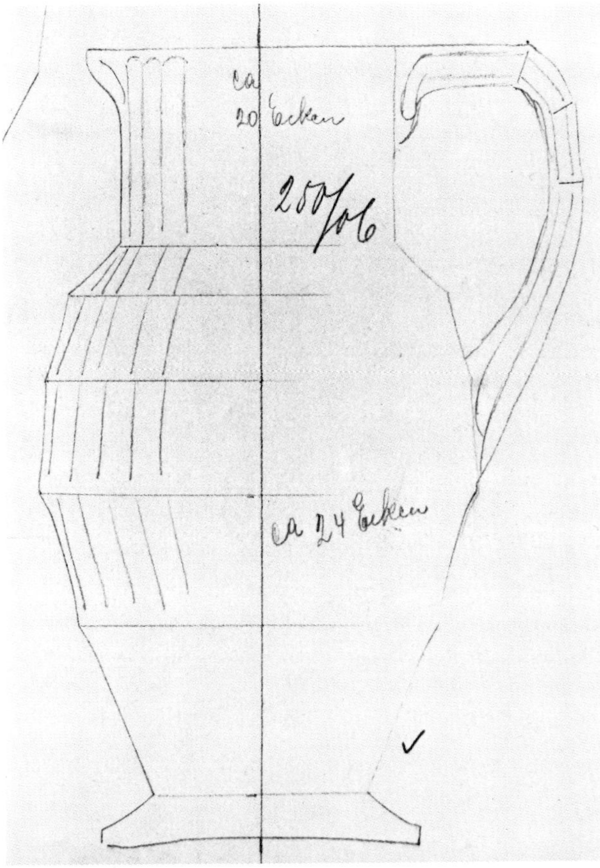

12

11
BECHER
aus dem Tafelservice
Nr. 130 von Bakalowits
Werkskizze Nr. 253/12
Entwurf: Emil Hoppe
H 10
Inv.: ÖMAK, B.I. 32066 c

11
BEAKER
from the table service
no. 130 by Bakalowits
Working sketch no. 253/12
Design: Emil Hoppe
H 10
Inv.: ÖMAK, B.I. 32066 c

12
KRUG
aus dem Tafelservice
Nr. 130 von Bakalowits
Werkskizze Nr. 250/06
Form: ca. 20 Ecken (Hals),
ca. 24 Ecken (Körper)
H 20
Inv.: ÖMAK, B.I. 32066 c

12
JUG
from the table service
no. 130 by Bakalowits
Working sketch no. 250/06
Shape:
approx. 20 sides (neck)
approx. 24 sides (body)
H 20
Inv.: ÖMAK, B.I. 32066 c

13
SECHS
CHAMPAGNERFLÖTEN
aus dem Tafelservice
Nr. 130 von Bakalowits
Entwurf: Emil Hoppe
Werknummer 251/06
Glas mit Facettenschliff
Form: 12 Ecken
Maße: H 18,9-19,
Do 5,4-5,5, Du 6,7-6,9
Inv.:
ÖMAK, Gl 3444/7-12
(1984 erworben)

13
SIX CHAMPAGNE
GLASSES
from the table service
no. 130 by Bakalowits
Design: Emil Hoppe
Serial number 251/06
Bevel-cut glass
Shape: 12 sides
H 18.9-19, Dt 5.4-5.5,
Db 6.7-6.9
Inv.: ÖMAK, Gl 3444/7-12
(acquired 1984)

14
CHAMPAGNERFLÖTE
aus dem Tafelservice
Nr. 130 von Bakalowits
Werkskizze Nr. 251/06
Entwurf: Emil Hoppe
H 19
Inv.: ÖMAK, B.I. 32066 c

14
CHAMPAGNE GLASSES
from the table service
no. 130 by Bakalowits
Working sketch no. 251/06
Design: Emil Hoppe
H 19
Inv.: ÖMAK, B.I. 32066 c

13

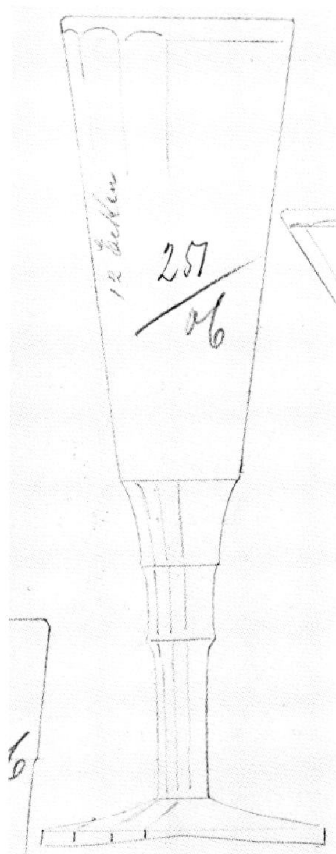

14

15
BIERGLAS
aus dem Tafelservice
Nr. 130 von Bakalowits
Werkskizze Nr. 259/06
Entwurf: Emil Hoppe
H 16,3
Inv.: ÖMAK, B.I. 32066 c

16
FIVE BEER GLASSES
from the table service
no. 130 by Bakalowits
Design: Emil Hoppe
Serial number 259/06
Bevel-cut glass
Shape: 16 sides
H 16-16.3, Dt 7.5-7.7
Db 6.4-6.7
Inv.: ÖMAK, Gl 3444/13-17

16
FÜNF BIERGLÄSER
aus dem Tafelservice
Nr. 130 von Bakalowits
Entwurf: Emil Hoppe
Werknummer 259/06
Kristallglas
mit Facettenschliff
Form: 16 Ecken
H 16-16,3, Do 7,5-7,7
Du 6,4-6,7
Inv.: ÖMAK, Gl 3444/13-17

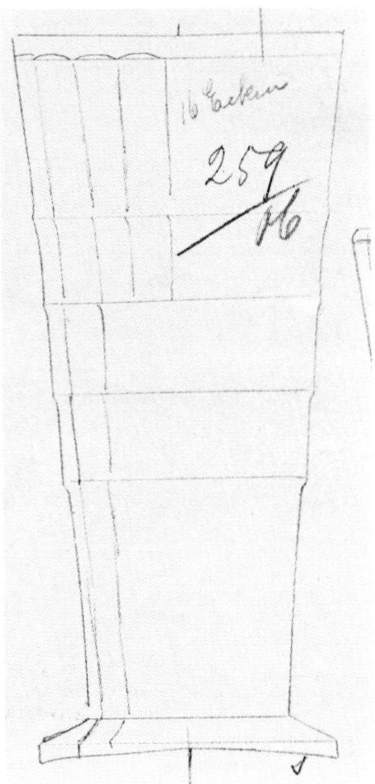

15

16

15
BEER GLASS
from the table service
no. 130 by Bakalowits
Working sketch no. 259/06
Design: Emil Hoppe
H 16.3
Inv.: ÖMAK, B.I. 32066 c

17
SIX GOBLETS
from the table service
no. 130 by Bakalowits
Design: Emil Hoppe
Serial number 253/06
Bevel-cut glass
Shape: 12 sides
H 17.7, Dt 7.4, Db 7.4
Inv.: ÖMAK, Gl 3473/5
(donated by
Neuner & Henzl,
Vienna 1984)

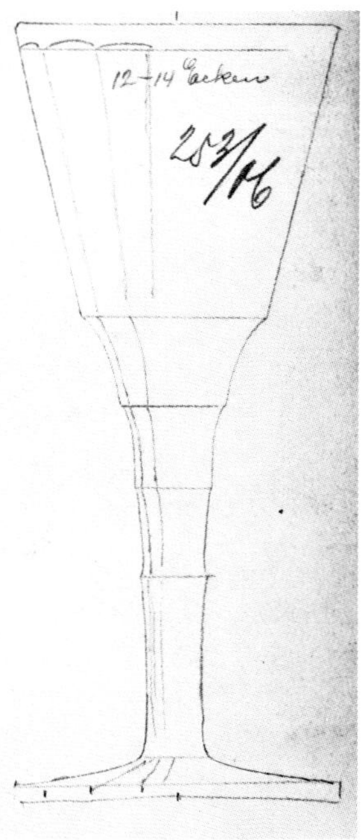

18

17

17
SECHS KELCHGLÄSER
aus dem Tafelservice
Nr. 130 von Bakalowits
Entwurf: Emil Hoppe
Werknummer 253/06
Glas mit Facettenschliff
Form: 12 Ecken
H 17,7, Do 7,4, Du 7,4
Inv.: ÖMAK, Gl 3473/5
(Widmung Neuner & Henzl,
Wien, 1984)

18
KELCHGLAS
aus dem Tafelservice
Nr. 130 von Bakalowits
Werkskizze Nr. 253/06
Entwurf: Emil Hoppe
H 17,6
Inv.: ÖMAK, B.I. 32066 c

18
GOBLET
from the table service
no. 130 by Bakalowits
Working sketch no. 253/06
Design: Emil Hoppe
H 17.6
Inv.: ÖMAK, B.I. 32066 c

19
GOBLET
from the table service
no. 130 by Bakalowits
Working sketch no. 254/06
Design: Emil Hoppe
H 15.9
Inv.: ÖMAK, B.I. 32066 c

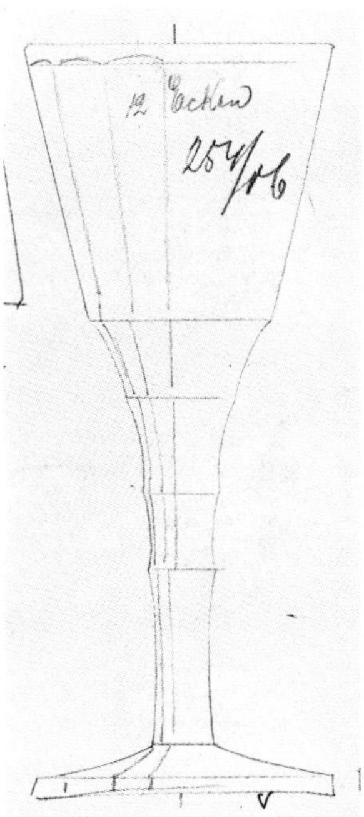

19

19
KELCHGLAS
aus dem Tafelservice
Nr. 130 von Bakalowits
Werkskizze Nr. 254/06
Entwurf: Emil Hoppe
H 15,9
Inv.: ÖMAK, B.I. 32066 c

20

20
FÜNF KELCHGLÄSER
aus dem Tafelservice
Nr. 130 von Bakalowits
Entwurf: Emil Hoppe
Werknummer 254/06
Glas mit Facettenschliff
H 15,7-15,8, Do 6,4-6,7,
Du 6,4-6,6
Inv.: ÖMAK, Gl 3444/18-22
(erworben 1984)

20
FIVE GOBLETS
from the table service
no. 130 by Bakalowits
Design: Emil Hoppe
Serial number 254/06
Bevel-cut glass
H 15.7-15.8, Dt 6.4-6.7,
Db 6.4-6.6
Inv.: ÖMAK, Gl 3444/18-22
(acquired 1984)

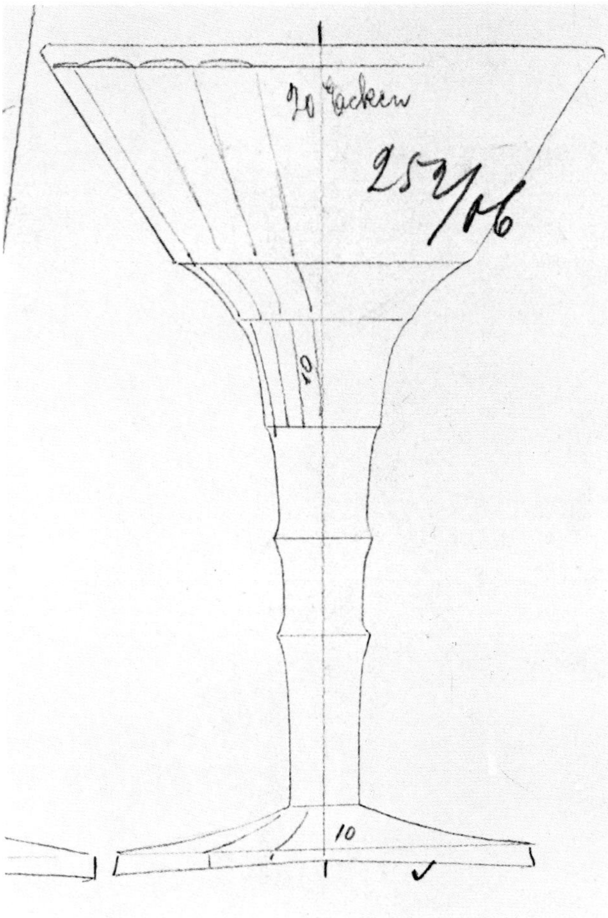

21

22
SECHS CHAMPAGNER-GLÄSER, FLACH
aus dem Tafelservice
Nr. 130 von Bakalowits
Entwurf: Emil Hoppe
Werknummer 252/06
(„Champagnercoupe“)
Glas mit Facettenschliff
Form: Kuppa 20 Ecken,
Fuß 10 Ecken
H 14,4, Do 9,9, Du 7,6-8
Inv.: ÖMAK, Gl 3444/1-6
(1984 erworben)

22
SIX CHAMPAGNE GLASSES, SHALLOW
from the table service
no. 130 by Bakalowits
Design: Emil Hoppe
Serial number 252/06
("Champagnercoupe")
Bevel-cut glass
Shape: bowl 20 sides,
foot 10 sides
H 14.4, Dt 9.9, Db 7.6-8
Inv.: ÖMAK, Gl 3444/1-6
(acquired 1984)

21
CHAMPAGNERGLÄSER, FLACH
aus dem Tafelservice
Nr. 130 von Bakalowits
Werkskizze Nr. 252/06
Entwurf: Emil Hoppe
H 14,6
Inv.: ÖMAK, B.I. 32066 c

21
CHAMPAGNE GLASSES, SHALLOW
from the table service
no. 130 by Bakalowits
Working sketch no. 252/06
Design: Emil Hoppe
H 14.6
Inv.: ÖMAK, B.I. 32066 c

22

23

24
GOBLET
from the table service
no. 130 by Bakalowits
Working sketch no. 255/06
Design: Emil Hoppe
H 15.2
Inv.: ÖMAK, B.I. 32066 c

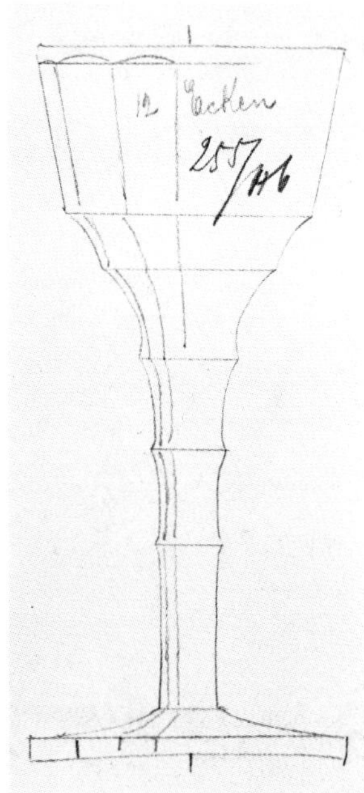

24

23
ZWEI KELCHGLÄSER
aus dem Tafelservice
Nr. 130 von Bakalowits
Entwurf: Emil Hoppe
Werknummer 255/06
Glas mit Facettenschliff
Form: 12 Ecken
H 15,3, Du 6,7 bzw. 6,8,
Du 6,5 bzw. 6,9
Inv.: ÖMAK, Gl 3473/3,4
(Widmung Neuner & Henzl,
Wien, 1984)

24
KELCHGLAS
aus dem Tafelservice
Nr. 130 von Bakalowits
Werkskizze Nr. 255/06
Entwurf: Emil Hoppe
H 15,2
Inv.: ÖMAK, B.I. 32066 c

23
TWO GOBLETS
from the table service
no. 130 by Bakalowits
Design: Emil Hoppe
Serial number 255/06
Bevel-cut glass
Shape: 12 sides
H 15.3, Db 6.7 and 6.8,
Db 6.5 and 6.9
Inv.: ÖMAK, Gl 3473/3,4
(donated by
Neuner & Henzl,
Vienna 1984)

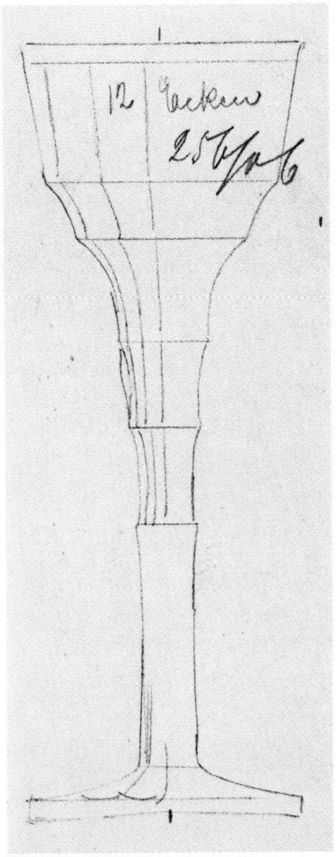

25

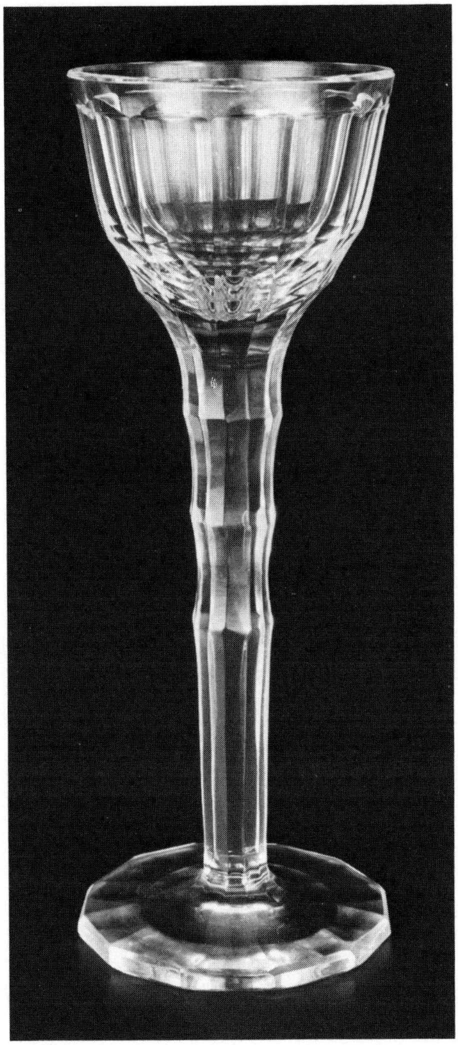

26

25
KELCHGLAS
aus dem Tafelservice
Nr. 130 von Bakalowits
Werkskizze Nr. 256/06
Entwurf: Emil Hoppe
H 15,4
Inv.: ÖMAK, B.I. 32066 c

25
GOBLET
from the table service
no. 130 by Bakalowits
Working sketch no. 256/06
Design: Emil Hoppe
H 15.4
Inv.: ÖMAK, B.I. 32066 c

26
SECHS KELCHGLÄSER
aus dem Tafelservice
Nr. 130 von Bakalowits
Entwurf: Emil Hoppe
Werknummer 256/06
Glas mit Facettenschliff
Form: 12 Ecken
H 15,3-15,4, Do 5,6-5,7,
Du 5,5-5,9
Inv.: ÖMAK, Gl 3444/29-34
(erworben 1984)

26
SIX GOBLETS
from the table service
no. 130 by Bakalowits
Design: Emil Hoppe
Serial number 256/06
Bevel-cut glass
Shape: 12 sides
H 15.3-15.4, Dt 5.6-5.7,
Db 5.5-5.9
Inv.: ÖMAK, Gl 3444/29-34
(acquired 1984)

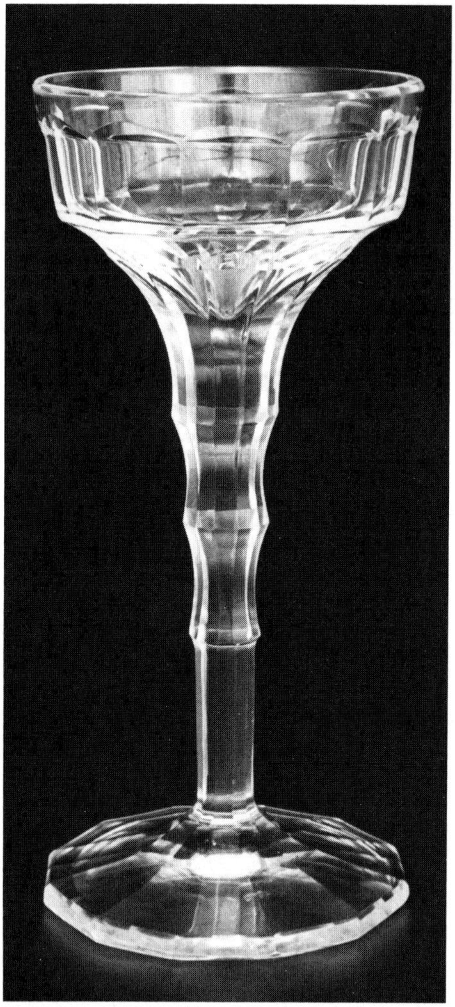

27

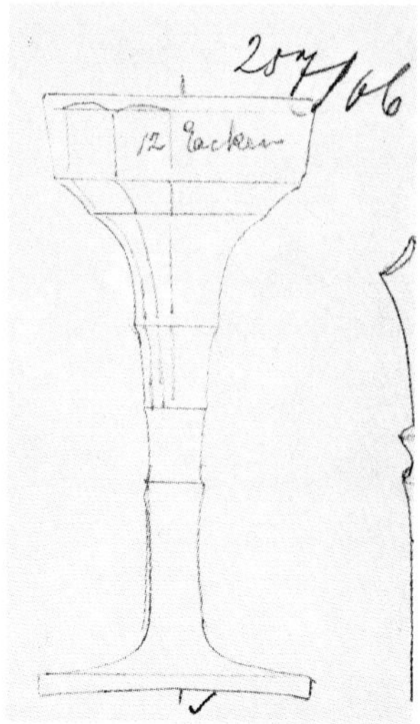

28

28
LIKÖRGLAS
aus dem Tafelservice
Nr. 130 von Bakalowits
Werkskizze Nr. 257/06
Entwurf: Emil Hoppe
H 10,7
Inv.: ÖMAK, B.I. 32066 c

28
LIQUEUR GLASS
from the table service
no. 130 by Bakalowits
Working sketch no. 257/06
Design: Emil Hoppe
H 10.7
Inv.: ÖMAK, B.I. 32066 c

27
SECHS LIKÖRGLÄSER
aus dem Tafelservice
Nr. 130 von Bakalowits
Entwurf: Emil Hoppe
Werknummer 257/06
Glas mit Facettenschliff
Form: 12 Ecken
H 10,6-10,7, Do 4,9-5,
Du 4,8-5,1
Inv.: ÖMAK, Gl 3444/35-40
(erworben 1984)

27
SIX LIQUEUR GLASSES
from the table service
no. 130 by Bakalowits
Design: Emil Hoppe
Serial number 257/06
Bevel-cut glass
Shape: 12 sides
H 10.6-10.7, Dt 4.9-5,
Db 4.8-5.1
Inv.: ÖMAK, Gl 3444/35-40
(acquired 1984)

29
LIKÖRFLASCHE
Werknummer unbekannt
Viereckige Grundform,
Facettenschliff mit
24 Ecken
H 19,4
Leihgabe
(Wiener Privatbesitz)

29

29
LIQUEUR DECANTER
Serial number unknown
Square basic shape,
bevel cut with 24 sides
H 19.4
On loan (private
collection in Vienna

30

30
WASSERGLAS
aus dem Tafelservice
Nr. 130 von Bakalowits
Werkskizze Nr. 258/06
Entwurf: Emil Hoppe
H 11,7
Inv.: ÖMAK, B.I. 32066 c

30
WATER GLASS
from the table service
no. 130 by Bakalowits
Working sketch no. 258/06
Design: Emil Hoppe
H 11.7
Inv.: ÖMAK, B.I. 32066 c

31
SECHS WASSERGLÄSER
aus dem Tafelservice
Nr. 130 von Bakalowits
Entwurf: Emil Hoppe
Werknummer 258/06
Kristallglas mit
Facettenschliff
Form: 14 Ecken
H 11,6-11,8, Do 7,5-7,7,
Du 6,6-6,7
Inv.: ÖMAK, Gl 3444/23-27
(erworben 1984)

31
SIX WATER GLASSES
from the table service
no. 130 by Bakalowits
Design: Emil Hoppe
Serial number 258/06
Bevel cut crystal glass
Shape: 14 sides
H 11.6-11.8, Dt 7.5-7.7,
Db 6.6-6.7
Inv.: ÖMAK, Gl 3444/23-27
(acquired 1984)

31

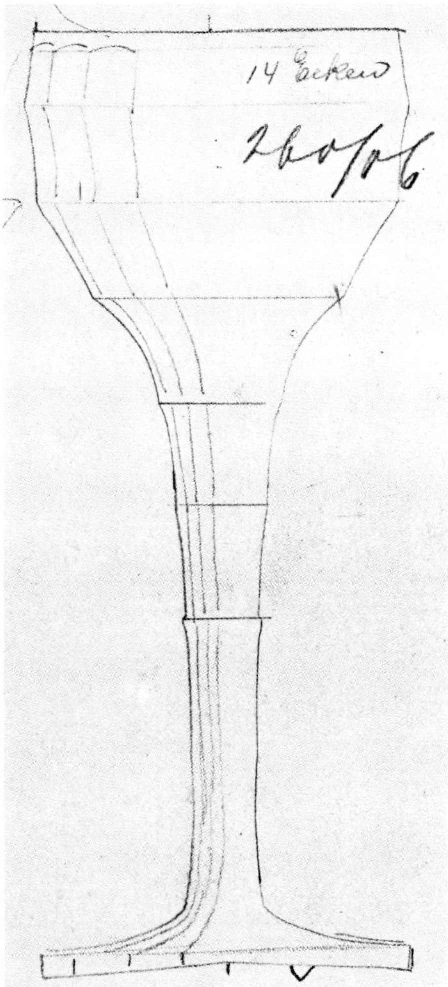

32

33
ZWEI
MOSELWEINGLÄSER
aus dem Tafelservice
Nr. 130 von Bakalowits
Entwurf: Emil Hoppe
Werknummer 260/06
Kristallglas mit
Facettenschliff,
Kuppa grünlich (helleres
und dunkleres Grün)
Form: 14 Ecken
H 17,5,Do 6,9 bzw. 7
Du 6,9 bzw. 7,3
Inv.: ÖMAK, Gl 3480, 3481
(Widmung Neuner & Henzl,
Wien, 1985)

33
TWO MOSELLE
WINE GLASSES
from the table service
no. 130 by Bakalowits
Design: Emil Hoppe
Serial number 260/06
Bevel cut crystal glass,
bowl greenish (pale and
darker green)
Shape: 14 sides
H 17.5, Dt 6.9 bzw. 7
Db 6.9 bzw. 7.3
Inv.: ÖMAK, Gl 3480, 3481
(donated by
Neuner & Henzl,
Vienna 1985)

32
MOSELWEINGLAS
aus dem Tafelservice
Nr. 130 von Bakalowits
Werkskizze Nr. 260/06
Entwurf: Emil Hoppe
H 17,5
Inv.: ÖMAK, B.I. 32066 c

32
MOSELLE WINE GLASS
from the table service
no. 130 by Bakalowits
Working sketch no. 260/06
Design: Emil Hoppe
H 17.5
Inv.: ÖMAK, B.I. 32066 c

33

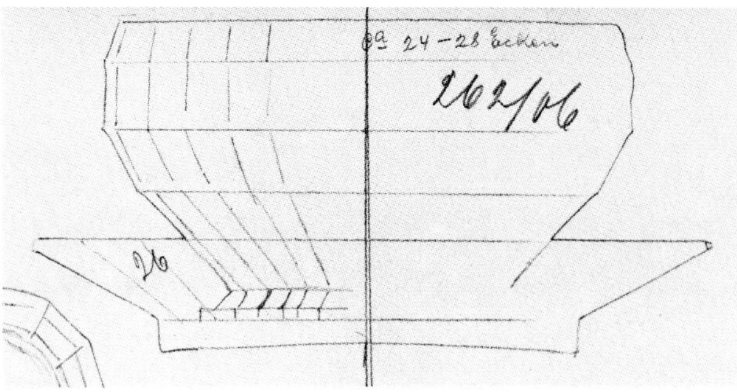

34

34
KOMPOTTSCHALE
MIT UNTERTASSE
aus dem Tafelservice
Nr. 130 von Bakalowits
Werkskizze Nr. 262/06
Form: Schale 24-28 Ecken,
Untertasse: 26 Ecken
Schale: H 6,9, Dg 12,7
Untertasse: D 16
Inv.: ÖMAK, B.I. 32066 c

34
FRUIT BOWL
WITH SAUCER
from the table service
no. 130 by Bakalowits
Working sketch no. 262/06
Shape: bowl 24-28 sides,
saucer: 26 sides
Bowl: H 6.9, Dm 12.7
Saucer: D 16
Inv.: ÖMAK, B.I. 32066 c

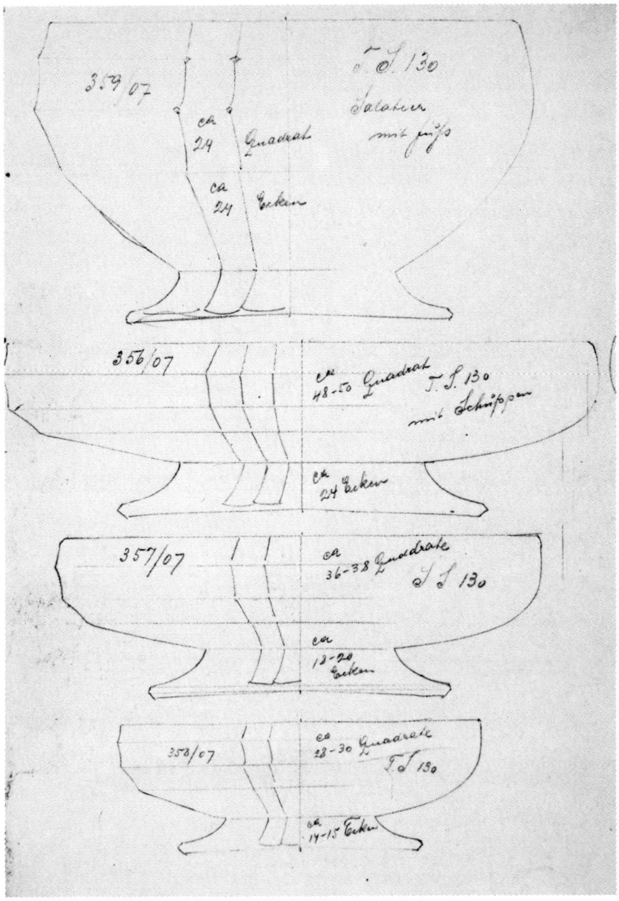

35

35
TEILE DES TAFELSERVICES
No. 130 von Bakalowits
Werkskizzen
Nr. 359/07 („Salatier“),
356/07-358/07
356/07: H 7,4
357/07: H 6,8
357/07: H 5,5
359/07: H 12,5
Inv.: ÖMAK, B.I. 32066 c

35
PARTS OF
TABLE SERVICE NO. 130
OF BAKALOWITS
Working sketch
no. 359/07 ("Salatier"),
356/07-358/07
356/07: H 7.4
357/07: H 6.8
357/07: H 5.5
359/07: H 12.5
Inv.: ÖMAK, B.I. 32066 c

36

36
ZWEI KELCHGLÄSER
Entwurf: Otto Prutscher
Ausführung: vermutlich
Meyr's Neffe, Adolf
Kristallglas mit Schliff
(Kuppa 24teilig, Fuß und
Stiel 12teilig) und
Silbergelb
ÖMAK, Gl 3265 g:
H 21,2, Do 8,6, Du 8,3
ÖMAK, Gl 3265 h:
H 20,9, Do 9,1, Du 8,7
Ausst.: WW 1967, Nr. 309
Lit.:
DKD 25/1909-10, S. 376
Kat. Neuwirth 1973,
Nr. 172, S. 308-309
Inv.: ÖMAK, Gl 3265 g, h

36
TWO GOBLETS
Design: Otto Prutscher
Manufacturer: probably
Meyr's Neffe, Adolf
Cut crystal glass and
silver-yellow
(bowl 24 sides, foot and
stem 12 sides)
ÖMAK, Gl 3265 g:
H 21.2, Dt 8.6, Db 8.3
ÖMAK, Gl 3265 h:
H 20.9, Dt 9.1, Db 8.7
Exhibition(s):
WW 1967, no. 309
Lit.:
DKD 25/1909-10, p. 376
Kat. Neuwirth 1973,
no. 172, pp. 308-309
Inv.: ÖMAK, Gl 3265 g, h

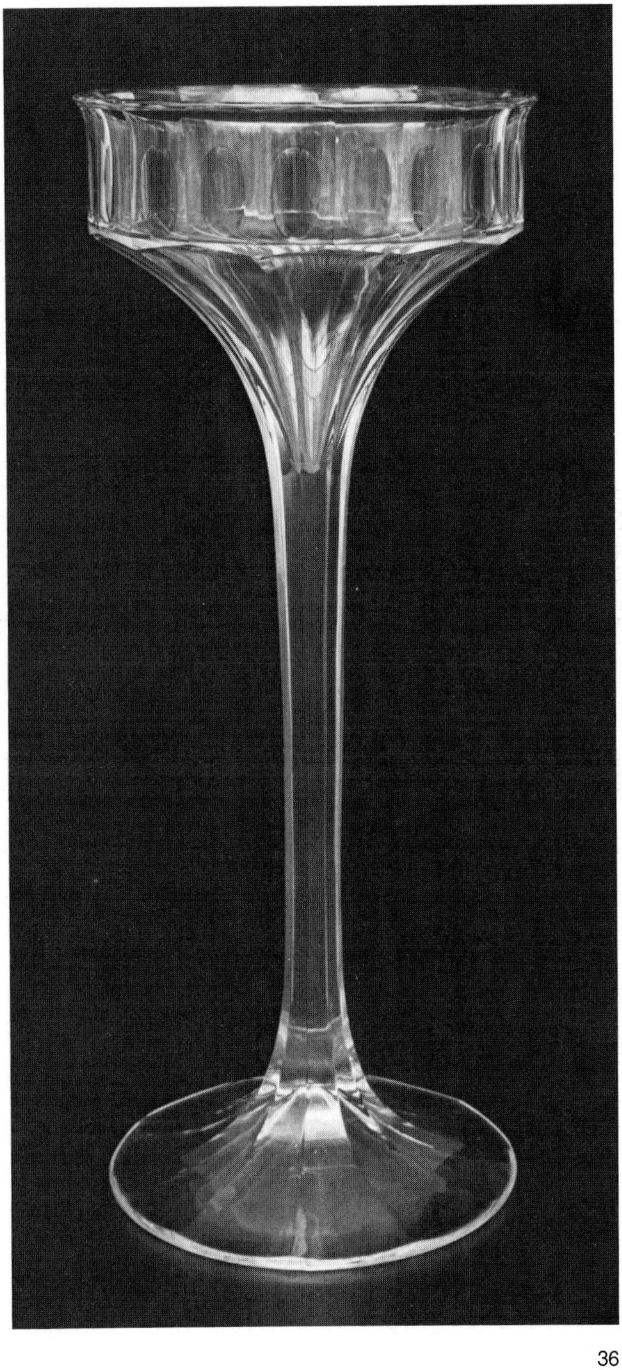

36

37
KELCHGLAS
Entwurf: Otto Prutscher
Ausführung: vermutlich
Meyr's Neffe, Adolf
Kristallglas mit Schliff
(Kuppa 24teilig, Fuß und
Stiel 12teilig)
H 21, Do 8,6, Du 8,4
Ausst.: WW 1967, Nr. 309
Kat. Neuwirth 1973, Nr. 172,
S. 308-309
Inv.: ÖMAK, Gl 3265 b
(inventarisiert 1964)

37
GOBLET
Design: Otto Prutscher
Manufacturer: probably
Meyr's Neffe, Adolf
Cut crystal glass
(bowl 24 sides, foot and
stem 12 sides)
H 21, Dt 8.6, Db 8.4
Exhibition(s):
WW 1967, no. 309
Kat. Neuwirth 1973,
no. 172, pp. 308-309
Inv.: ÖMAK, Gl 3265 b
(inventoried 1964)

37

38
DREI KELCHGLÄSER
Entwurf: Otto Prutscher
Ausführung: vermutlich
Meyr's Neffe, Adolf
Kristallglas mit Schliff
(Kuppa 24teilig, Fuß und
Stiel 12teilig)
H 20,7-21, Do 8,4-8,7,
Du 8-8,2
Ausst.:
WW 1967, Nr. 309
Lit.:
Kat. Neuwirth 1973,
Nr. 172, S. 308-309
Inv.: ÖMAK, Gl 3265 a
(inventarisiert 1964),
Gl 3451 a,b (erworben
1984)

38
THREE GOBLETS
Design: Otto Prutscher
Manufacturer: probably
Meyr's Neffe, Adolf
Cut crystal glass
(bowl 24 sides, foot and
stem 12 sides)
H 20.7-21, Dt 8.4-8.7,
Db 8-8.2
Exhibition(s):
WW 1967, no. 309
Lit.:
Kat. Neuwirth 1973,
no. 172, pp. 308-309
Inv.: ÖMAK, Gl 3265 a
(inventoried 1964),
Gl 3451 a,b (acquired
1984)

38

39

40

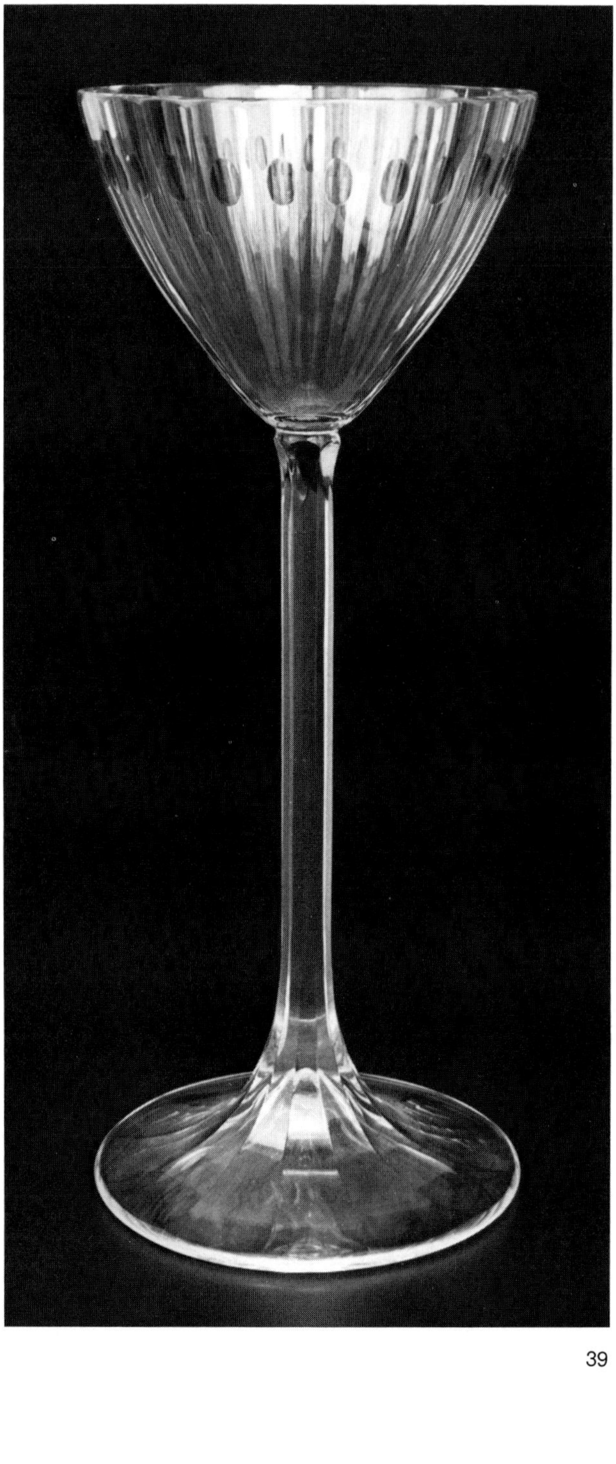

39
KELCHGLAS
Entwurf: Otto Prutscher
Ausführung: vermutlich
Meyr's Neffe, Adolf
Kristallglas mit Schliff
(Kuppa 24teilig, Fuß und
Stiel 12teilig),
Silbergelb
H 21, Do 8,5, Du 8,6
Ausst.:
WW 1967, Nr. 309
Lit.:
Kat. Neuwirth 1973,
Nr. 172, S. 308-309
Inv.: ÖMAK, Gl 3265 d
(inventarisiert 1964)

39
GOBLET
Design: Otto Prutscher
Manufacturer: probably
Meyr's Neffe, Adolf
Cut crystal glass,
silver-yellow
(bowl 24 sides, foot and
stem 12 sides)
H 21, Dt 8.5, Db 8.6
Exhibition(s):
WW 1967, no. 309
Lit.:
Kat. Neuwirth 1973,
no. 172, pp. 308-309
Inv.: ÖMAK, Gl 3265 d
(inventoried 1964)

39

40
ZWEI KELCHGLÄSER
Entwurf: Otto Prutscher
Ausführung: vermutlich
Meyr's Neffe, Adolf
Kristallglas mit Schliff
(Kuppa 20teilig, Fuß
und Stiel 10teilig),
Silbergelb
H 21, Do 8,4 bzw. 8,5,
Du 8,5 bzw. 8,6
Ausst.:
WW 1967, Nr. 309
Lit.:
DKD 25/1909-10, S. 376
Kat. Neuwirth 1973,
Nr. 172, S. 308-309
Inv.: ÖMAK, Gl 3265 e,f
(inventarisiert 1964)

40
TWO GOBLETS
Design: Otto Prutscher
Manufacturer: probably
Meyr's Neffe, Adolf
Cut crystal glass,
silver-yellow
(bowl 20 sides, foot
and stem 10 sides),
H 21, Dt 8.4 bzw. 8.5,
Db 8.5 bzw. 8.6
Exhibition(s):
WW 1967, no. 309
Lit.:
DKD 25/1909-10, p. 376
Kat. Neuwirth 1973,
no. 172, pp. 308-309
Inv.: ÖMAK, Gl 3265 e,f
(inventoried 1964)

40

41

41
KELCHGLAS
Entwurf: Otto Prutscher
Ausführung: vermutlich
Meyr's Neffe, Adolf
Kristallglas mit Schliff
(Kuppa 24teilig, Fuß und
Stiel 12teilig)
H 20,9, Do 8,5, Du 8,8
Ausst.:
WW 1967, Nr. 309
Lit.:
Kat. Neuwirth 1973,
Nr. 172, S. 308-309
Inv.: ÖMAK, Gl 3265 c
(inventarisiert 1964)

41
GOBLET
Design: Otto Prutscher
Manufacturer: probably
Meyr's Neffe, Adolf
Cut crystal glass
(bowl 24 sides, foot and
stem 12 sides)
H 20.9, Dt 8.5, Db 8.8
Exhibition(s):
WW 1967, no. 309
Lit.:
Kat. Neuwirth 1973,
no. 172, pp. 308-309
Inv.: ÖMAK, Gl 3265 c
(inventoried 1964)

42

42
AUFSATZ
Entwurf: Oscar Strnad
Verleger: Lobmeyr, Wien
Kristallglas, oval,
20 Ecken
H 16,7, oben: 9,4 × 13,4,
unten: 14,5 × 20
Lit.: Neuwirth 1973,
Kat. Nr. 90, S. 214-215
Inv.: ÖMAK, W.I. 898
(inventarisiert am
21. 2. 1911, erworben um
73,50 Kronen von Lobmeyr)

42
CENTREPIECE
Design: Oscar Strnad
Commissioned by:
Lobmeyr, Vienna
Cut crystal glass, oval,
20 sides
H 16.7, 9.4 × 13.4 (top),
14.5 × 20 (bottom)
Lit.: Neuwirth 1973,
no. 90, pp. 214-215
Inv.: ÖMAK, W.I. 898
(inventoried 21/02/11;
acquired for 73.50 crowns
from Lobmeyr)

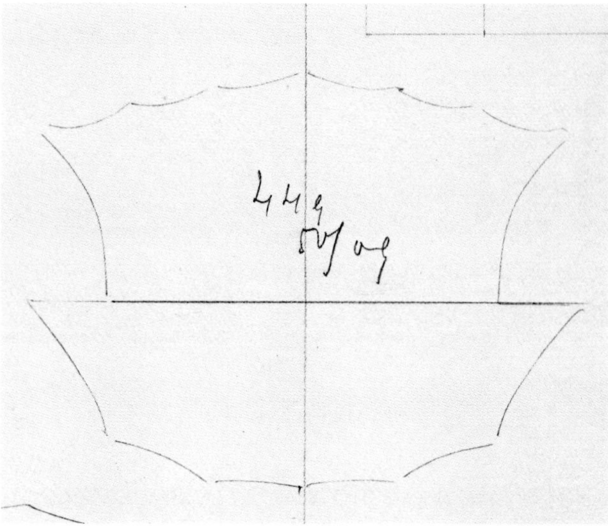

43
JARDINIERE
Werkskizze Nr. 449/09
bzw. 450/09
(Bakalowits, Wien)
H 5,8, L 14
Inv.: ÖMAK, B.I. 32066 c

43
JARDINIERE
Working sketch no. 449/09
and 450/09
(Bakalowits, Vienna)
H 5.8, L 14
Inv.: ÖMAK, B.I. 32066 c

43

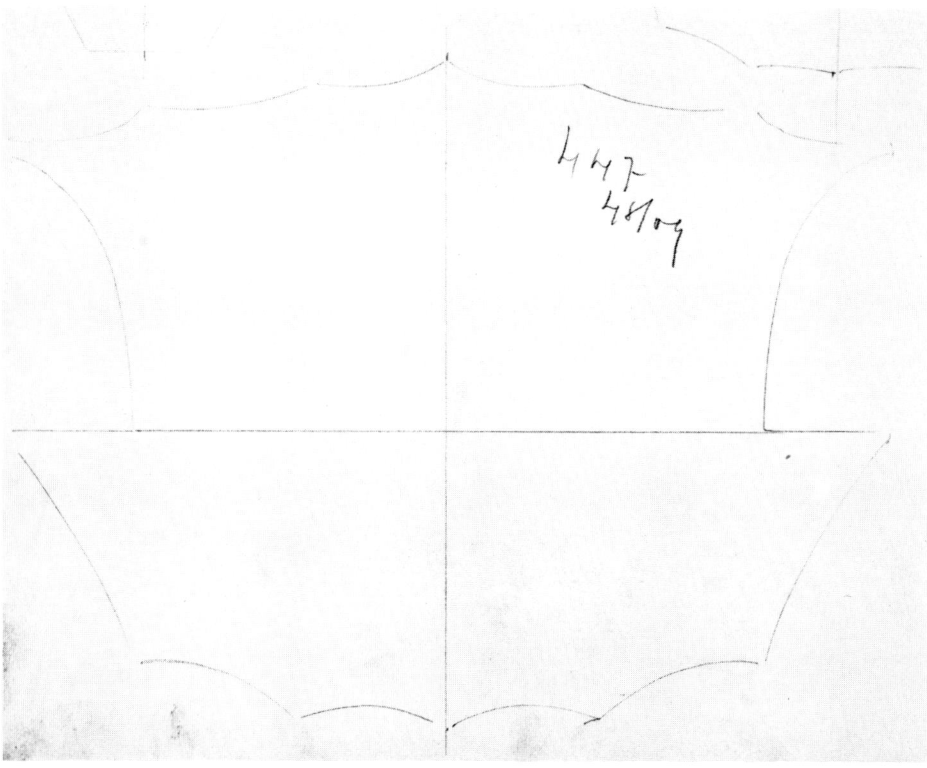

44

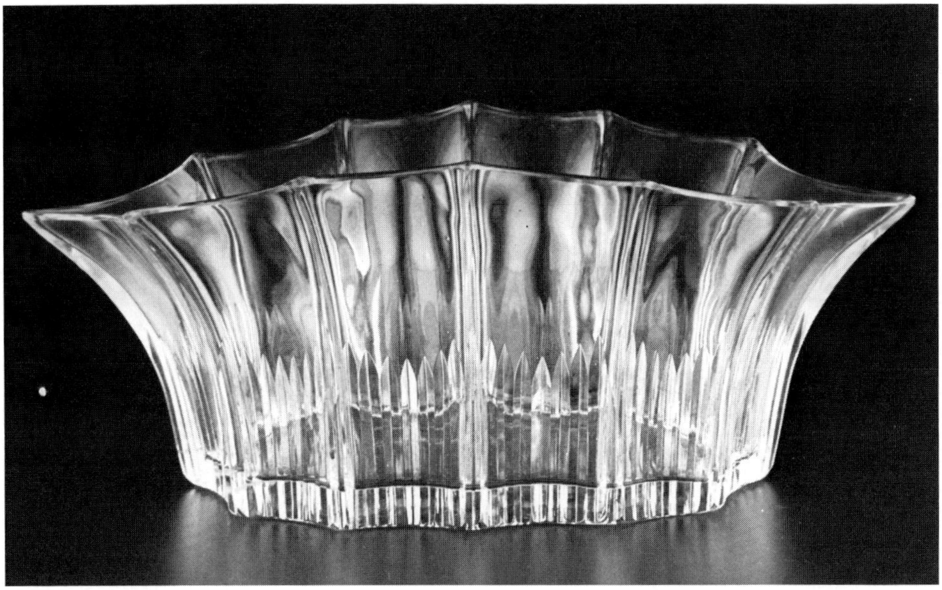

45

44
JARDINIERE
Werkskizze Nr. 447/09 bzw.
448/09 (Bakalowits, Wien)
H 10,3, L 25,5
Inv.: ÖMAK, B.I. 32066 c

44
JARDINIERE
Working sketch no. 447/09
and 448/09
(Bakalowits, Vienna)
H 10.3, L 25.5
Inv.: ÖMAK, B.I. 32066 c

45
JARDINIERE
Verleger: Bakalowits, Wien
Form: 12 Ecken
H 10,5, unten: 10,2 × 17,5
oben: 17,2 × 26
Lit.: Neuwirth 1973,
Kat. Nr. 21, S. 120-121
Inv.: ÖMAK, W.I. 755
(inventarisiert am
19. 4. 1910, erworben um
28 Kronen von Bakalowits)

45
JARDINIERE
Commissioned by:
Bakalowits, Vienna
Shape: 12 sides
H 10.5, 17.2 × 26 (top)
10.2 × 17.5 (bottom)
Lit.: Neuwirth 1973,
no. 21, pp. 120-121
Inv.: ÖMAK, W.I. 755
(inventoried 19/04/10;
acquired for 28 crowns
from Bakalowits)

PROFESSOR JOSEF HOFFMANN. »KRISTALLGLAS MIT REICHEM SCHLIFF« AUSFÜHRUNG: J. & L. LOBMEYR WIEN.

46

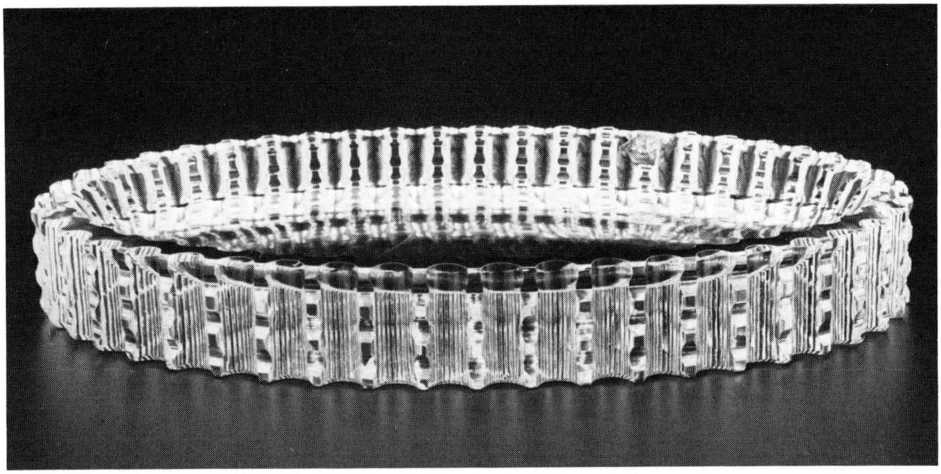

47

47
SCHALE
Entwurf:
Otto Hofner (Inventar)
oder Josef Hoffmann (DKD)
Verleger: Lobmeyr, Wien
Form: oval, geschliffen
H 3,1, oben 15,2 × 24
Ausst.: Köln 1914
Lit.: Neuwirth 1973,
Kat. Nr. 105, S. 230-231
Inv.: ÖMAK, W.I. 1629
(inventarisiert am
7. 7. 1915, erworben von
Lobmeyr um 50 Kronen)

47
BOWL
Design:
Otto Hofner (inventory)
or Josef Hoffmann (DKD)
Commissioned by:
Lobmeyr, Vienna
Shape: oval, cutting
H 3.1, top 15.2 × 24
Exhibition(s): Köln 1914
Lit.: Neuwirth 1973,
no. 105, pp. 230-231
Inv.: ÖMAK, W.I. 1629
(inventoried 07/07/15;
acquired for 50 crowns
from Lobmeyr)

46
GLASSES
Design: Josef Hoffmann
Commissioned by:
Lobmeyr, Vienna
Exhibition(s): Köln 1914
Reproduced from:
DKD 34/1914, p. 376

46
GLÄSER
Entwurf: Josef Hoffmann
Verleger: Lobmeyr, Wien
Ausst.: Köln 1914
Reproduktion aus:
DKD 34/1914, S. 376

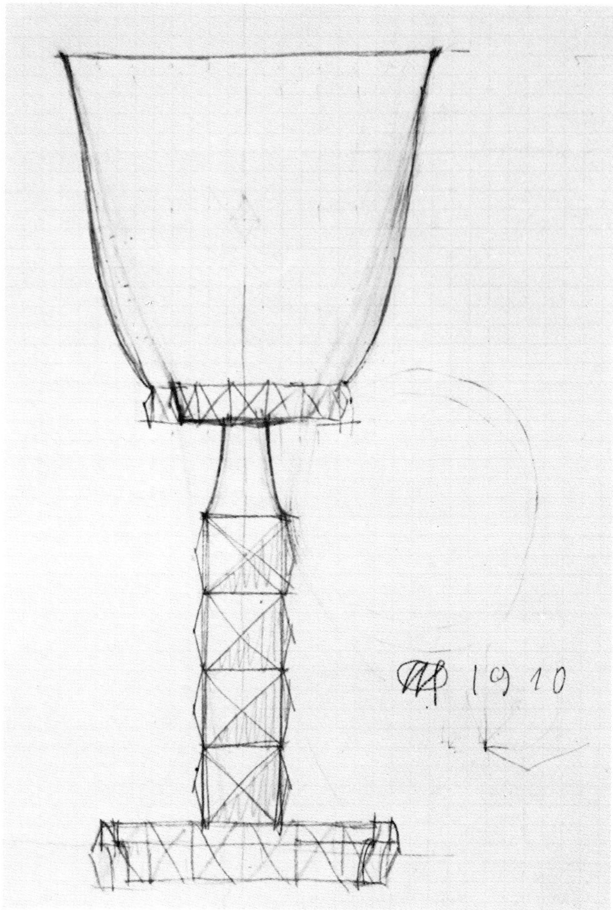

48

48
KELCHGLAS
Entwurf: Josef Hoffmann
sign. und dat.: JH 1910
H 21,5
Archiv Lobmeyr, Wien

48
GOBLET
Design: Josef Hoffmann
Signed and dated: JH 1910
H 21.5
Lobmeyr archives, Vienna

49
KELCHGLAS
Entwurf: Josef Hoffmann
Verleger: Lobmeyr, Wien
Diamantschliff
H 21,1, Do 9,7,
Fußplatte 8 × 8
Ausst.: Köln 1914
Lit.: WWMB 61, S. 455
(„Pokal Nr. 10“,Kommission von Lobmeyr 1914)
DKD 34/1914, S 376
Eisler 1916, S. 160
Neuwirth 1973, Nr. 111, S. 238
Inv.: ÖMAK, W.I. 1630/2
(inventarisiert am 7. 7. 1915, fünf Gläser – W.I. 1630/1-5 – erworben um 108 Kronen von Lobmeyr)

49
GOBLET
Design: Josef Hoffmann
Commissioned by: Lobmeyr, Vienna
Diamond cutting
H 21.1, Dt 9.7, base 8 × 8
Exhibition(s): Köln 1914
Lit.: WWMB 61, p. 455
("Goblet no. 10", commissioned by Lobmeyr 1914)
DKD 34/1914, S 376
Eisler 1916, p. 160
Neuwirth 1973, no. 111, p. 238
Inv.: ÖMAK, W.I. 1630/2
(inventoried 07/07/15; five glasses – W.I. 1630/1-5 – acquired for 108 crowns from Lobmeyr)

49

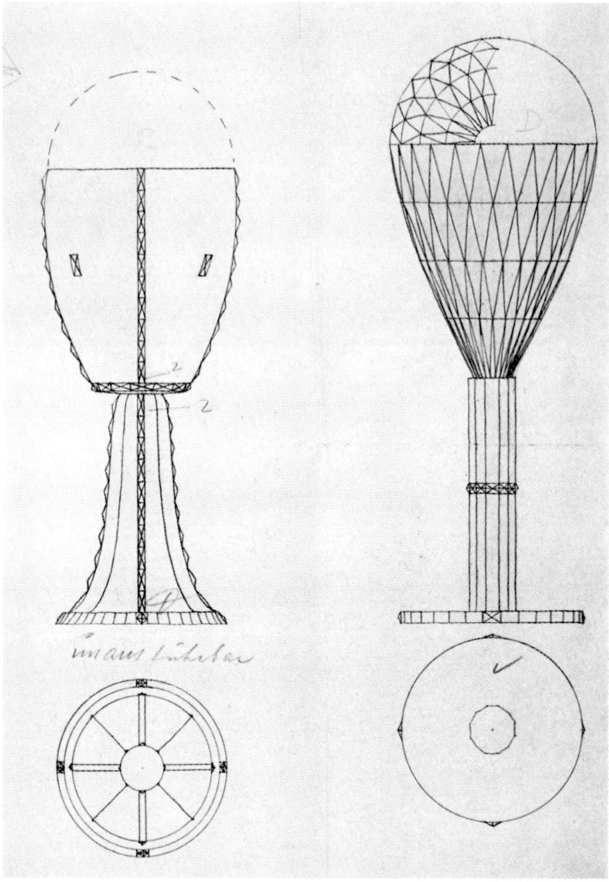

50

51
GOBLET
Design: Josef Hoffmann
Commissioned by:
Lobmeyr, Vienna
bowl bevel cut,
stem: 12 sides
H 20.7, Dt 9.2, Db 8.5
Exhibition(s):
Köln 1914. – ÖMAK 1973
Lit.:
WWMB 61, p. 456
(commissioned by
Lobmeyr 1914, "goblet
no. 11")
DKD 34/1914, p. 376
Eisler 1916, p. 160
Neuwirth 1973, no. 110,
p. 236
Inv.: ÖMAK, W.I. 1267
(inventoried 07/01/14;
acquired for 31.5 crowns
from Lobmeyr)

50
ZWEI KELCHGLÄSER
Entwurf: Josef Hoffmann
Verleger: Lobmeyr, Wien
Bez.: „unausführbar"
(Glas links)
H 19,4 bzw. 20,5
Archiv Lobmeyr, Wien

50
TWO GOBLETS
Design: Josef Hoffmann
Commissioned by:
Lobmeyr, Vienna
Description: "unmakeable"
(left-hand glass)
H 19.4 and 20.5
Lobmeyr archives, Vienna

51
KELCHGLAS
Entwurf: Josef Hoffmann
Verleger: Lobmeyr, Wien
Stiel: 12 Ecken, Kuppa facettiert geschliffen
H 20,7, Do 9,2, Du 8,5
Ausst.:
Köln 1914. – ÖMAK 1973
Lit.:
WWMB 61, S. 456 (Kommission Lobmeyr 1914, „Pokal No 11")
DKD 34/1914, S. 376
Eisler 1916, S. 160
Neuwirth 1973, Nr. 110, S. 236
Inv.: ÖMAK, W.I. 1267 (inventarisiert am 7. 1. 1914, erworben um 31,5 Kronen von Lobmeyr)

51

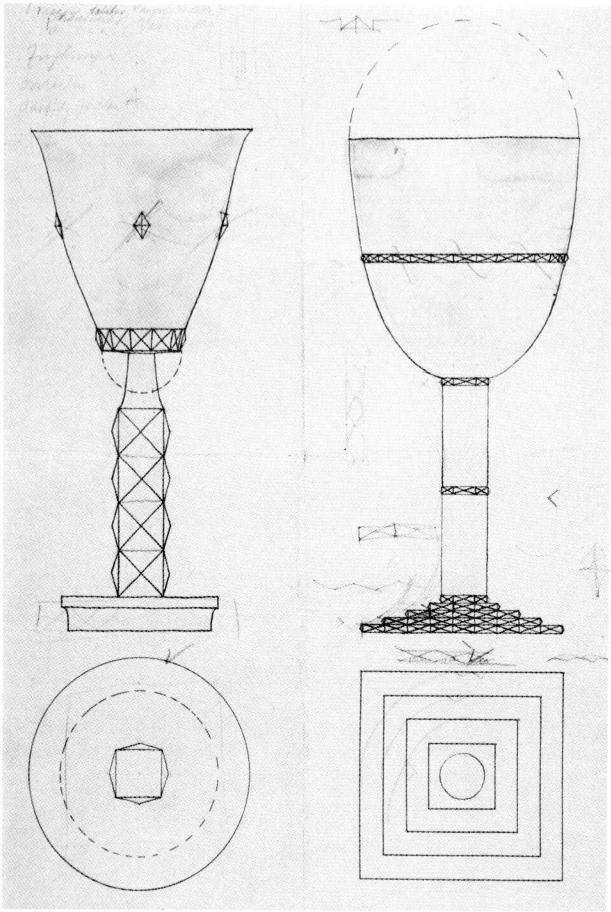

52

52
ZWEI KELCHGLÄSER
Entwurf: Josef Hoffmann
Verleger: Lobmeyr, Wien
H 21,4 bzw. 21
Archiv Lobmeyr, Wien

52
TWO GOBLETS
Design: Josef Hoffmann
Commissioned by:
Lobmeyr, Vienna
H 21.4 and 21
Lobmeyr archives, Vienna

53
GOBLET
Design: Josef Hoffmann
Commissioned by:
Lobmeyr, Vienna
Shape: square foot, four steps, cutting
H 20.9, Dt 9.4,
foot 8.6 × 8.6
Exhibition(s):
Köln 1914. – ÖMAK 1973
Lit.:
WWMB 61, p. 454 ("Goblet no. 9", commissioned by Lobmeyr 1914)
DKD 34/1914, p. 376
Eisler 1916, p. 160
Neuwirth 1973, no. 111, p. 238
Inv.: ÖMAK, W.I. 1630/5 (inventoried 07/07/15; five glasses – W.I. 1630/1-5 – acquired for 108 crowns from Lobmeyr)

53
KELCHGLAS
Entwurf: Josef Hoffmann
Verleger: Lobmeyr, Wien
Fuß quadratisch, vierfach abgetreppt, geschliffen
H 20,9, Do 9,4,
Fuß 8,6 × 8,6
Ausst.:
Köln 1914. – ÖMAK 1973
Lit.:
WWMB 61, S. 454 („Pokal No 9", Kommission Lobmeyr 1914)
DKD 34/1914, S. 376
Eisler 1916, S. 160
Neuwirth 1973, Nr. 111, S. 238
Inv.: ÖMAK, W.I. 1630/5 (inventarisiert am 7. 7. 1915, fünf Gläser – W.I. 1630/1-5 – erworben um 108 Kronen von Lobmeyr)

53

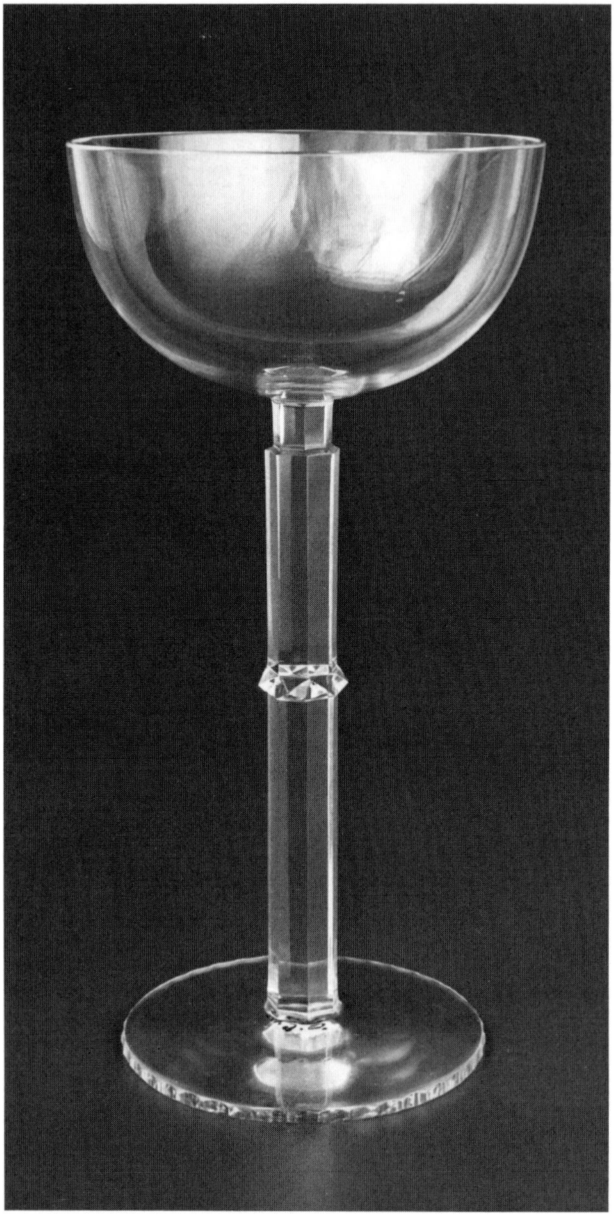

54

54
KELCHGLAS
Entwurf: Josef Hoffmann
Verleger: Lobmeyr, Wien
Stiel sechsseitig geschliffen
H 19,3, Do 9,8, Du 8,2
Ausst.:
Köln 1914. – ÖMAK 1973
Lit.:
WWMB 61, S. 457 („Weinglas No 12", Kommission Lobmeyr 1914)
DKD 34/1914, S. 376
Eisler 1916, S. 160
Neuwirth 1973, Nr. 111, S. 238-239
Inv.: ÖMAK, W.I. 1630/1 (inventarisiert am 7. 7. 1915, fünf Gläser – W.I. 1630/1-5 – erworben um 108 Kronen von Lobmeyr)

54
GOBLET
Design: Josef Hoffmann
Commissioned by: Lobmeyr, Vienna
Shape: hexagonal cut stem
H 19.3, Dt 9.8, Db 8.2
Exhibition(s):
Köln 1914. – ÖMAK 1973
Lit.:
WWMB 61, p. 457 ("Wine glass no. 12", commissioned by Lobmeyr 1914)
DKD 34/1914, p. 376
Eisler 1916, p. 160
Neuwirth 1973, no. 111, pp. 238-239
Inv.: ÖMAK, W.I. 1630/1 (inventoried 07/07/15; five glasses – W.I. 1630/1-5 – acquired for 108 crowns from Lobmeyr)

55
BLUMENGLAS
Entwurf: Josef Hoffmann
Verleger: Lobmeyr, Wien
Form: runder Querschnitt, Fuß geschliffen
H 18,1, Do 14,9, Du 10
Ausst.:
Köln 1914. – ÖMAK 1973
Lit.:
WWMB 61, S. 452 („Vase No 7", Kommission Lobmeyr 1914)
DKD 34/1914, S. 376
Eisler 1916, S. 160
Robert Schmidt, 100 Jahre österreichische Glaskunst Lobmeyr 1823-1923, Wien 1925, Taf. 18
Neuwirth 1973, Nr. 111, S. 237-238
Inv.: ÖMAK, W.I. 1630/4 (inventarisiert am 7. 7. 1915, fünf Gläser – W.I. 1630/1-5 – erworben um 108 Kronen von Lobmeyr)

55

55
FLOWER VASE
Design: Josef Hoffmann
Commissioned by: Lobmeyr, Vienna
Shape: round cross-section, cut foot
H 18.1, Dt 14.9, Db 10
Exhibition(s):
Köln 1914. – ÖMAK 1973
Lit.:
WWMB 61, p. 452 ("Vase no. 7", commissioned by Lobmeyr 1914)
DKD 34/1914, p. 376
Eisler 1916, p. 160
Robert Schmidt, 100 Jahre österreichische Glaskunst Lobmeyr 1823-1923, Vienna 1925, Taf. 18
Neuwirth 1973, no. 111, pp. 237-238
Inv.: ÖMAK, W.I. 1630/4 (inventoried 07/07/15; five glasses – W.I. 1630/1-5 – acquired for 108 crowns from Lobmeyr)

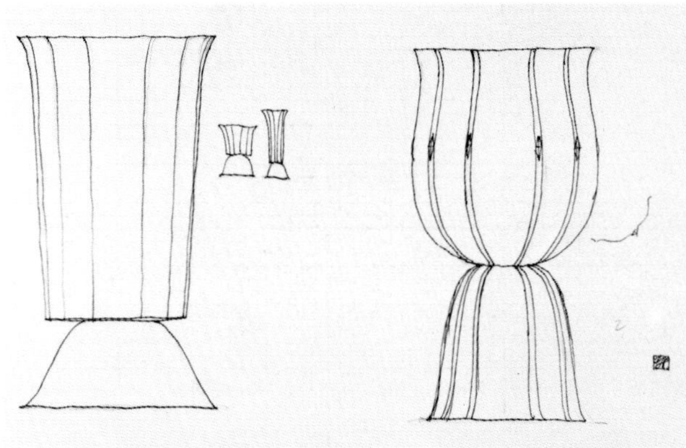

56

56
ZWEI VASEN
Entwurf: Josef Hoffmann
Verleger: Lobmeyr, Wien
Sign.: Monogramm JH
H 14,5 (beide)
Archiv Lobmeyr, Wien

56
TWO VASES
Design: Josef Hoffmann
Commissioned by:
Lobmeyr, Vienna
Singed: monogram JH
H 14.5 (both)
Lobmeyr archives, Vienna

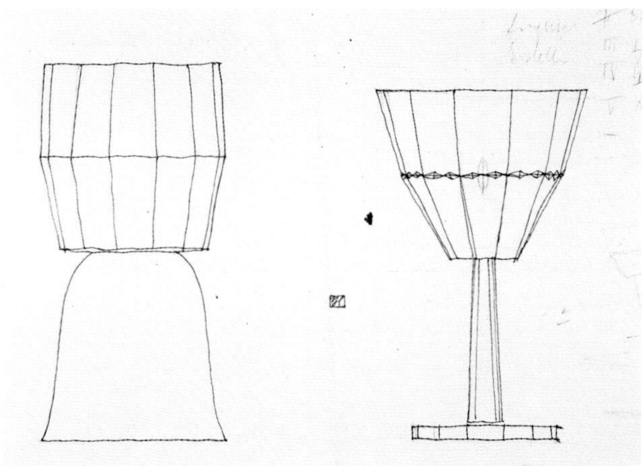

57

57
VASEN
Entwurf: Josef Hoffmann
Verleger: Lobmeyr, Wien
Sign.: JH-Monogramm
H 15,6 bzw. 14,5
Archiv Lobmeyr, Wien

57
VASES
Design: Josef Hoffmann
Commissioned by:
Lobmeyr, Vienna
Signed: monogram JH
H 15.6 and 14.5
Lobmeyr archives, Vienna

58
ZWEI VASEN
Entwurf: Josef Hoffmann
Verleger: Lobmeyr, Wien
Sign.: Monogramm JH
H 11,5 bzw. 13,5
Die Vase rechts
ursprünglich in der
Sammlung des ÖMAK
(W.I. 1630/3)
Archiv Lobmeyr, Wien

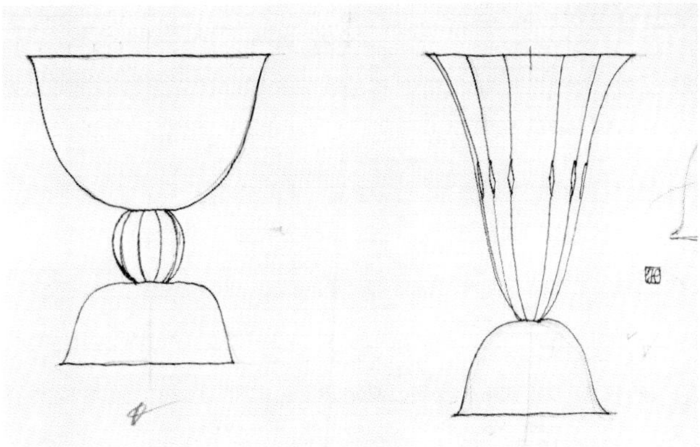

58

58
TWO VASES
Design: Josef Hoffmann
Commissioned by:
Lobmeyr, Vienna
Signed: monogram JH
H 11.5 and 13.5
Right-hand vase
originally in the
ÖMAK collection
(Inv. W.I. 1630/3)
Lobmeyr archives, Vienna

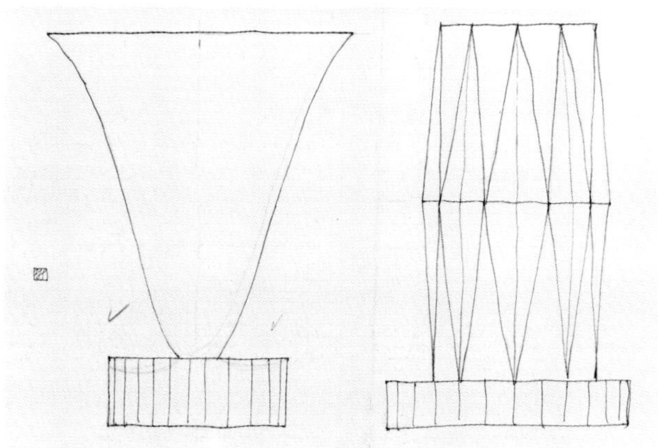

59

59
ZWEI VASEN
Entwurf: Josef Hoffmann
Verleger: Lobmeyr, Wien
Sign.: Monogramm JH
H 17,5 bzw. 18
Archiv Lobmeyr, Wien

59
TWO VASES
Design: Josef Hoffmann
Commissioned by:
Lobmeyr, Vienna
Signed: monogram JH
H 17.5 and 18
Lobmeyr archives, Vienna

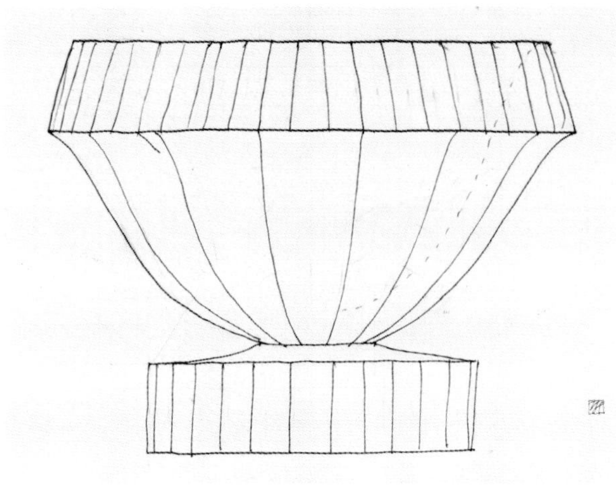

60

60
JARDINIERE
Entwurf: Josef Hoffmann
Verleger: Lobmeyr, Wien
Sign.: Monogramm JH
H 16
Archiv Lobmeyr, Wien

60
JARDINIERE
Design: Josef Hoffmann
Commissioned by:
Lobmeyr, Vienna
Signed: monogram JH
H 16
Lobmeyr archives, Vienna

61
VERSCHIEDENE OBJEKTE
Entwurf: Josef Hoffmann
Verleger: Lobmeyr, Wien
Sign.: Monogramm JH
H (Deckeldose Mitte): 10,5
Archiv Lobmeyr, Wien

61
VARIOUS OBJECTS
Design: Josef Hoffmann
Commissioned by:
Lobmeyr, Vienna
Signed: monogram JH
H (middle box): 10.5
Lobmeyr archives, Vienna

62
STEHLAMPE
Entwurf von
Josef Hoffmann
H 9
Detail aus Kat. Nr. 61

62
TABLE LAMP
Design by Josef Hoffmann
H 9
Detail from cat. no. 61

63
STEHLAMPE
Entwurf: Josef Hoffmann
Verleger: Lobmeyr, Wien
Ursprünglich in der Sammlung des ÖMAK (W.I. 1634, inventarisiert am 7. 7. 1915, erworben um 300 Kronen von Lobmeyr, Leihgabe an die Gesandtschaft in Bukarest, von dort nicht mehr zurückerhalten)
Ausst.: Köln 1914
Lit.: WWMB 61, S. 481 („Stehlampe No 40", Kommission Lobmeyr 1914, Schirm „Wasserfall")
Reproduktion aus:
DKD 34/1914, S. 375

63
TABLE LAMP
Design: Josef Hoffmann
Commissioned by:
Lobmeyr, Vienna
Originally in the ÖMAK collection (W.I. 1634, inventoried 07/07/15, acquired for 300 crowns from Lobmeyr, loaned to the embassy in Bucharest, not returned from there)
Exhibition(s): Köln 1914
Lit.: WWMB 61, p. 481 ("Table lamp no. 40", commissioned by Lobmeyr 1914, lampshade "waterfall")
Reproduced from:
DKD 34/1914, p. 375

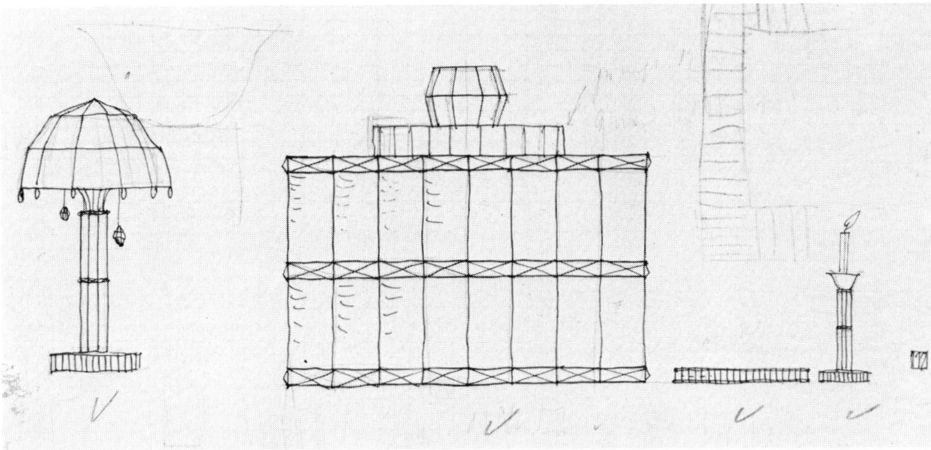

61

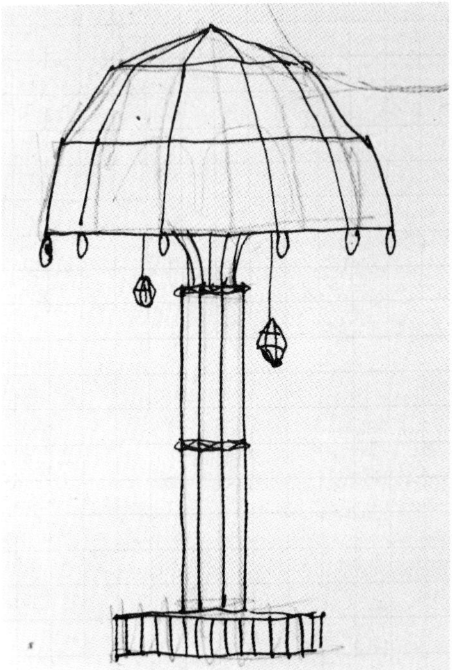

62

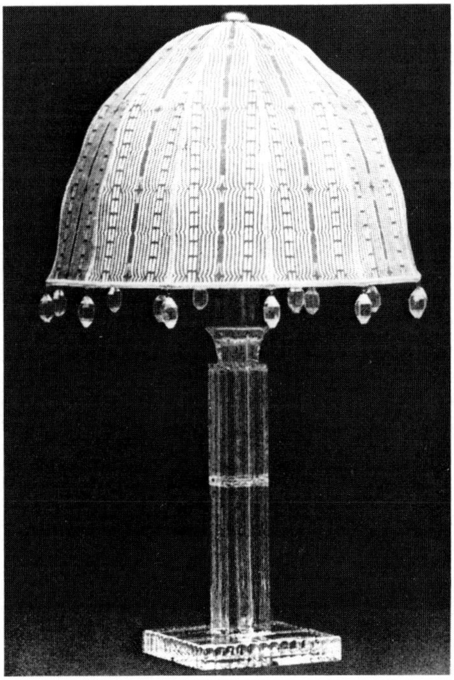

63

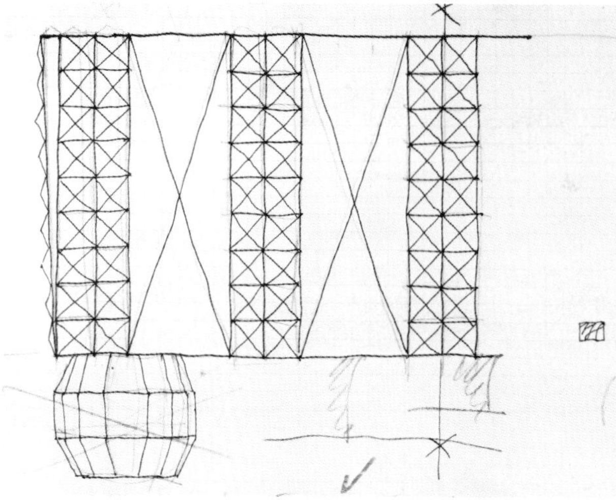

64

64
JARDINIERE
Entwurf: Josef Hoffmann
Verleger: Lobmeyr, Wien
Sign.: Monogramm JH,
bez.: „Hiezu 1 Seitenstück"
H 12,4 (mit Fuß) bzw. 9
Archiv Lobmeyr, Wien

65
JARDINIERE MIT PLATTE
Entwurf: Josef Hoffmann
Verleger: Lobmeyr, Wien
Viereckige Form, Diamantschliff (Jardinière)
Jardinière: H 10,5,
oben 8,2 × 13,7,
unten 7,3 × 12,7
Platte: H 1,7, 12,4 × 18,1
Ausst.: Köln 1914
Lit.: Neuwirth 1973,
Nr. 107, S. 232-233
Inv.: ÖMAK, W.I. 1626/3
(Jardinière),
W.I. 1626/4 (Platte)
(inventarisiert am
7. 7. 1915, Kat. Nrn.
65-66 erworben um
243 Kronen von Lobmeyr)

64
JARDINIERE
Design: Josef Hoffmann
Commissioned by:
Lobmeyr, Vienna
Signed: monogram JH
Description:
"with matching side piece"
H 12.4 (with foot) and 9
Lobmeyr archives, Vienna

66

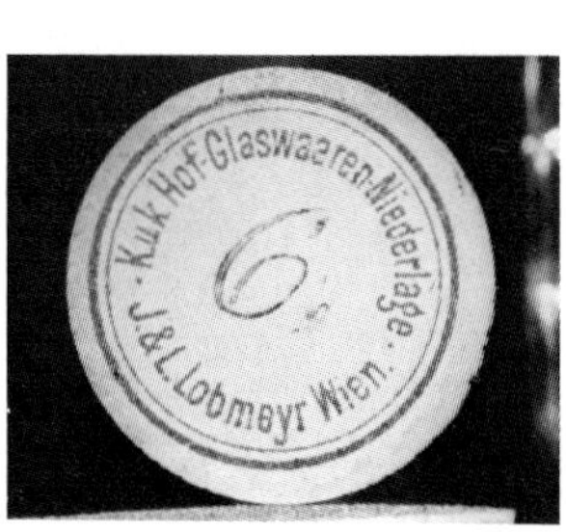

65

65
JARDINIERE WITH PLATE
Design: Josef Hoffmann
Commissioned by:
Lobmeyr, Vienna
Square shape, diamond
cutting (jardinière)
Jardinière: H 10.5,
8.2 × 13.7 (top),
7.3 × 12.7 (bottom)
Plate: H 1.7, 12.4 × 18.1
Exhibition(s): Köln 1914
Lit.: Neuwirth 1973,
no. 107, pp. 232-233
Inv.: ÖMAK, W.I. 1626/3
(jardinière),
W.I. 1626/4 (plate)
(inventoried 07/07/15;
cat. nos. 65-66 acquired
for 243 crowns from
Lobmeyr)

66
JARDINIERE WITH PLATE
Design: Josef Hoffmann
Commissioned by:
Lobmeyr, Vienna
Square shape, diamond
cutting (jardinière)
Jardinière: H 10.5,
13.7 × 24.7 (top),
23.2 × 12.7 (bottom)
Plate: H 1.7, 19.1 × 30.2
Exhibition(s): Köln 1914
Lit.: WWMB 61, p. 458
("jardinière no 13",
commissioned by
Lobmeyr 1914)
Neuwirth 1973, no. 107,
pp. 232-233
Inv.: ÖMAK, W.I. 1626/1
(Jardinière),
W.I. 1626/2 (plate)
(inventoried 07/07/15;
cat. nos. 65-66 acquired
for 243 crowns from
Lobmeyr)

65

67
PUNCH GLASS,
Design: Josef Hoffmann
Commissioned by:
Lobmeyr, Vienna
Shape: round bowl,
cut foot, seven-sided
H 13, Dt 9.3, Db 6.3
Exhibition(s):
Köln 1914. – ÖMAK 1973
Lit.:
DKD 34/1914, p. 376
Neuwirth 1973, no. 109,
p. 234
Inv.: ÖMAK, W.I. 1631/1
(inventoried 07/07/15;
acquired from Lobmeyr,
Vienna; no prices given)

66
JARDINIERE MIT PLATTE
Entwurf: Josef Hoffmann
Verleger: Lobmeyr, Wien
Viereckige Form, Diamantschliff (Jardinière)
Jardinière: H 10,5,
oben 13,7 × 24,7,
unten 23,2 × 12,7
Platte: H 1,7, 19,1 × 30,2
Ausst.: Köln 1914
Lit.: WWMB 61, S. 458
(„Blumenschale No 13",
Kommission Lobmeyr 1914)
Neuwirth 1973, Nr. 107,
S. 232-233
Inv.: ÖMAK, W.I. 1626/1
(Jardinière),
W.I. 1626/2 (Platte)
(inventarisiert am
7. 7. 1915, Kat. Nrn.
65-66 erworben um
243 Kronen von Lobmeyr)

66

67

68

67
PUNSCHGLAS
Entwurf: Josef Hoffmann
Verleger: Lobmeyr, Wien
Form: runde Kuppa,
Fuß siebenmal geschliffen
H 13, Do 9,3, Du 6,3
Ausst.:
Köln 1914. – ÖMAK 1973
Lit.: DKD 34/1914, S. 376
Neuwirth 1973, Nr. 109,
S. 234
Inv.: ÖMAK, W.I. 1631/1
(inventar. am 7. 7. 1915,
erworben von Lobmeyr,
Wien; keine Preisangabe)

68
BONBONSCHALE
Entwurf: Josef Hoffmann
Verleger: Lobmeyr, Wien
Form: runde Kuppa, Fuß
zehnmal geschliffen
H 12,2, Do 15, Du 9,7
Ausst. und Lit. wie
Kat. Nr. 67
Inv.: ÖMAK, W.I. 1631/2
(vgl. Kat. Nr. 67)

68
CHOCOLATE DISH
Design: Josef Hoffmann
Commissioned by:
Lobmeyr, Vienna
Shape: round bowl, cut
foot, ten-sided
H 12.2, Dt 15, Db 9.7
Exhibition(s) and
Lit.: cf. cat. no. 67
Inv.: ÖMAK, W.I. 1631/2
(cf. cat. no. 67)

69
PUNSCHBOWLE
Entwurf: Josef Hoffmann
Verleger: Lobmeyr, Wien
Form: Bowle mit Deckel,
massiver Fuß zehnmal
geschliffen
H 34,1, Dg 23,5, Du 14,2
Lit. und Ausst.: wie
Kat. Nr. 76
Inv.: ÖMAK, W.I. 1631/3
(vgl. Kat. Nr. 67)

69
PUNCH BOWL
Design: Josef Hoffmann
Commissioned by:
Lobmeyr, Vienna
Shape: bowl with lid,
solid foot, cut ten-sided
H 34.1, Dm 23.5, Db 14.2
Exhibition(s) and
Lit.: cf. cat. no. 67
Inv.: ÖMAK, W.I. 1631/3
(cf. cat. no. 67)

69

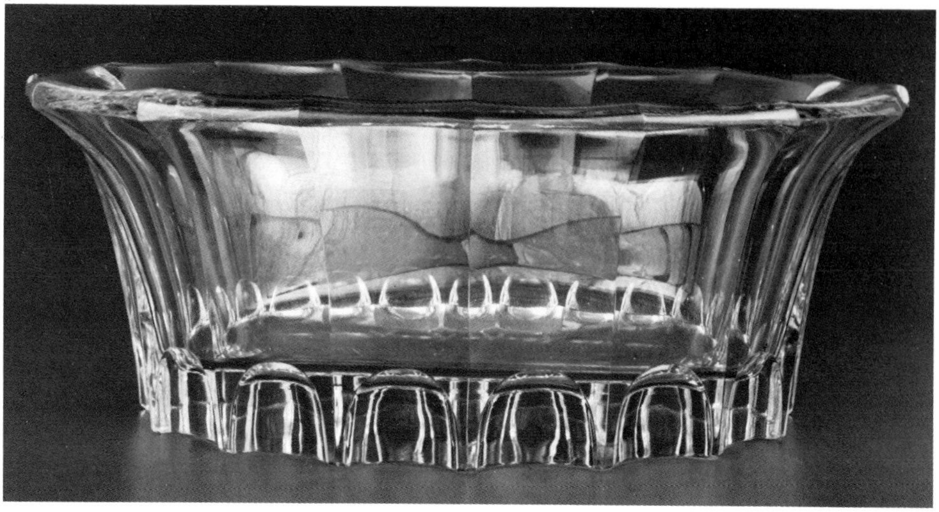

70

70
JARDINIERE
Entwurf: Stephan Rath, 1912
Verleger: Lobmeyr, Wien
Form: oval, geschliffener Fuß (16 Ecken)
H 14,2, 23,8 × 37,7
Ausst.: Stockholm 1916

Lit.:
DKD 35/1914-15, S. 435
Eisler 1916, S. 160
Robert Schmidt, 100 Jahre österreichische Glaskunst, Lobmeyr 1823-1923, Wien 1925, Taf. 18
Neuwirth 1973, Nr. 108, S. 232-233

Inv.: ÖMAK, W.I. 1165 (inventarisiert am 15. 7. 1912, erworben um 262,50 Kronen von Lobmeyr, Wien)

71

70
JARDINIERE
Design: Stephan Rath, 1912
Commissioned by: Lobmeyr, Vienna
Shape: oval, cut foot (16 sides)
H 14.2, 23.8 × 37.7
Exhibition(s): Stockholm 1916
Lit.:
DKD 35/1914-15, p. 435
Eisler 1916, p. 160
Robert Schmidt, 100 Jahre österreichische Glaskunst, Lobmeyr 1823-1923, Vienna 1925, Taf. 18
Neuwirth 1973, no. 108, pp. 232-233
Inv.: ÖMAK, W.I. 1165 (inventoried 15/07/12; acquired for 262.50 crowns from Lobmeyr, Vienna)

72
VASE
Verleger: Lobmeyr, Wien
Form: 8 Ecken, geschliffen
H 35,7, Do 15,2, Du 10,5
Ausst.:
ÖMKI 1915. – ÖMAK 1973
Lit.:
DKD 35/1914-15, S. 435
Neuwirth 1973, Nr. 106,
S. 232
Inv.: ÖMAK, W.I. 1671
(inventarisiert am
1. 4. 1916, erworben um
103 Kronen von Lobmeyr)

72
VASE
Commissioned by:
Lobmeyr, Vienna
Cut crystal glass
Shape: 8 sides
H 35.7, Dt 15.2, Db 10.5
Exhibition(s):
ÖMKI 1915. – ÖMAK 1973
Lit.:
DKD 35/1914-15, p. 435
Neuwirth 1973, no. 106,
p. 232
Inv.: ÖMAK, W.I. 1671
(inventoried 01/04/16;
acquired for 103 crowns
from Lobmeyr)

71
ZWEI AUFSÄTZE
Verleger: Lobmeyr, Wien
Inv.: ÖMAK, VS 173 C
(zeitgenössisches Foto)

71
TWO CENTREPIECES
Commissioned by:
Lobmeyr, Vienna
Inv.: ÖMAK, VS 173 C
(contemporary photograph)

72

73
DECKELGEFÄSS
Gebrüder Lorenz, Steinschönau
„Deckelgefäß in Krystallschliff"
Reproduktion aus: Pazaurek 1925, S. 129

73
LIDDED JAR
Gebrüder Lorenz, Steinschönau
("Lidded jar with crystal cutting")
Reproduced from: Pazaurek 1925, p. 129

73

74

74
BECHER
Entwurf: Philipp (lt. Inventar)
Verleger: Lobmeyr, Wien
Form: unten geschliffen (16 Ecken), Motiv auf der Wandung zweimal wiederholt
H 10,8, Do 7, Du 5,4
Inv.: ÖMAK, W.I. 902 (inventarisiert am 21. 1. 1911, erworben um 24,30 Kronen von Lobmeyr)

75
DECKELPOKAL
Entwurf: Fritz Alber
Verleger: Lobmeyr, Wien
Form: massives Glas, abgestuft geschliffenes Motiv der Wandung in viermaliger Wiederholung
H 23,9, Du 8,5,
D Mundrand 9,2, Dg 11,7
Klebeetikett: „No. 41 M“
Ausst.: ÖMKI 1909/10
(Foto ÖMAK Inv. VS 174 B)
ÖMAK 1973
Lit.: KKH 13/1910, S. 676
DK XIX/1911, S. 232
Neuwirth 1973, Nr. 84, S. 208-209
Inv.: ÖMAK, W.I. 901
(inventarisiert am 21. 2. 1911, erworben um 86 Kronen von Lobmeyr)

75

74
BEAKER
Design: Philipp (inventory)
Commissioned by: Lobmeyr, Vienna
Shape: cut bottom (16 sides), motif on side repeated twice
H 10.8, Dt 7, Db 5.4
Inv.: ÖMAK, W.I. 902
(inventoried 21/01/11; acquired for 24.30 crowns from Lobmeyr)

75
LIDDED GOBLET
Design: Fritz Alber
Commissioned by: Lobmeyr, Vienna
Shape: solid glass, stepped, cut motif on side repeated four times
H 23.9, Db 8.5,
D (lip) 9.2, Dm 11.7
Label with "No. 41 M"

Exhibition(s):
ÖMKI 1909/10 (photograph ÖMAK, VS 174 B)
ÖMAK 1973
Lit.: KKH 13/1910, p. 676
DK XIX/1911, p. 232
Neuwirth 1973, no. 84, pp. 208-209
Inv.: ÖMAK, W.I. 901
(inventoried 21/02/11; acquired for 86 crowns from Lobmeyr)

76
VASE UND SCHALE
Entwurf: Otto Hofner
Verleger: Lobmeyr, Wien
Reproduktion aus:
DKD 34/1914, S. 374

76
VASE AND DISH
Design: Otto Hofner
Commissioned by:
Lobmeyr, Vienna
Reproduced from:
DKD 34/1914, p. 374

76

77
SCHALE
Entwurf: Otto Hofner
Verleger: Lobmeyr, Wien
Form: massives Glas mit
11teiligem Schliff
H 11, Do 20, Du 14
Ausst.:
Köln 1914. – ÖMAK 1973
Lit.: DKD 34/1914, S. 374
Eisler 1916, S. 160
Neuwirth 1973, Nr. 112,
S. 240
Inv.: ÖMAK, Gl 3135
(1954 nachträglich
inventarisiert)

77
DISH
Design: Otto Hofner
Commissioned by:
Lobmeyr, Vienna
Shape: solid glass, cut,
11 sides
H 11, Dt 20, Db 14
Exhibition(s):
Köln 1914. – ÖMAK 1973
Lit.: DKD 34/1914, p. 374
Eisler 1916, p. 160
Neuwirth 1973, no. 112,
p. 240
Inv.: ÖMAK, Gl 3135
(inventoried only 1954)

77

78
BOTTLE
FROM A TOILET SET
Design: Lobmeyr
company's own design
Commissioned by:
Lobmeyr, Vienna
Cut crystal glass
Shape: oval,
22-sided (bottle) and
12-sided (stopper)
H 13, 6.7 × 9.5 (bottom),
7.1 × 10 (shoulder)
Exhibition(s): Köln 1914
Lit.: Neuwirth 1973,
no. 104, p. 230
Inv.: ÖMAK, W.I. 1628/3
(inventoried 07/07/15;
cat. nos. 78-81 acquired
for 104.50 crowns from
Lobmeyr, Vienna)

78

78
FLAKON AUS EINER TOILETTEGARNITUR
Entwurf: eigener Entwurf Firma Lobmeyr
Verleger: Lobmeyr, Wien
Form: oval, 22teiliger (Gefäß) bzw. 12 teiliger (Stöpsel) Schliff
H 13, unten 6,7 × 9,5, Schulter 7,1 × 10
Ausst.: Köln 1914
Lit.: Neuwirth 1973, Nr. 104, S. 230

Inv.: ÖMAK, W.I. 1628/3 (inventarisiert am 7. 7. 1915, Kat. Nrn. 78-81 erworben um 104,50 Kronen von Lobmeyr, Wien)

79

79
POWDER PUFF
FROM A TOILET SET
Design: Lobmeyr
company's own design
Commissioned by:
Lobmeyr, Vienna
Cut crystal glass
Shape: oval, 26 sides
H 7.5, 8 × 11 (bottom),
8.7 × 12 (lid)
Exhibition(s): Köln 1914
Lit.: Neuwirth 1973,
no. 104, p. 230
Inv.: ÖMAK, W.I. 1628/4
(inventoried 07/07/15;
cat. nos. 78-81 acquired
for 104.50 crowns from
Lobmeyr, Vienna)

79
PUDERDOSE AUS EINER
TOILETTEGARNITUR
Entwurf: eigener Entwurf
Firma Lobmeyr
Verleger: Lobmeyr, Wien
Form: oval,
Schliff (26 Ecken)
H 7,5, unten 8 × 11,
Deckel 8,7 × 12
Ausst.: Köln 1914
Lit.: Neuwirth 1973,
Nr. 104, S. 230
Inv.: ÖMAK, W.I. 1628/4
(inventarisiert am
7. 7. 1915, Kat. Nrn.
78-81 erworben um
104,50 Kronen von
Lobmeyr, Wien)

80
NEEDLE BOWL
FROM A TOILET SET
Design: Lobmeyr
company's own design
Commissioned by:
Lobmeyr, Vienna
Cut crystal glass
Shape: oval, 32 sides
H 3.9 × 15
Exhibition(s): Köln 1914
Lit.: Neuwirth 1973,
no. 104, pp. 230-231
Inv.: ÖMAK, W.I. 1628/2
(inventoried 07/07/15;
cat. nos. 78-81 acquired
for 104.50 crowns from
Lobmeyr, Vienna)

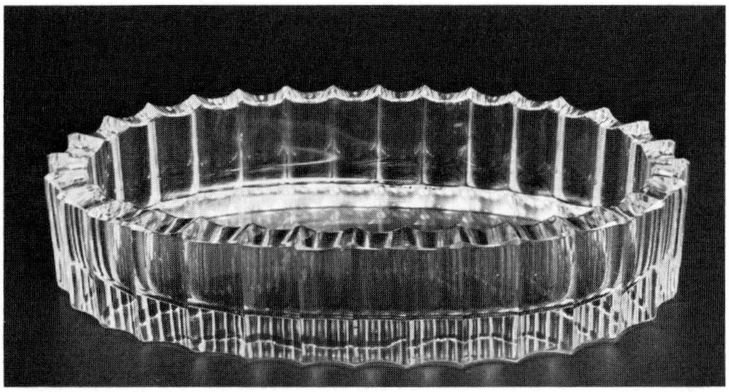

80

80
NADELSCHALE AUS EINER TOILETTEGARNITUR
Entwurf: eigener Entwurf Firma Lobmeyr
Verleger: Lobmeyr, Wien
Form: oval,
Schliff (32 Ecken)
H 3, 9 × 15
Ausst.: Köln 1914
Lit.: Neuwirth 1973, Nr. 104, S. 230-231
Inv.: ÖMAK, W.I. 1628/2 (inventarisiert am 7. 7. 1915, Kat. Nrn. 78-81 erworben um 104,50 Kronen von Lobmeyr, Wien)

81
KAMMSCHALE AUS EINER TOILETTEGARNITUR
Entwurf: eigener Entwurf Firma Lobmeyr
Verleger: Lobmeyr, Wien
Form: oval,
Schliff (44 Ecken)
H 36, 11 × 25
Ausst.: Köln 1914
Lit.:
Neuwirth 1973, Nr. 104, S. 230-231
Inv.: ÖMAK, W.I. 1628/1 (inventarisiert am 7. 7. 1915, Kat. Nrn. 78-81 erworben um 104,50 Kronen von Lobmeyr, Wien)

81
COMB BOWL FROM A TOILET SET
Design: Lobmeyr company's own design
Commissioned by: Lobmeyr, Vienna
Cut crystal glass
Shape: oval, 44 sides
H 36, 11 × 25
Exhibition(s): Köln 1914
Lit.:
Neuwirth 1973, no. 104, pp. 230-231
Inv.: ÖMAK, W.I. 1628/1 (inventoried 07/07/15; cat. nos. 78-81 acquired for 104.50 crowns from Lobmeyr, Vienna)

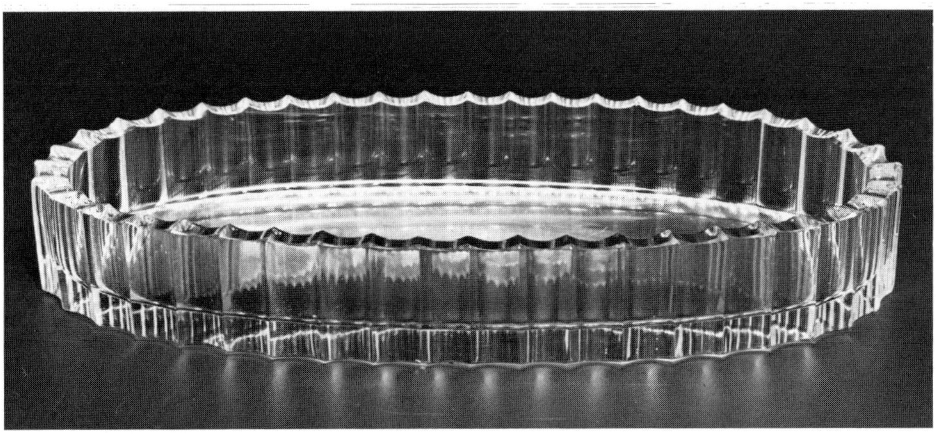

81

82

82
ABLUTION BOWL
Design: Stephan Rath
Commissioned by: Lobmeyr, Vienna
Cut crystal glass
Shape: round, knob cross-shaped, shaft cut (10 sides)
H 13.5
Labels: "N 58 / K 41.-" and round company label from Lobmeyr
Exhibition(s): ÖMKI 1912 (Religious Art)
Inv.: ÖMAK, W.I. 1188 (inventoried 13/02/13; acquired for 41 crowns from Lobmeyr)

82

82
ABLUTIONSDOSE
Entwurf: Stephan Rath
Verleger: Lobmeyr, Wien
Form: rund, Knauf kreuzförmig geschliffen, Schaft geschliffen (10 Ecken)
H 13,5
Klebeetiketten: „N 58 / K 41.-" bzw. rundes Firmenetikett von Lobmeyr
Ausst.: ÖMKI 1912 (Ausstellung kirchlicher Kunst)
Inv.: ÖMAK, W.I. 1188 (inventarisiert am 13. 2. 1913, erworben um 41 Kronen von Lobmeyr)

83
ABLUTION BOWL
Design: Stephan Rath
Commissioned by: Lobmeyr, Vienna
Cut crystal glass
Shape: round cross-section, 14 sides, knob cut cross-shaped
H 13, Dt (lip) 11, Db 10.5
Labels: "N 58 / K 41.-" and round company label from Lobmeyr
Exhibition(s): ÖMKI 1912 (Religious Art)
Inv.: ÖMAK, W.I. 1189 (inventoried 13/02/13; acquired for 46 crowns from Lobmeyr)

83

83
ABLUTIONSDOSE
Entwurf: Stephan Rath
Verleger: Lobmeyr, Wien
Form: runder Querschnitt, Wandung geschliffen (14 Ecken), Knauf kreuzförmig geschliffen
H 13, Do (Mundrand) 11, Du 10,5
Klebeetiketten: „N 58 / K 41.-" bzw. rundes Firmenetikett von Lobmeyr
Ausst.: ÖMKI 1912 (Ausstellung kirchlicher Kunst)
Inv.: ÖMAK, W.I. 1189 (inventarisiert am 13. 2. 1913, erworben um 46 Kronen von Lobmeyr)

84

84
DECKELDOSE
Verleger: Lobmeyr, Wien
Form: runder Querschnitt, Deckel geschliffen
H 10,5, Du 7,9, Dg 8,4
Ausst.: ÖMAK 1973
Lit.:
Neuwirth 1973, Nr. 87, S. 212-213
Inv.: ÖMAK, W.I. 1263 (inventarisiert am 7. 1. 1914, erworben um 13,80 Kronen von Lobmeyr)

84
COVERED BOWL
Commissioned by: Lobmeyr, Vienna
Shape: round cross-section, cut lid
H 10.5, Db 7.9, Dm 8.4
Exhibition(s): ÖMAK 1973
Lit.:
Neuwirth 1973, no. 87, pp. 212-213
Inv.: ÖMAK, W.I. 1263 (inventoried 07/01/14; acquired for 13.80 crowns from Lobmeyr)

85

85
DECKELDOSE
Verleger: Lobmeyr, Wien
Form: runder Querschnitt, Schliff von Deckel und Wandung
H 10, Du 8,5, Dg 9,1
Ausst.: ÖMAK 1973
Lit.:
Neuwirth 1973, Nr. 87, S. 212-213
Inv.: ÖMAK, W.I. 1264 (inventarisiert am 7. 1. 1914, erworben um 16,30 Kronen von Lobmeyr)

85
COVERED BOWL
Commissioned by: Lobmeyr, Vienna
Shape: round cross-section, cut lid and side
H 10, Db 8.5, Dm 9.1
Exhibition(s): ÖMAK 1973
Lit.:
Neuwirth 1973, no. 87, pp. 212-213
Inv.: ÖMAK, W.I. 1264 (inventoried 07/01/14; acquired for 16.30 crowns from Lobmeyr)

86

86
DECKELDOSE
Entwurf: Oscar Strnad
Verleger: Lobmeyr, Wien
Form: ovaler Querschnitt, Schliff (abwechselnd schmälere und breitere Flächen)
H 11,9, 7,6 × 9,8 (größte Ausdehnung)
Ausst.: ÖMAK 1973
Lit.:
Neuwirth 1973, Nr. 86, S. 212-213
Inv.: ÖMAK, W.I. 1029 (inventarisiert am 10. 2. 1912, erworben um 50,50 Kronen von Lobmeyr)

86
COVERED BOWL
Design: Oscar Strnad
Commissioned by: Lobmeyr, Vienna
Shape: oval cross-section, cutting (alternate narrow and wide surfaces)
H 11.9, 7.6 × 9.8 (max. extent)
Exhibition(s): ÖMAK 1973
Lit.:
Neuwirth 1973, no. 86, pp. 212-213
Inv.: ÖMAK, W.I. 1029 (inventoried 10/02/12; acquired for 50.50 crowns from Lobmeyr)

87

87
DECKELDOSE
Entwurf: Oscar Strnad
Verleger: Lobmeyr, Wien
Form: runder Querschnitt, Schliff (abwechselnd schmälere und breitere Flächen, 12 Ecken), Kantenschliff
H 12,6, Dg 9,4
Ausst.: ÖMAK 1973
Lit.:
Neuwirth 1973, Nr. 86, S. 212-213
Inv.: ÖMAK, W.I. 1030 (inventarisiert am 10. 2. 1912, erworben um 30,50 Kronen von Lobmeyr)

87
COVERED BOWL
Design: Oscar Strnad
Commissioned by: Lobmeyr, Vienna
Shape: round cross-section, cutting (alternate narrow and wide surfaces), 12 sides, cut edges
H 12.6, Dm 9.4
Exhibition(s): ÖMAK 1973
Lit.:
Neuwirth 1973, no. 86, pp. 212-213
Inv.: ÖMAK, W.I. 1030 (inventoried 10/02/12; acquired for 30.50 crowns from Lobmeyr)

88

88
DECKELPOKAL
Fachschule Haida
Kantenschliff (6 Ecken)
H 22,2, Do 7,2, Du 6,8,
D Deckel 7,9
Ausst.:
ÖMKI 1910/11, Nr. 256
(Foto ÖMAK, Inv. VS 178 B)
ÖMAK 1973
Lit.:
Neuwirth 1973, Nr. 47,
S. 148, 151
Inv.: ÖMAK, W.I. 884
(inventarisiert am
21. 2. 1911, erworben um
50 Kronen von der
Fachschule Haida)

88
LIDDED GOBLET
Haida school
of glassmaking
Cut edges (6 sides)
H 22.2, Dt 7.2, Db 6.8,
D (lid) 7.9
Exhibition(s):
ÖMKI 1910/11, no. 256
(photograph ÖMAK,
VS 178 B). – ÖMAK 1973
Lit.:
Neuwirth 1973, no. 47,
pp. 148, 151
Inv.: ÖMAK, W.I. 884
(inventoried 21/02/11;
acquired for 50 crowns
from the Haida school of
glassmaking)

89
VASE
Fachschule Haida
Kantenschliff (6 Ecken)
H 25,9, Do 5,5, Du 7,8
Ausst.: ÖMKI 1910/11
ÖMAK 1973
Lit.:
Neuwirth 1973, Nr. 46,
S. 148, 151
Inv.: ÖMAK, W.I. 885
(inventarisiert am
21. 2. 1911, erworben um
50 Kronen von der
Fachschule Haida)

89
VASE
Haida school
of glassmaking
Cut edges (6 sides)
H 25.9, Dt 5.5, Db 7.8
Exhibition(s):
ÖMKI 1910/11
ÖMAK 1973
Lit.:
Neuwirth 1973, no. 46,
pp. 148, 151
Inv.: ÖMAK, W.I. 885
(inventoried 21/02/11;
acquired for 50 crowns
from the Haida school of
glassmaking)

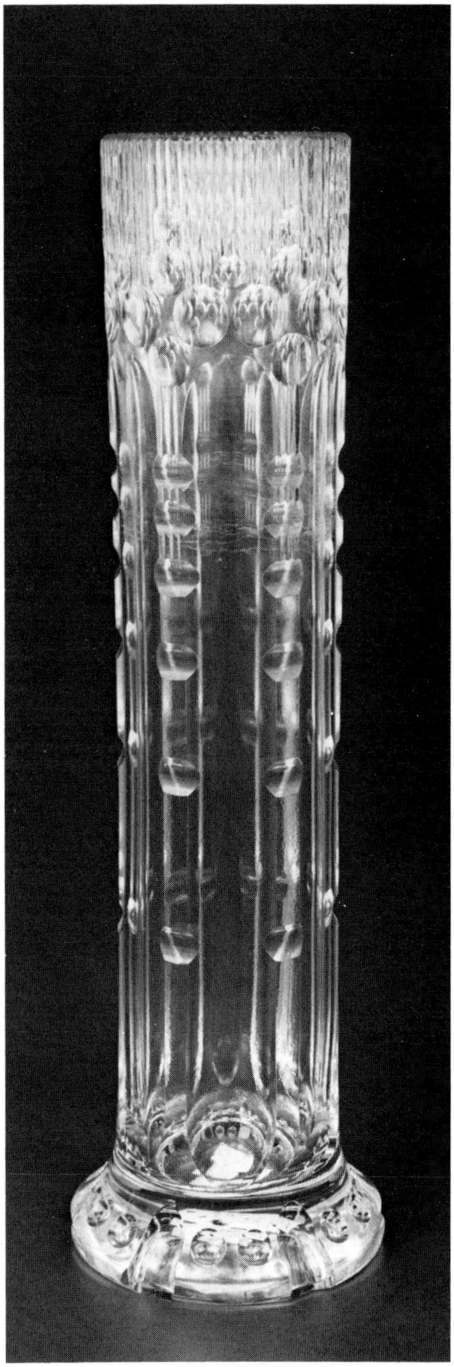

89

90

90
ZIERGLÄSER UND VASEN
Fachschule Haida
Reproduktion aus:
DKD 34/1914, S. 377

90
DECORATIVE JARS
AND VASES
Haida school
of glassmaking
Reproduced from:
DKD 34/1914, p. 377

91
DECKELPOKAL
Entwurf: Fachschule Haida
Ausführung: Oertel, Haida
Werknummer 2742 (Oertel)
Schliff (12 Ecken)
H 46,5, D 10,4, D (Fuß) 14
Ausst.: ÖMKI 1915
Lit.:
Neuwirth 1973, Nr. 181, S. 316, 319
Inv.: ÖMAK, W.I. 1661 (inventarisiert am 1. 4. 1916, erworben um 110 Kronen von Oertel, Haida)

91
LIDDED GOBLET
Design: Haida school of glassmaking
Manufacturer: Oertel, Haida
Serial number 2742 (Oertel)
Cut crystal glass (12 sides)
H 46.5, D 10.4, D (foot) 14
Exhibition(s): ÖMKI 1915
Lit.:
Neuwirth 1973, no. 181, pp. 316, 319
Inv.: ÖMAK, W.I. 1661 (inventoried 01/04/16; acquired for 110 crowns from Oertel, Haida)

91

92
BOWLEGARNITUR
bestehend aus einer Bowle mit Deckel und 6 Gläsern
Werknummer 16 K (Artěl)
Entwurf: Jan Kotěra
(Artěl, Prag)
Form: Bowle 22 Ecken, Gläser 8 Ecken
Bowle: H 40,5, Dg 26,8, D Fuß 17,2
Gläser: H 11,8, Du 5,8-6 Do 6,7-6,8
Ausst.: St. Louis 1904
ÖMKI 1913/14, Nr. 6
(Foto ÖMAK, Inv. VS 174 B)
ÖMAK 1973
Lit.:
Volné směry 8/1904, S. 137
KKH 16/1913, S. 619
F. X. Jiřík, České Sklo, Prag 1934, Taf. XXXIX (1905 datiert)
Kat. Czechoslovakian Glass 1350-1980, Corning, New York, 1981, Nr. 74, S. 91 (entworfen 1903, vereinfacht 1910)
Kat. Tschechische Kunst 1878-1914, Darmstadt 1984-1985, Nr. 234, S. 157 (1903-1910 datiert)
Neuwirth 1973, Nr. 1, S. 108-109
Inv.: ÖMAK, W.I. 1524/1-7 (inventarisiert am 24. 3. 1915, erworben um 100 Kronen von Artěl, Prag)

92
PUNCH SET
Consisting of a bowl with lid and six glasses
Serial number 16 K (Artěl)
Design: Jan Kotěra
(Artěl, Prague)
Shape: bowl 22 sides, glasses 8 sides
Bowl: H 40.5, Dm 26.8, D (foot) 17.2
Glasses: H 11.8, Db 5.8-6 Dt 6.7-6.8
Exhibition(s): St. Louis 1904
ÖMKI 1913/14, no. 6
(photograph ÖMAK, VS 174 B). – ÖMAK 1973
Lit.:
Volné směry 8/1904, p. 137
KKH 16/1913, p. 619
F. X. Jiřík, České Sklo, Prague 1934, Taf. XXXIX (dated 1905)
Kat. Czechoslovakian Glass 1350-1980, Corning, New York, 1981, no. 74, p. 91 (designed 1903, simplified 1910)
Kat. Tschechische Kunst 1878-1914, Darmstadt 1984-1985, no. 234, p. 157 (dated 1903-1910)
Neuwirth 1973, no. 1, pp. 108-109
Inv.: ÖMAK, W.I. 1524/1-7 (inventoried 24/03/15; acquired for 100 crowns from Artěl, Prague)

92

93

93
COVERED BOWL
Design: Jaroslav Horejc
(Artěl, Prague)
Serial number 15 H (Artěl)
Cut crystal glass
(foot 12 sides, lid 14 sides,
wall 15 sides)
H 14.2, Dm 9.2, D (foot) 5.9
Label with "15 H K 6.-"
Lit.: Jana Hornekova,
Jaroslav Horejc,
Prague 1971, no. 1
(Harrach, 1912)
Inv.: ÖMAK, W.I. 1512
(inventoried 24/03/15;
acquired for 6 crowns
from Artěl)

93

93
DECKELDOSE
Entwurf: Jaroslav Horejc
(Artěl, Prag)
Werknummer 15 H (Artěl)
Schliff (Fuß 12 Ecken,
Wandung 15 Ecken,
Deckel 14 Ecken)
H 14,2, Dg 9,2, D Fuß 5,9
Klebeetikett: 15 H K 6.-
Lit.: Jana Hornekova,
Jaroslav Horejc,
Prag 1971, Kat. Nr. 1
(Harrach, 1912)
Inv.: ÖMAK, W.I. 1512
(inventarisiert am
24. 3. 1915, erworben um
6 Kronen von Artěl)

94
COVERED BOWL
Design: Jaroslav Horejc
(Artěl, Prague)
Serial number 14 H (Artěl)
Cut crystal glass
(foot 11 sides, wall and lid
14 sides)
H 12,1, Dm 8,6, D (foot) 4,8
Label with "H 14 K 5.50"
Lit.: Jana Hornekova,
Jaroslav Horejc,
Prague 1971, no. 1
(Harrach, 1912)
Inv.: ÖMAK, W.I. 1511
(inventoried 24/03/15;
acquired for 5.5 crowns
from Artěl)

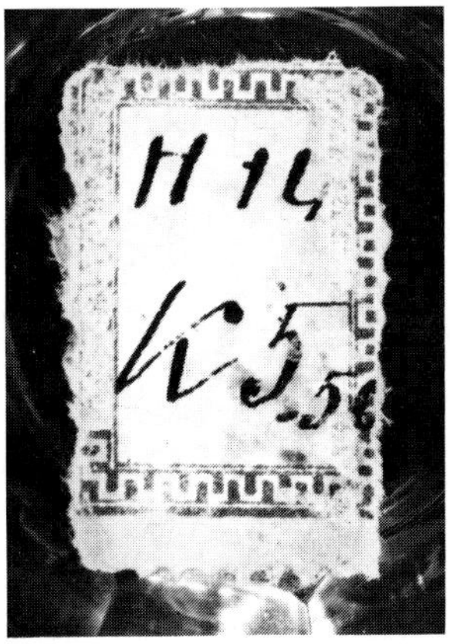

94

94

94
DECKELDOSE
Entwurf: Jaroslav Horejc
(Artěl, Prag)
Werknummer 14 H (Artěl)
Schliff (Fuß 11 Ecken,
Wandung und Deckel
14 Ecken)
H 12,1, Dg 8,6, D Fuß 4,8
Klebeetikett: H 14 K 5.5
Lit.: Jana Hornekova,
Jaroslav Horejc,
Prag 1971, Kat. Nr. 1
(Harrach, 1912)
Inv.: ÖMAK, W.I. 1511
(inventarisiert am
24. 3. 1915, erworben um
5,50 Kronen von Artěl)

95

95
VASE
Entwurf: Josef Rosipal
(Artěl, Prag)
Werknummer 2 R (Artěl)
Form: siebenfach gebaucht, geschliffen
H 35, Du 9, Do 4
Ausst.: ÖMAK 1973
Lit.:
Neuwirth 1973, Nr. 9, S. 110
Inv.: ÖMAK, W.I. 1517
(inventarisiert am 24. 3. 1915, erworben um 15 Kronen von Artěl, Prag)

95
VASE
Design: Josef Rosipal
(Artěl, Prague)
Serial number 2 R (Artěl)
Cut crystal glass
Shape: seven bulges
H 35, Db 9, Dt 4
Exhibition(s): ÖMAK 1973
Lit.:
Neuwirth 1973, no. 9, p. 110
Inv.: ÖMAK, W.I. 1517
(inventoried 24/03/15; acquired for 15 crowns from Artěl, Prague)

96

96
AUFSATZ
Entwurf: Rudolf Stockar
(Artěl, Prag)
Werknummer 9 St (Artěl)
Form: runder Fuß (optisch geblasen) und zackig geschliffener Rand
H 15,6, Du 21,7,
Do 30,6 (unregelmäßig)
Ausst.: ÖMAK 1973
Lit.:
Neuwirth 1973, Nr. 18, S. 116
Inv.: ÖMAK, W.I. 1513
(inventarisiert am 24. 3. 1915, erworben um 12 Kronen von Artěl, Prag)

96
CENTREPIECE
Design: Rudolf Stockar
(Artěl, Prague)
Serial number 9 St (Artěl)
Shape: round foot (optically blown) and serrated cut edge
H 15.6, Db 21.7,
Dt 30.6 (irregular)
Exhibition(s): ÖMAK 1973
Lit.:
Neuwirth 1973, no. 18, p. 116
Inv.: ÖMAK, W.I. 1513
(inventoried 24/03/15; acquired for 12 crowns from Artěl, Prague)

97

97
SECHS CHAMPAGNERGLÄSER
Entwurf: Rudolf Stockar (Artěl, Prag)
Form: Stiel geschliffen (6 Ecken), Kuppa mit zwei geschliffenen Linien
H 13,1-13,2, Do 9,3-9,5, Du 7-7,5
Inv.: ÖMAK, W.I. 1535/1-6 (inventarisiert am 24. 3. 1915, erworben um 14 Kronen von Artěl, Prag)

97
SIX CHAMPAGNE GLASSES
Design: Rudolf Stockar (Artěl, Prague)
Cut crystal glass
Shape: stem (6 sides), bowl with two cut lines
H 13.1-13.2, Dt 9.3-9.5, Db 7-7.5
Inv.: ÖMAK, W.I. 1535/1-6 (inventoried 24/03/15; acquired for 14 crowns from Artěl, Prague)

98
FÜNF WEINGLÄSER
Entwurf: Rudolf Stockar (Artěl, Prag)
Form: Stiel geschliffen (6 Ecken), Kuppa mit zwei geschliffenen Linien
Weinflasche ursprünglich vorhanden, ebenso ein sechstes Weinglas
H 14,9-15, Do 6,6, Du 6,4-6,6
Ausst.: ÖMAK 1973
Lit.:
Neuwirth 1973, Nr. 16, S. 116
Inv.: ÖMAK, W.I. 1514/2-6 (inventarisiert am 24.3.1915, erworben um 12 Kronen von Artěl, Prag)

98
FIVE WINE GLASSES
Design: Rudolf Stockar (Artěl, Prague)
Cut crystal glass
Shape: stem (6 sides), bowl with two cut lines
The set originally included a wine decanter and a sixth wine glass
H 14.9-15, Dt 6.6, Db 6.4-6.6
Exhibition(s): ÖMAK 1973
Lit.:
Neuwirth 1973, no. 16, p. 116
Inv.: ÖMAK, W.I. 1514/2-6 (inventoried 24/03/15; acquired for 12 crowns from Artěl, Prague)

99
THREE MOSELLE WINE GLASSES
Design: Rudolf Stockar (Artěl, Prague)
Cut crystal glass
Shape: stem (6 sides) and green bowl
H 14.9-15, Dt 6.5-6.6, Db 6.4-6.8
Only three of the original six glasses still survive (three glasses lost in war)
Inv.: ÖMAK, W.I. 1537/1-3 (inventoried 24/03/15; six glasses acquired for 14 crowns from Artěl, Prague)

98 99

99
DREI
MOSELWEINGLÄSER
Entwurf: Rudolf Stockar
(Artěl, Prag)
Glas mit geschliffenem
Stiel (6 Ecken) und
grüner Kuppa
H 14,9-15, Do 6,5-6,6,
Du 6,4-6,8

Von ursprünglich sechs
Gläsern nur mehr drei
erhalten (drei weitere:
Kriegsverlust)
Inv.: ÖMAK, W.I. 1537/1-3
(inventarisiert am
24. 3. 1915, erworben um
14 Kronen (6 Stück) von
Artěl, Prag)

100

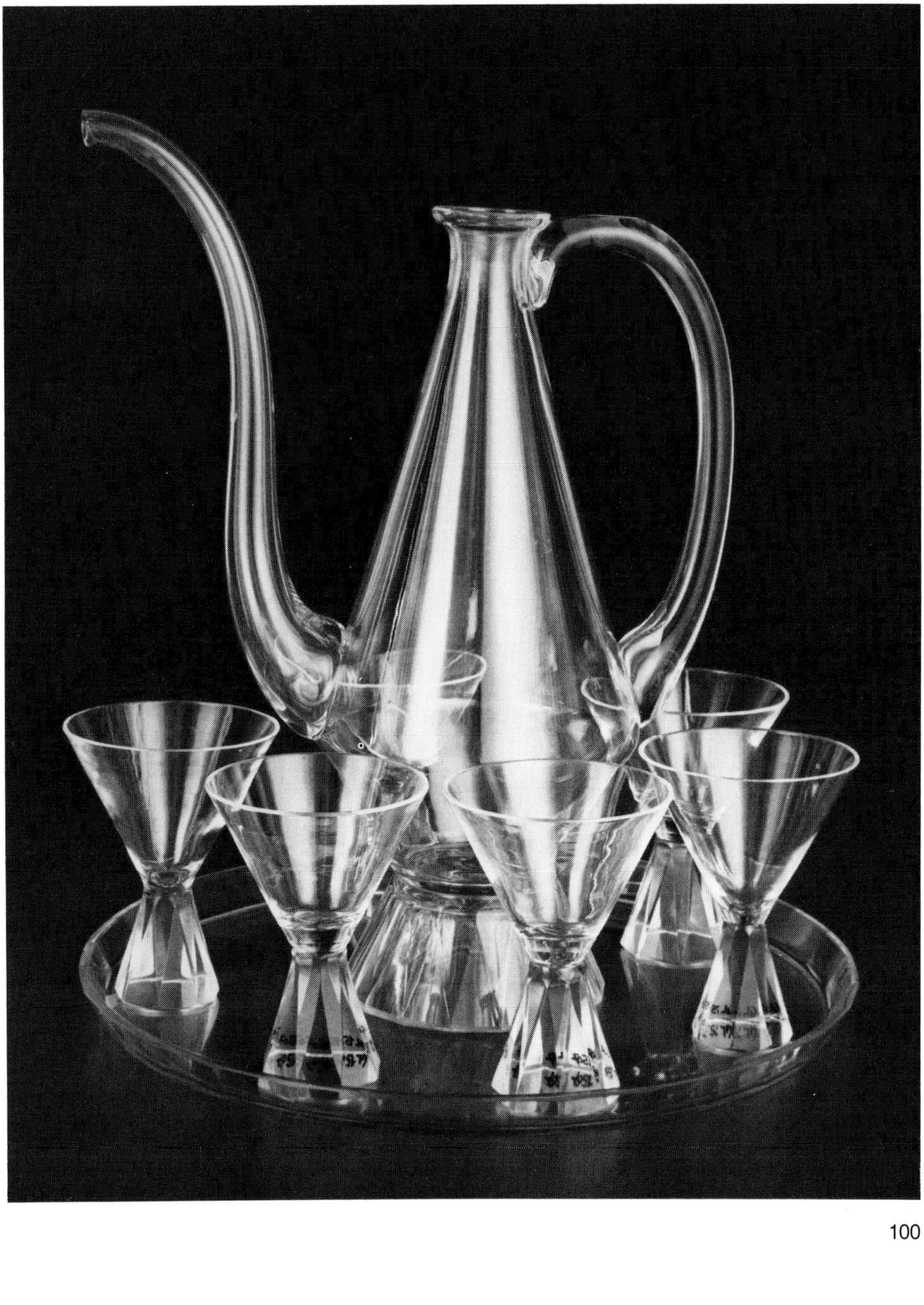

100

100
LIKÖRSERVICE
Henkelflasche, Platte,
sechs Gläser
Entwurf: Otakar Novotný
(Artěl, Prag)
Werknummer 12 N (Artěl)
Dreieckiger Facettenschliff (Füße von Henkelkanne und Gläsern), Plattenrand gerade geschliffen
Kanne: H 22,5 (Ausguß)
Platte: Do 20,8, H 1,3
Gläser: H 7,2-7,3,
Do 5,4-5,7, Du 2,7-3,1
Ausst.: ÖMAK 1973
Lit.:
Neuwirth 1973, Nr. 2,
S. 108
Inv.: ÖMAK, W.I. 1507/1-8
(inventarisiert am
24. 3. 1915, erworben um
14 Kronen von Artěl, Prag)

100
LIQUEUR SERVICE
Handled jug, salver,
six glasses
Design: Otakar Novotný
(Artěl, Prague)
Serial number 12 N (Artěl)
Three-sided bevel cut (bases of jug and glasses), edge of plate cut straight
Jug: H 22.5 (spout)
Plate: Dt 20.8, H 1.3
Glasses: H 7.2-7.3,
Dt 5.4-5.7, Db 2.7-3.1
Exhibition(s): ÖMAK 1973
Lit.:
Neuwirth 1973, no. 2,
p. 108
Inv.: ÖMAK, W.I. 1507/1-8
(inventoried 24/03/15;
acquired for 14 crowns
from Artěl, Prague)

101
LIKÖRSERVICE
Henkelflasche, Platte,
sechs Gläser
Entwurf: Josef Rosipal
(Artěl, Prag)
Werknummer 7 R oder 17 R
Optisches Glas, Stiele der Gläser geschliffen, Platte auf vier Kugelfüßchen
Kanne: H 15, Du 9,4
Platte: Do 23,1, H 2,1
Gläser: H 11-11,3,
Do 4-4,2, Du 4,3-4,5
Ausst.: ÖMAK 1973
Lit.:
Neuwirth 1973, Nr. 5,
S. 110
Inv.: ÖMAK, W.I. 1505/1-8
(inventarisiert am
24. 3. 1915, erworben um
11 Kronen von Artěl, Prag)

101
LIQUEUR SERVICE
Handled jug, salver,
six glasses
Design: Josef Rosipal
(Artěl, Prague)
Serial number 7 R or 17 R
Optical glass, cut stems of glasses, plate on four balls
Jug H 15, Db 9.4
Plate: Dt 23.1, H 2.1
Glasses H 11-11.3,
Dt 4-4.2, Db 4.3-4.5
Exhibition(s): ÖMAK 1973
Lit.:
Neuwirth 1973, no. 5,
p. 110
Inv.: ÖMAK, W.I. 1505/1-8
(inventoried 24/03/15;
acquired for 11 crowns
from Artěl, Prague)

101

102
LIKÖRSERVICE
Henkelkanne, Platte, fünf
Gläser
Entwurf: Josef Rosipal
(Artěl, Prag)
Werknummer 7 R oder 17 R
Optisches Glas, Stiele und
Fuß der Gläser sowie Hals
des Kännchens geschliffen,
Platte auf vier
Kugelfüßchen
Kanne: H 16,6, Du 10,1
Platte: Do 23,2, H 2
Gläser: H 10,6-10,9,
Do 4,4-4,6, Du 5,1-5,2
Ausst.: ÖMAK 1973
Lit.: Neuwirth 1973, Nr. 8,
S. 110
Inv.: ÖMAK, W.I. 1508/1-7
(inventarisiert am
24. 3. 1915, erworben um
11 Kronen von Artěl, Prag)

102
LIQUEUR SERVICE
Handled jug, salver,
six glasses
Design: Josef Rosipal
(Artěl, Prague)
Serial number 7 R or 17 R
Optical glass, cut stems
and feet of glasses,
cut neck of jug, plate on
four balls
Jug: H 16.6, Db 10.1
Plate: Dt 23.2, H 2
Glasses: H 10.6-10.9,
Dt 4.4-4.6, Db 5.1-5.2
Exhibition(s): ÖMAK 1973
Lit.: Neuwirth 1973, no. 8,
p. 110
Inv.: ÖMAK, W.I. 1508/1-7
(inventoried 24/03/15;
acquired for 11 crowns
from Artěl, Prague)

102

103
TEILE EINES
LIKÖRSERVICES
Entwurf: Otto Prutscher
Ausführung:
Carl Schappel, Haida
„Likörsatz, feinstes
Kristall mit feinem
Schliff und
Hochglanzpolitur"
Reproduktion aus:
Kat. Schappel, Kunstgläser

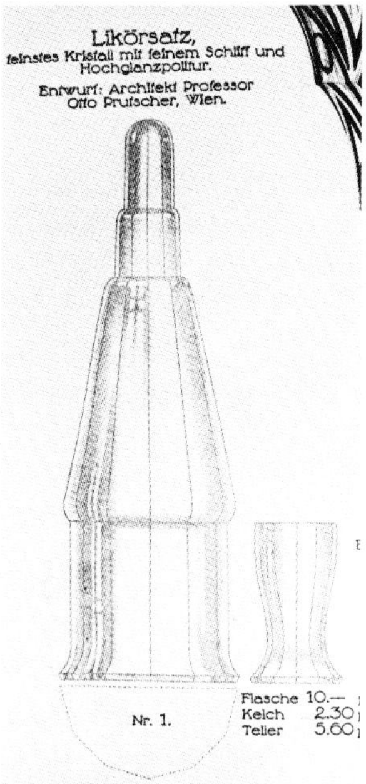

103

104

103
PART OF
A LIQUEUR SERVICE
Design: Otto Prutscher
Manufacturer:
Carl Schappel, Haida
"Liqueur set, finest
crystal with fine cutting
and high-lustre polish"
Reproduced from:
Kat. Schappel, Kunstgläser

104

104
LIKÖRSERVICE
Flasche, Platte,
sechs Gläser
Entwurf: Otto Prutscher
Ausführung:
Carl Schappel, Haida
Geschliffenes Glas
(Flasche: 12 Ecken,
Platte: 20 Ecken,
Gläser: 8 Ecken)
Flasche mit Stöpsel:
H 25,7, Du 8
Platte: D 25,5, H 3,1
Gläser: H 7,4-7,5
Do 3,3-3,7, Du 3,7-3,8
Firmenetikett Schappel
(Flasche)
Lit.: Kunstgewerbeblatt
NF/27. Jg. 1916, S. 195
DKD 41/1917-18, S. 318
Inv.: ÖMAK, W.I. 1476/1-8
(inventarisiert am
24. 3. 1915, erworben
um 35,90 Kronen von
Schappel, Haida)

104

104
LIQUEUR SERVICE
Decanter, salver,
six glasses
Design: Otto Prutscher
Manufacturer:
Carl Schappel, Haida
Cut crystal glass
(decanter: 12 sides,
plate: 20 sides,
glasses: 8 sides)
Decanter with stopper:
H 25.7, Db 8
Plate D 25.5, H 3.1
Glasses: H 7.4-7.5
Dt 3.3-3.7, Db 3.7-3.8
Schappel company label
(decanter)
Lit.: Kunstgewerbeblatt
NF/27th year, 1916, p. 195
DKD 41/1917-18, p. 318
Inv.: ÖMAK, W.I. 1476/1-8
(inventoried 24/03/15;
acquired for 35.90 crowns
from Schappel, Haida)

105

106

105
KELCHGLAS
Verleger: Lobmeyr, Wien
Werknummer 35 (Lobmeyr)
Geschliffenes Glas
(6 Ecken)
H 12,3, Do 6,8, D Fuß 6,8
Ausst.: ÖMKI 1915
(Foto ÖMAK Inv. VS 176 B)
Lit.:
KKH XVIII/1915, S. 429
Inv.: ÖMAK, W.I. 1673
(inventarisiert am
1. 4. 1916, erworben um
5,30 Kronen von Lobmeyr)

105
GOBLET
Commissioned by:
Lobmeyr, Vienna
Serial number 35 (Lobmeyr)
Cut crystal glass
(6 sides)
H 12.3, Dt 6.8,
D (foot) 6.8
Exhibition(s): ÖMKI 1915
(photograph ÖMAK,
VS 176 B)
Lit.:
KKH XVIII/1915, p. 429
Inv.: ÖMAK, W.I. 1673
(inventoried 01/04/16
acquired for 5.30 crowns
from Lobmeyr)

106
VASE
Entwurf: Otto Prutscher
Ausführung:
Carl Schappel, Haida
Schliff (6 Ecken)
H 19,4, Du 10,6, Do 8
Inv.: ÖMAK, W.I. 1475
(inventarisiert am
24. 3. 1915, erworben um
15 Kronen von Schappel,
Haida)

106
VASE
Design: Otto Prutscher
Manufacturer:
Carl Schappel, Haida
Cut crystal glass (6 sides)
H 19.4, Db 10.6, Dt 8
Inv.: ÖMAK, W.I. 1475
(inventoried 24/03/15;
acquired for 15 crowns
from Schappel, Haida)

107
VASE
Entwurf: Otto Prutscher
Ausführung:
Carl Schappel, Haida
Werknummer 4403
Schliff (6 Ecken)
H 26,2, Do 11,4, Du 14
Ausst.: ÖMKI 1915
Inv.: ÖMAK, W.I. 1711
(inventarisiert am
1. 4. 1916, erworben um
34 Kronen von Schappel,
Haida)

107
VASE
Design: Otto Prutscher
Manufacturer:
Carl Schappel, Haida
Serial number 4403
Cut crystal glass (6 sides)
H 26.2, Dt 11.4, Db 14
Exhibition(s): ÖMKI 1915
Inv.: ÖMAK, W.I. 1711
(inventoried 01/04/16;
acquired for 34 crowns
from Schappel, Haida)

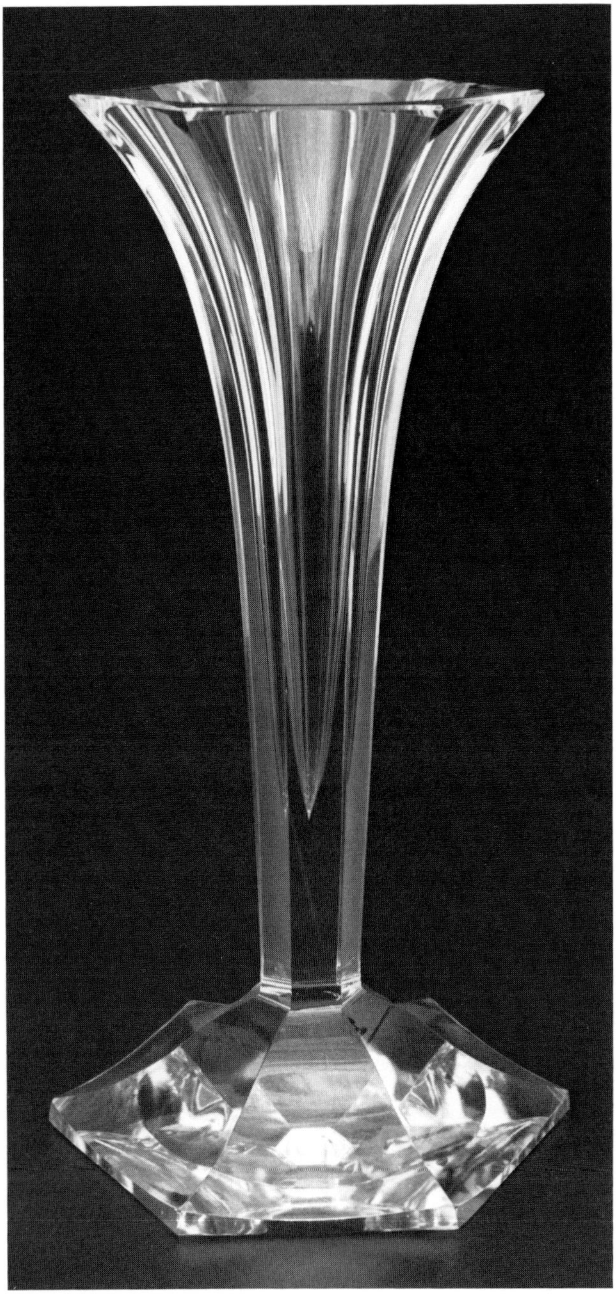

107

108

108
DECKELPOKAL
UND AUFSATZ
Entwurf: Otto Prutscher
Ausführung:
Carl Schappel, Haida
Ausst.: Berlin 1916
Reproduktion aus:
DKD 38/1916, S. 276

108
LIDDED GOBLET
AND CENTREPIECE
Design: Otto Prutscher
Manufacturer:
Carl Schappel, Haida
Exhibition(s): Berlin 1916
Reproduced from:
DKD 38/1916, p. 276

109

109
VASEN
Entwurf: Otto Prutscher
Ausführung:
Carl Schappel, Haida
Ausst.: Berlin 1916
Reproduktion aus:
DKD 38/1916, S. 276

109
VASES
Design: Otto Prutscher
Manufacturer:
Carl Schappel, Haida
Exhibition(s): Berlin 1916
Reproduced from:
DKD 38/1916, p. 276

110
DECKELPOKAL
Entwurf: Otto Prutscher
Ausführung:
Carl Schappel, Haida
Werknummer 4429
Schliff: Fuß und Stiel
6 Ecken, Kuppa 10 Rippen
H 27,8
Ausst.: ÖMKI 1915
(Foto ÖMAK Inv. VS 178 A)
Berlin 1916
Lit.:
KKH XVIII/1915, S. 428
DKD 38/1916, S. 276
Brigitte Klesse – Gisela Reineking-von Bock, Kat. Glas, Köln 1973, Nr. 624, S. 282
Inv.: ÖMAK, W.I. 1712
(inventarisiert am 1. 4. 1916, erworben um 40 Kronen von Schappel, Haida)

110
LIDDED GOBLET
Design: Otto Prutscher
Manufacturer:
Carl Schappel, Haida
Serial number 4429
Cut crystal glass:
foot und stem 6 sides, bowl 10 ribs
H 27.8
Exhibition(s): ÖMKI 1915
(photograph ÖMAK, VS 178 A). – Berlin 1916
Lit.:
KKH XVIII/1915, p. 428
DKD 38/1916, p. 276
Brigitte Klesse – Gisela Reineking-von Bock, Kat. Glas, Köln 1973, no. 624, p. 282
Inv.: ÖMAK, W.I. 1712
(inventoried 01/04/16; acquired for 40 crowns from Schappel, Haida)

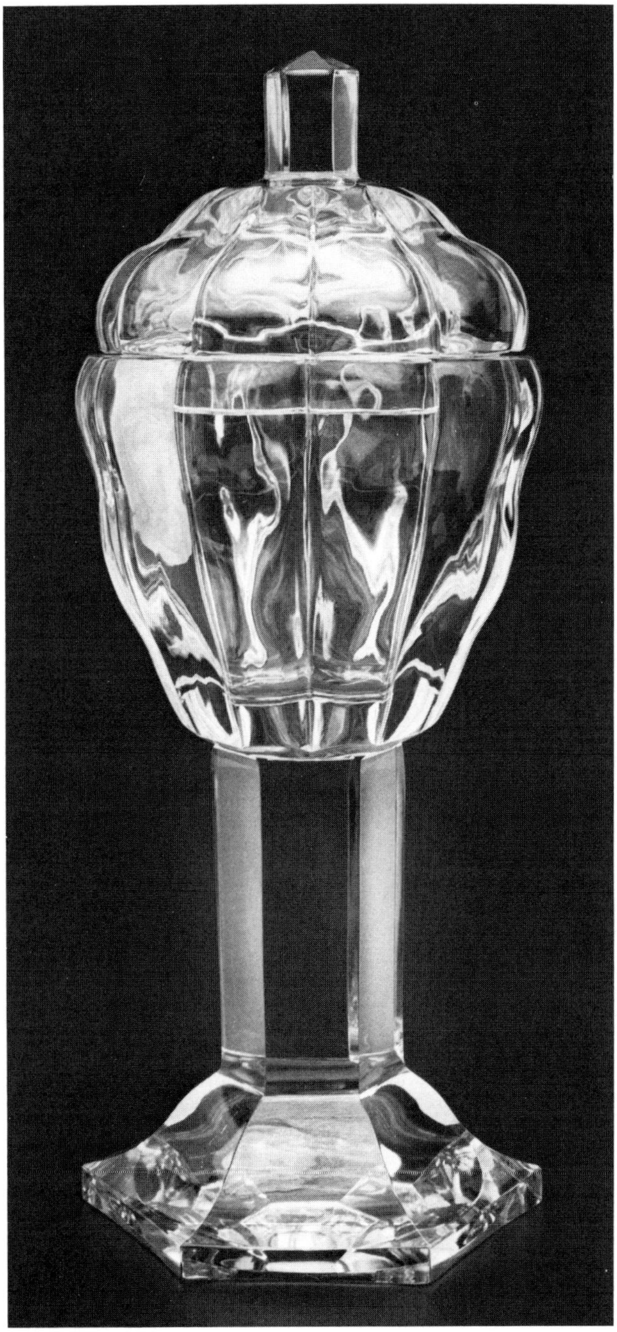

110

111

111
DECKELPOKAL
Entwurf: Carl Thomas
Verleger: Lobmeyr, Wien
Stiel und Knauf
geschliffen (6 Ecken)
H 26,5, D Mundrand 9,6,
D Fuß 9, D Deckel 9,9
Ausst.:
ÖMKI 1913/14, Nr. 564
(Foto ÖMAK Inv. VS 174 A)
Lit.: DK XXIII, S. 30
Eisler 1916, S. 28
Inv.: ÖMAK, W.I. 1265
(inventarisiert am
7. 1. 1914, erworben um
23,10 Kronen von Lobmeyr)

111
LIDDED GOBLET
Design: Carl Thomas
Commissioned by:
Lobmeyr, Vienna
Cut crystal glass:
stem and knob (6 sides)
H 26.5, D (lip) 9.6,
D (foot) 9, D (lid) 9.9
Exhibition(s):
ÖMKI 1913/14, no. 564
(photograph ÖMAK,
VS 174 A)
Lit.: DK XXIII, p. 30
Eisler 1916, p. 28
Inv.: ÖMAK, W.I. 1265
(inventoried 07/01/14;
acquired for 23.10 crowns
from Lobmeyr)

112

113

112
DECKELPOKAL
Entwurf: Otto Prutscher
Ausführung:
Carl Schappel, Haida
Ausst.: Berlin 1916
Reproduktion aus:
DKD 38/1916, S. 277

112
LIDDED GOBLET
Design: Otto Prutscher
Manufacturer:
Carl Schappel, Haida
Exhibition(s): Berlin 1916
Reproduced from:
DKD 38/1916, p. 277

113
TEILE EINES
WEINSERVICES
Fachschule Haida
Reproduktion aus:
DKD 41/1917-18, S. 106

113
PARTS OF
A WINE SERVICE
Haida school
of glassmaking
Reproduced from:
DKD 41/1917-18, p. 106

114

115

115

114
DECKELDOSE
Entwurf:
Josef Emanuel Margold
Ausführung:
Carl Schappel, Haida
Werknummer 4440
Schliff (16 Ecken sowie Oliven)
H 28,5, D Fuß 13, D Deckel und Mundrand 22,7
Doppelseitiges Klebeetikett (Firmensignet Schappel sowie Entwerfer)
Ausst.: ÖMKI 1915
(Foto ÖMAK Inv. VS 174 B)
Lit.:
KKH XVIII/1915, S. 427
Inv.: ÖMAK, W.I. 1715
(inventarisiert am 1. 4. 1916, erworben um 100 Kronen von Schappel, Haida)

114
LIDDED JAR
Design:
Josef Emanuel Margold
Manufacturer:
Carl Schappel, Haida
Serial number 4440
Cut crystal glass
(16 sides and olives)
H 28.5, D (foot) 13,
D (lid and lip) 22.7
Double-sided label
(Schappel company signet and designer)
Exhibition(s): ÖMKI 1915
(photograph ÖMAK, VS 174 B)
Lit.:
KKH XVIII/1915, p. 427
Inv.: ÖMAK, W.I. 1715
(inventoried 01/04/16; acquired for 100 crowns from Schappel, Haida)

114

115

115
LIDDED JAR
Design:
Josef Emanuel Margold
Manufacturer:
Carl Schappel, Haida
Serial number 4450
Cut crystal glass
H 19.7, lid 13.5 × 13.5
Double-sided label
(Schappel company signet
and designer and no. 4450)
Exhibition(s): ÖMKI 1915
(photograph ÖMAK,
VS 174 B)
Inv.:
Joanneum, AKGW, no. 16645
(acquired 12/08/15 for
45 crowns from ÖMKI)

115
DECKELDOSE
Entwurf:
Josef Emanuel Margold
Ausführung:
Carl Schappel, Haida
Werknummer 4450
Schliff
H 19,7, Deckel 13,5 × 13,5
Doppelseitiges Klebeetikett (Firmensignet
Schappel sowie Entwerfer
und Nr. 4450)
Ausst.: ÖMKI 1915
(Foto ÖMAK Inv. VS 174 B)
Inv.:
Joanneum, AKGW, Nr. 16645
(erworben am 12. 8. 1915
um 45 Kronen vom ÖMKI)

115

116

116
KASSETTE
aus vier Teilen bestehend
(Gefäß, zwei Deckel,
vertikale Trennwand)
Ausführung: Meyr's Neffe,
Adolf
Kästchenartige Form mit
vertikalen Schliffmotiven
H 13,5, oben 12,4 × 23,
unten 11,5 × 22,7
Inv.: ÖMAK, W.I. 1613
(inventarisiert am
1. 6. 1915, erworben um
30 Kronen von Meyr's
Neffe)

116
CASKET
consisting of four parts
(container, two lids,
vertical partition)
Manufacturer: Meyr's Neffe,
Adolf
Box-shaped with vertical
cut motifs
H 13.5, 12.4 × 23 (top),
11.5 × 22.7 (bottom)
Inv.: ÖMAK, W.I. 1613
(inventoried 01/06/15;
acquired for 30 crowns
from Meyr's Neffe)

117
FLAKON
Verleger: Lobmeyr, Wien
Viereckig geschliffen
H 24,4, unten 6,7 × 6,7
Klebeetikett: No 9
Ausst.: ÖMKI 1915
Inv.: ÖMAK, W.I. 1672
(inventarisiert am
1. 4. 1916, erworben um
33,60 Kronen von Lobmeyr)

117
BOTTLE
Commissioned by:
Lobmeyr, Vienna
Cut crystal glass, square
shape
H 24.4, 6.7 × 6.7 (bottom)
Label with "No 9"
Exhibition(s): ÖMKI 1915
Inv.: ÖMAK, W.I. 1672
(inventoried 01/04/16;
acquired for 33.60 crowns
from Lobmeyr)

117

117

118

118

118
LEUCHTER
Meyr's Neffe, Adolf
Schliff (8 Ecken,
Kantenschliff)
H 25,8
Preisetikett: 19.50
Ausst.:
ÖMKI 1912, Kat. 559
Inv.: Joanneum,
AKGW, Nr. 14021
(erworben am 10. 7. 1912
um 19,50 Kronen vom ÖMKI)

118
CANDLESTICK
Meyr's Neffe, Adolf
Cut crystal glass
(8 sides, cut edges)
H 25.8
Label with "19.50"
Exhibition(s):
ÖMKI 1912, Kat. 559
Inv.: Joanneum,
AKGW, no. 14021
(acquired 10/07/12 for
19.50 crowns from ÖMKI)

119
LEUCHTER
Ausführung: Meyr's Neffe,
Adolf
Schliff (8 Ecken)
H 24,4
Ausst.: Stockholm 1916
Inv.: ÖMAK, W.I. 1603
(inventarisiert am
1. 6. 1915, erworben um
22 Kronen von Meyr's Neffe)

119
CANDLESTICK
Manufacturer:
Meyr's Neffe, Adolf
Cut crystal glass (8 sides)
H 24.4
Exhibition(s):
Stockholm 1916
Inv.: ÖMAK, W.I. 1603
(inventoried 01/06/15;
acquired for 22 crowns
from Meyr's Neffe)

119

120
LEUCHTER
Ausführung: Meyr's Neffe, Adolf
Schliff (8 Ecken)
H 31,5
Ausst.: Stockholm 1916
Inv.: ÖMAK, W.I. 1602 (inventarisiert am 1. 6. 1915, erworben um 22 Kronen von Meyr's Neffe)

120
CANDLESTICK
Manufacturer:
Meyr's Neffe, Adolf
Cut crystal glass (8 sides)
H 31.5
Exhibition(s):
Stockholm 1916
Inv.: ÖMAK, W.I. 1602 (inventoried 01/06/15; acquired for 22 crowns from Meyr's Neffe)

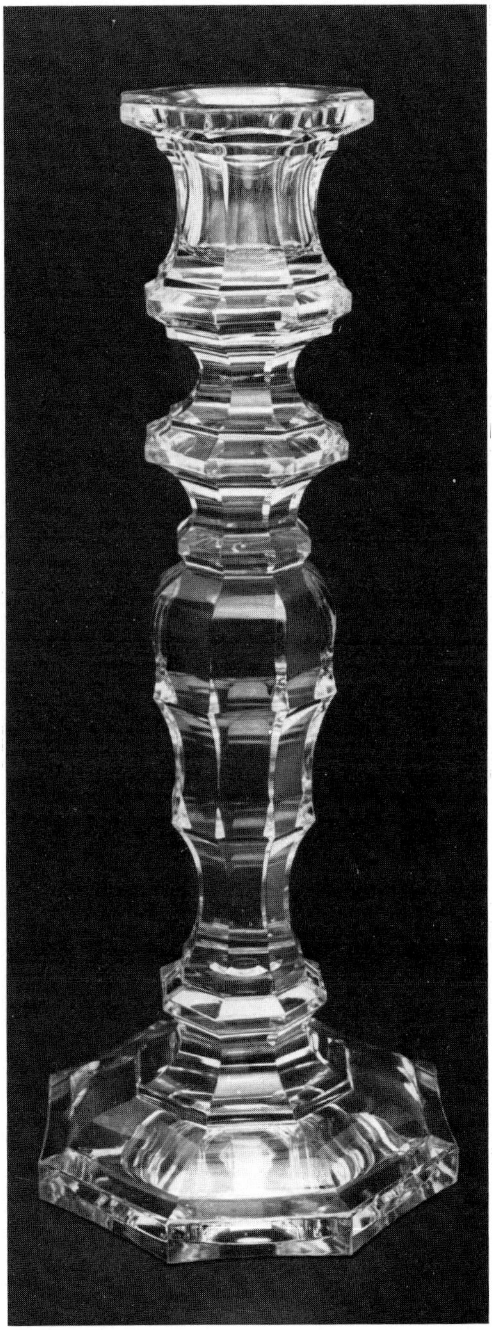

120

121

121
DOSE MIT LEUCHTER
Ausführung: Meyr's Neffe, Adolf
Schliff (12 Ecken)
H 17,2, Du 7,8,
D Tropftasse 8,7
Inv.: ÖMAK, W.I. 1607
(inventarisiert am
1. 6. 1915, erworben um
6,50 Kronen von
Meyr's Neffe)

121
BOX WITH CANDLESTICK
Manufacturer:
Meyr's Neffe, Adolf
Cut crystal glass
(12 sides)
H 17.2, Db 7.8,
D (drip tray) 8.7
Inv.: ÖMAK, W.I. 1607
(inventoried 01/06/15;
acquired for 6.50 crowns
from Meyr's Neffe)

122
WRITING SET
consisting of ink-well,
tray and two candlesticks
Design: Oswald Dittrich
Commissioned by:
Lobmeyr, Vienna
Originally ÖMAK,
W.I. 1625/1-4
(inventoried 07/07/15;
acquired for 116 crowns
from Lobmeyr,
loaned to embassy in
Berlin and not returned)
Exhibition(s): Köln 1914
DKD 34/1914, p. 374
Inv.: ÖMAK Inv. VS 173 C
(contemporary photograph)

122
SCHREIBTISCHGARNITUR
bestehend aus Tintenfaß, Untertasse und zwei Leuchtern
Entwurf: Oswald Dittrich
Verleger: Lobmeyr, Wien
Ursprünglich ÖMAK, W.I. 1625/1-4
(inventarisiert am 7. 7. 1915, erworben um 116 Kronen von Lobmeyr, als Leihgabe von der Gesandtschaft Berlin nicht zurückgekommen)
Ausst.: Köln 1914
DKD 34/1914, S. 374
Inv.: ÖMAK Inv. VS 173 C
(zeitgenössisches Photo)

123
DECKELDOSE
Entwurf: Fachschule Haida
Ausführung: Oertel, Haida
Werknummer (Oertel) 2695
Geschliffenes Glas
H 14,4, Du 9,2,
D Mundrand 9,7
Ausst.: ÖMKI 1915
Inv.: ÖMAK, W.I. 1659
(inventarisiert am 1. 4. 1916, erworben um 22 Kronen von Oertel, Haida)

123
COVERED JAR
Design: Haida school of glassmaking
Manufacturer: Oertel, Haida
Serial number 2695 (Oertel)
Cut crystal glass
H 14.4, Db 9.2,
D (lip) 9.7
Exhibition(s): ÖMKI 1915
Inv.: ÖMAK, W.I. 1659
(inventoried 01/04/16; acquired for 22 crowns from Oertel, Haida)

122

123

124

124

124
STURZFLASCHE
MIT BECHER
Meyr's Neffe
Schliff (10 Ecken)
Flasche: H 20,1
(mit Becher 22,3),
Dg 10,4, Do 4,8, Du 9,5
Becher: H 9,5, Do 7,5,
Du 5,5
Ausst.: Stockholm 1916
Inv.: ÖMAK, W.I. 1616/1-2
(inventarisiert am
1. 6. 1915, erworben um
12 Kronen von Meyr's
Neffe)

124
BOTTLE WITH BEAKER
Meyr's Neffe
Cut crystal glass
(10 sides)
Bottle: H 20.1
(with beaker 22.3),
Dm 10.4, Dt 4.8, Db 9.5
Beaker: H 9.5, Dt 7.5,
Db 5.5
Exhibition(s):
Stockholm 1916
Inv.: ÖMAK, W.I. 1616/1-2
(inventoried 01/06/15;
acquired for 12 crowns
from Meyr's Neffe)

124

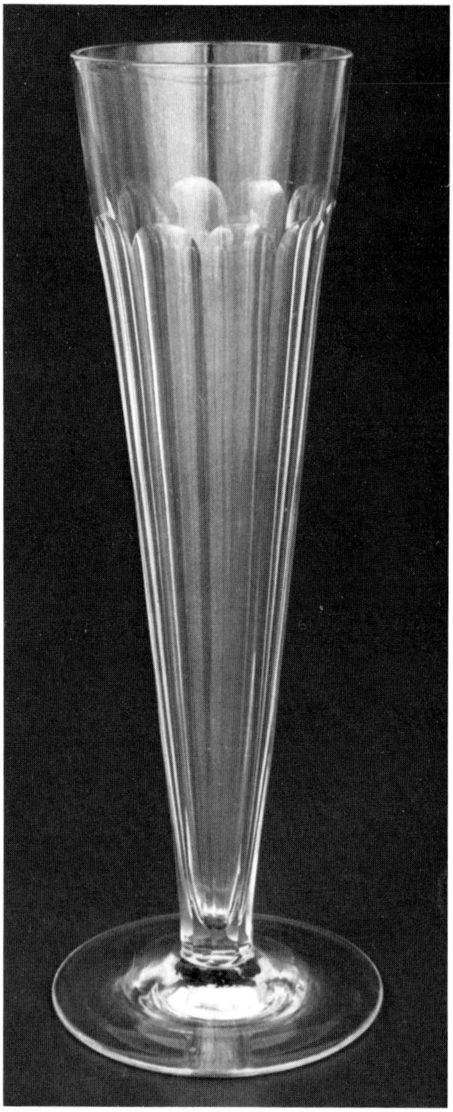

125

125
CHAMPAGNERFLÖTE
Gerner, Haida
Werknummer 4848
Schliff (10 Ecken)
H 20,4, Do 5,7, Du 7,5
Ausst.: ÖMKI 1915
Inv.: ÖMAK, W.I. 1696
(inventarisiert am
1. 4. 1916, erworben um
4,20 Kronen von Gerner,
Haida)

125
CHAMPAGNE GLASS
Gerner, Haida
Serial number 4848
Cut crystal glass
(10 sides)
H 20.4, Dt 5.7, Db 7.5
Exhibition(s): ÖMKI 1915
Inv.: ÖMAK, W.I. 1696
(inventoried 01/04/16;
acquired for 4.20 crowns
from Gerner, Haida)

126
KOMPOTTVASE
Gerner, Haida
Werknummer 4823
Schliff (8 Ecken)
H 21,5, D Mundrand 9,8,
D Deckel 10, Du 8,6
Ausst.: ÖMKI 1915
Inv.: ÖMAK, W.I. 1695
(inventarisiert am
1. 4. 1916, erworben um
24 Kronen von Gerner,
Haida)

126
FRUIT JAR
Gerner, Haida
Serial number 4823
Cut crystal glass (8 sides)
H 21.5, D (lip) 9.8,
D (lid) 10, Db 8.6
Exhibition(s): ÖMKI 1915
Inv.: ÖMAK, W.I. 1695
(inventoried 01/04/16;
acquired for 24 crowns
from Gerner, Haida)

126

127

127
VASE
Meyr's Neffe, Adolf
Schliff (8 Ecken)
H 29,6, Do 11,3, Du 12,1
Ausst.: Stockholm 1916
Inv.: ÖMAK, W.I. 1614
(inventarisiert am
1. 6. 1915, erworben um
27,50 Kronen von Meyr's
Neffe)

127
VASE
Meyr's Neffe, Adolf
Cut crystal glass (8 sides)
H 29.6, Dt 11.3, Db 12.1
Exhibition(s):
Stockholm 1916
Inv.: ÖMAK, W.I. 1614
(inventoried 01/06/15;
acquired for 27.50 crowns
from Meyr's Neffe)

128
VASE
Meyr's Neffe, Adolf
Schliff (8 Ecken)
H 32,6, Do 12,2, Du 11,6
Ausst.: Stockholm 1916
Inv.: ÖMAK, W.I. 1598
(inventarisiert am
1. 6. 1915, erworben um
29 Kronen von Meyr's
Neffe)

128
VASE
Meyr's Neffe, Adolf
Cut crystal glass (8 sides)
H 32.6, Dt 12.2, Db 11.6
Exhibition(s):
Stockholm 1916
Inv.: ÖMAK, W.I. 1598
(inventoried 01/06/15;
acquired for 29 crowns
from Meyr's Neffe)

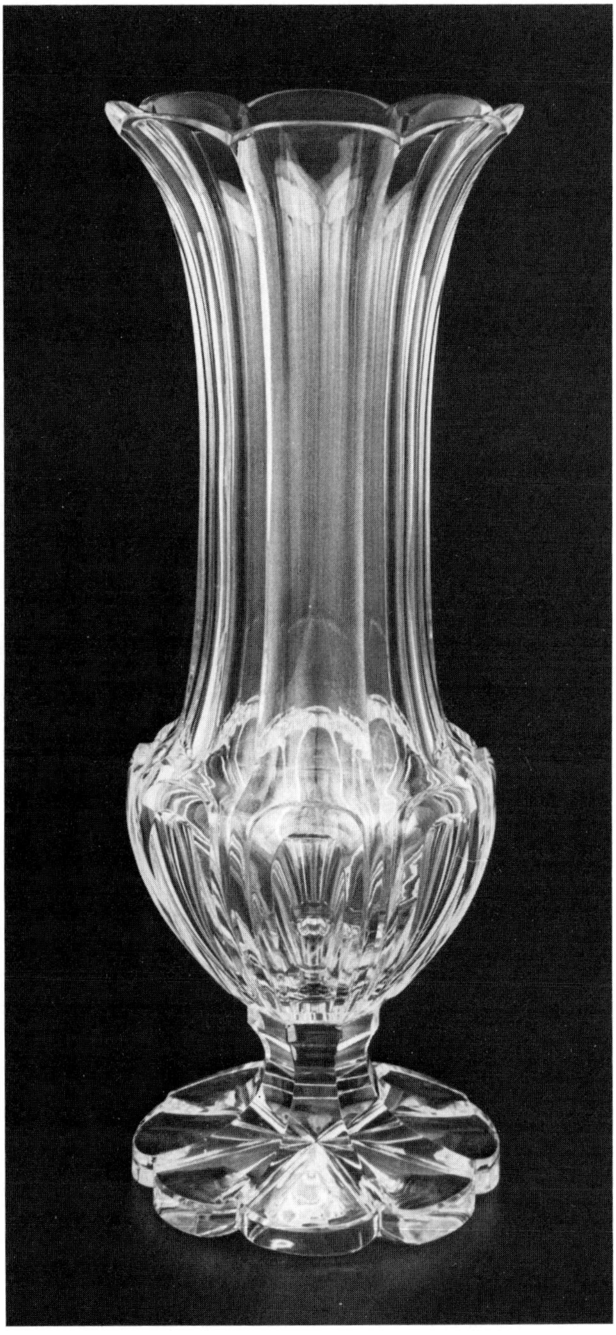

128

129

129
AUFSATZ
Meyr's Neffe, Adolf
Schliff (Fuß und Nodus 10 Ecken, Schale 20 Ecken)
H 11,2, Do 18,2, Du 10,1
Ausst.: Stockholm 1916
Inv.: ÖMAK, W.I. 1609 (inventarisiert am 1. 6. 1915, erworben um 10 Kronen von Meyr's Neffe)

129
CENTREPIECE
Meyr's Neffe, Adolf
Cut crystal glass (foot and knop 10 sides, bowl 20 sides)
H 11.2, Dt 18.2, Db 10.1
Exhibition(s): Stockholm 1916
Inv.: ÖMAK, W.I. 1609 (inventoried 01/06/15; acquired for 10 crowns from Meyr's Neffe)

130

130
AUFSATZ
Meyr's Neffe, Adolf
Schliff (10 Ecken)
H 14,6, Do 14,6, Du 10,8
Ausst.: Stockholm 1916
Inv.: ÖMAK, W.I. 1610
(inventarisiert am
1. 6. 1915, erworben um
13,50 Kronen von Meyr's
Neffe)

130
CENTREPIECE
Meyr's Neffe, Adolf
Cut crystal glass
(10 sides)
H 14.6, Dt 14.6, Db 10.8

Exhibition(s):
Stockholm 1916
Inv.: ÖMAK, W.I. 1610
(inventoried 01/06/15;
acquired for 13.50 crowns
from Meyr's Neffe)

131

131
FLAKON
Meyr's Neffe, Adolf
Schliff (8 Ecken)
H 17
Ausst.: Stockholm 1916
Inv.: ÖMAK, W.I. 1612
(inventarisiert am
1. 6. 1915, erworben um
6 Kronen von Meyr's Neffe)

131
BOTTLE
Meyr's Neffe, Adolf
Cut crystal glass (8 sides)
H 17
Exhibition(s):
Stockholm 1916
Inv.: ÖMAK, W.I. 1612
(inventoried 01/06/15;
acquired for 6 crowns
from Meyr's Neffe)

132
FLAKON
Meyr's Neffe, Adolf
Schliff (8 Ecken)
H 17,1
Inv.: ÖMAK, W.I. 1611
(inventarisiert am
1. 6. 1915, erworben um
6 Kronen von Meyr's Neffe)

132
BOTTLE
Meyr's Neffe, Adolf
Cut crystal glass (8 sides)
H 17.1
Inv.: ÖMAK, W.I. 1611
(inventoried 01/06/15;
acquired for 6 crowns
from Meyr's Neffe)

132

133

133
DECKELPOKAL
Rasch, Ulrichsthal
Werknummer 4207 (Rasch)
Schliff (8 Ecken)
H 39,9, D Deckel 11,4,
Do 11,2, Du 12
Auf der Deckelinnenseite:
Klebeetikett (Angaben
kaum leserlich: Nr.:
Künstler: Erzeuger:
Preis: 37 K 50)
Ausst.: ÖMKI 1915
(Foto ÖMAK Inv. VS 180 C)
Lit.:
KKH XVIII/1915, S. 428
Inv.: ÖMAK, W.I. 1704
(inventarisiert am
1. 4. 1916, erworben um
30,20 Kronen von Rasch,
Ulrichsthal)

133
LIDDED GOBLET
Rasch, Ulrichsthal
Serial number 4207
Cut crystal glass (8 sides)
H 39.9, D (lid) 11.4,
Dt 11.2, Db 12
On inside of lid: label
(details scarcely legible:
no: artist: manufacturer:
price: 37 K 50)
Exhibition(s): ÖMKI 1915
(photograph ÖMAK,
VS 180 C)
Lit.:
KKH XVIII/1915, p. 428
Inv.: ÖMAK, W.I. 1704
(inventoried 01/04/16;
acquired for 30.20 crowns
from Rasch, Ulrichsthal)

134
FLASCHE
Ausführung: Mühlhaus, Haida
Flasche mit Stöpsel, Schliff (8 Ecken), Bodenstern, Stöpsel mit Facettenschliff
H 43,4, Du 9,6
Ausst.: ÖMKI 1912
(Foto ÖMAK Inv. VS 175 A)
Lit.:
KKH XV/1912,S. 362
Inv.: ÖMAK, W.I. 1106
(inventarisiert am 15. 7. 1912, erworben um 13,50 Kronen von Mühlhaus, Haida)

134
BOTTLE
Manufacturer: Mühlhaus, Haida
Bottle with stopper
Cut crystal glass (8 sides) star in bottom, bevel-cut stopper
H 43.4, Db 9.6
Exhibition(s): ÖMKI 1912
(photograph ÖMAK, VS 175 A)
Lit.:
KKH XV/1912, p. 362
Inv.: ÖMAK, W.I. 1106
(inventoried 15/07/12; acquired for 13.50 crowns from Mühlhaus, Haida)

134

135
KELCHGLAS
Meyr's Neffe, Adolf
Schliff (12 Ecken),
runder Fuß
H 12,2, Do 5,5, Du 5,7
Inv.: ÖMAK, W.I. 1623
(inventarisiert am
1. 6. 1915, erworben um
4,75 Kronen von Meyr's
Neffe)

135
GOBLET
Meyr's Neffe, Adolf
Cut crystal glass (12 sides),
round foot
H 12.2, Dt 5.5, Db 5.7
Inv.: ÖMAK, W.I. 1623
(inventoried 01/06/15;
acquired for 4.75 crowns
from Meyr's Neffe)

135

136

136
KELCHGLAS
Meyr's Neffe, Adolf
Schliff (8 Ecken)
H 13,8, Do 8,2, Du 6,5
Ausst.: Stockholm 1916
Inv.: ÖMAK, W.I. 1624
(inventarisiert am
1. 6. 1915, erworben um
6,50 Kronen von Meyr's
Neffe)

136
GOBLET
Meyr's Neffe, Adolf
Cut crystal glass (8 sides)
H 13.8, Dt 8.2, Db 6.5
Exhibition(s):
Stockholm 1916
Inv.: ÖMAK, W.I. 1624
(inventoried 01/06/15;
acquired for 6.50 crowns
from Meyr's Neffe)

137

137
BECHER
Meyr's Neffe, Adolf
Schliff (8 Ecken)
H 11,2, Do 8, Du 4,7
Inv.: ÖMAK, W.I. 1605
(inventarisiert am
1. 6. 1915, erworben um
3,75 Kronen von Meyr's
Neffe)

137
BEAKER
Meyr's Neffe, Adolf
Cut crystal glass (8 sides)
H 11.2, Dt 8, Db 4.7
Inv.: ÖMAK, W.I. 1605
(inventoried 01/06/15;
acquired for 3.75 crowns
from Meyr's Neffe)

138
TEEFLAKON
mit Stöpsel
Meyr's Neffe, Adolf
Schliff (10 Ecken)
H 18,3, D Mundrand 6,3,
Du 7,6
Ausst.: Stockholm 1916
Inv.: ÖMAK, W.I. 1608
(inventarisiert am
1. 6. 1915, erworben um
5 Kronen von Meyr's Neffe)

138
TEA BOTTLE
with stopper
Meyr's Neffe, Adolf
Cut crystal glass (10 sides)
H 18.3, D (lip) 6.3,
Db 7.6
Exhibition(s):
Stockholm 1916
Inv.: ÖMAK, W.I. 1608
(inventoried 01/06/15;
acquired for 5 crowns
from Meyr's Neffe)

138

139

139
BECHER
Meyr's Neffe, Adolf
Schliff (8 Ecken),
runder Mundrand
H 12,2, Do 8,4, Du 6
Ausst.: Stockholm 1916
Inv.: ÖMAK, W.I. 1604
(inventarisiert am
1. 6. 1915, erworben um
5 Kronen von Meyr's Neffe)

139
BEAKER
Meyr's Neffe, Adolf
Cut crystal glass (8 sides),
round lip
H 12.2, Dt 8.4, Db 6
Exhibition(s):
Stockholm 1916
Inv.: ÖMAK, W.I. 1604
(inventoried 01/06/15;
acquired for 5 crowns
from Meyr's Neffe)

140

140
BECHER
Meyr's Neffe, Adolf
Schliff (8 Ecken),
runder Mundrand
H 12,6, Do 8,2, Du 6,8
Inv.: ÖMAK, W.I. 1606
(inventarisiert am
1. 6. 1915, erworben um
4,50 Kronen von Meyr's
Neffe)

140
BEAKER
Meyr's Neffe, Adolf
Cut crystal glass (8 sides),
round lip
H 12.6, Dt 8.2, Db 6.8
Inv.: ÖMAK, W.I. 1606
(inventoried 01/06/15;
acquired for 4.50 crowns
from Meyr's Neffe)

141

141
VASE
Verleger: Lobmeyr, Wien
Schliff (Schaft 12 Ecken), viereckige Fußplatte, Kuppa von rundem Querschnitt
H 21, Do 15,3, unten 8,8 × 8,8
Etikett: No 43 M
Ausst.:
ÖMAK 1913/14, Nr. 564 (Foto ÖMAK Inv. VS 174 A)
Inv.: ÖMAK, W.I. 1266 (inventarisiert am 7. 1. 1914, erworben um 27,30 Kronen von Lobmeyr)

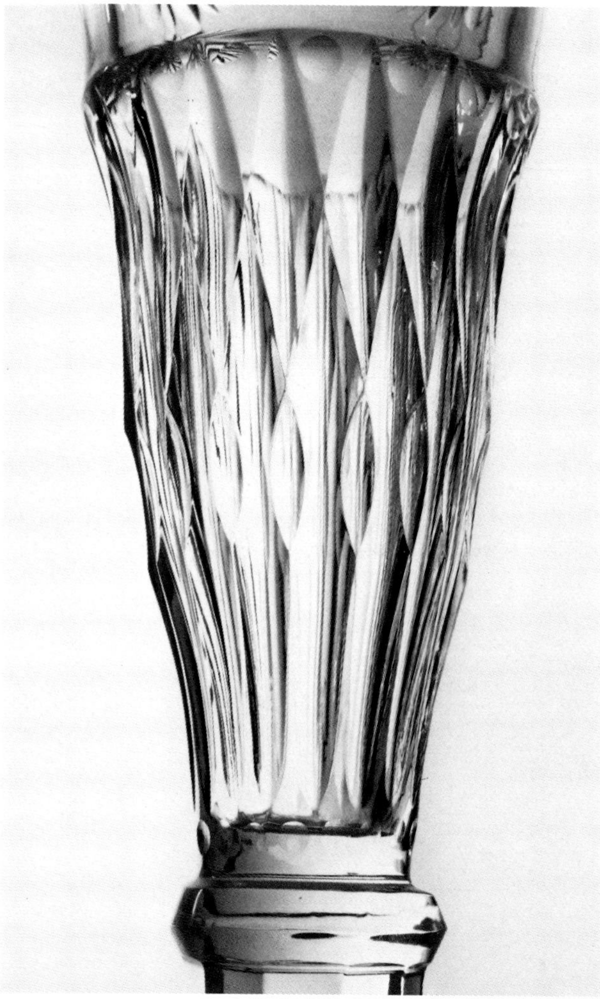

142

141
VASE
Commissioned by: Lobmeyr, Vienna
Cut crystal glass (stem 12-sided), square foot plate, bowl round in cross-section
H 21, Dt 15.3, 8.8 × 8.8 (bottom)
Label with "No 43 M"
Exhibition(s):
ÖMAK 1913/14, no. 564 (photograph ÖMAK, VS 174 A)
Inv.: ÖMAK, W.I. 1266 (inventoried 07/01/14; acquired for 27.30 crowns from Lobmeyr)

141

142

142
VASE
Meyr's Neffe, Adolf
Schliff (Fuß 10 Ecken)
H 32,4, Do 14,5,
D Fuß 13,1
Inv.: ÖMAK, W.I. 1615
(inventarisiert am
1. 6. 1915, erworben um
16 Kronen von Meyr's
Neffe)

142
VASE
Meyr's Neffe, Adolf
Cut crystal glass
(foot 10 sides)
H 32.4, Dt 14.5,
D foot 13.1
Inv.: ÖMAK, W.I. 1615
(inventoried 01/06/15;
acquired for 16 crowns
from Meyr's Neffe)

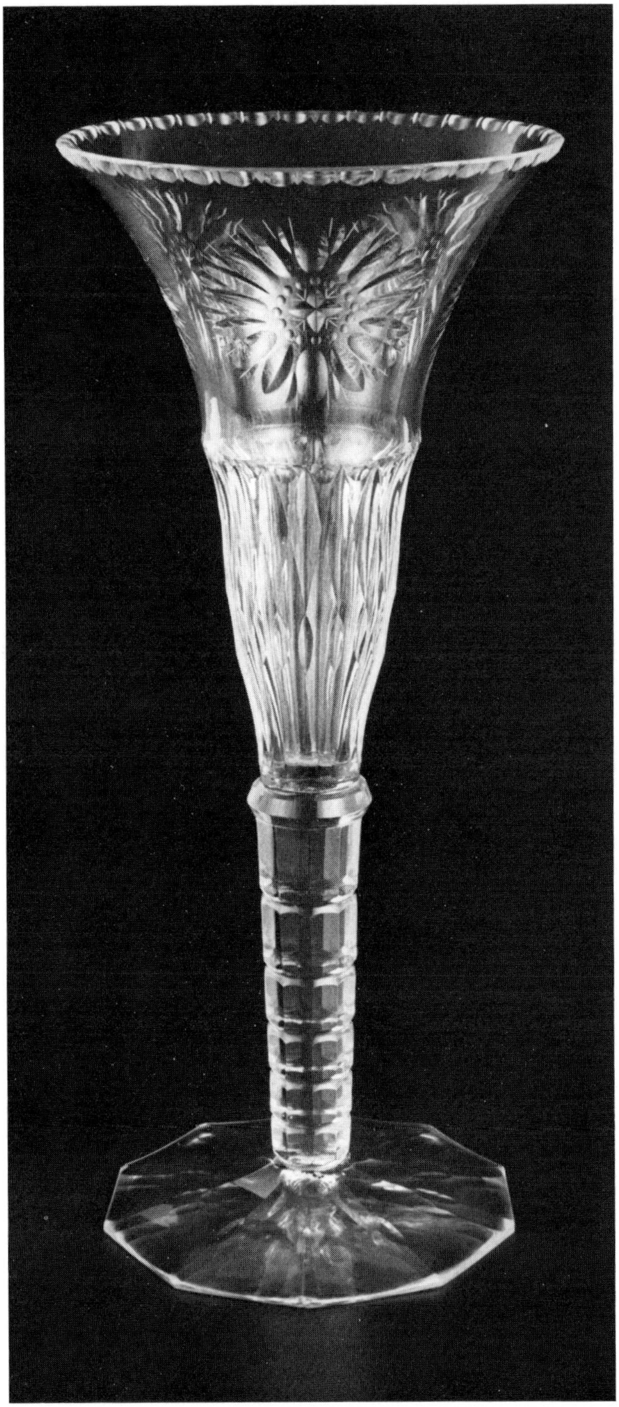

142

143

143
HENKELKRUG
MIT STÖPSEL
Gerner, Haida
Werknummer 4872 (Gerner)
Schliff (Boden, oberer
Teil der Wandung, Hals,
Stöpsel)
H 23,6
Ausst.: ÖMKI 1915
(Foto ÖMAK Inv. VS 177 C)
Lit.:
KKH XVIII/1915, S. 430
Inv.: ÖMAK, W.I. 1697
(inventarisiert am
1. 4. 1916, erworben um
8 Kronen von Gerner,
Haida)

143
HANDLED JUG
WITH STOPPER
Gerner, Haida
Serial number 4872
Cut crystal glass
(bottom, upper part of
side, neck, stopper)
H 23.6
Exhibition(s): ÖMKI 1915
(photograph ÖMAK,
VS 177 C)
Lit.:
KKH XVIII/1915, p. 430
Inv.: ÖMAK, W.I. 1697
(inventoried 01/04/16;
acquired for 8 crowns from
Gerner, Haida)

144

144
KRÜGLEIN
Meyr's Neffe, Adolf
Schliff (8 Ecken)
H 10,9 (Henkel)
Ausst.: ÖMKI 1915
Inv.: ÖMAK, W.I. 1691
(inventarisiert am
1. 4. 1916, erworben um
6 Kronen von Meyr's Neffe)

144
SMALL JUG
Meyr's Neffe, Adolf
Cut crystal glass (8 sides)
H 10.9 (handle)
Exhibition(s): ÖMKI 1915
Inv.: ÖMAK, W.I. 1691
(inventoried 01/04/16;
acquired for 6 crowns
from Meyr's Neffe)

145

145
VASE
Meyr's Neffe, Adolf
Schliff (Schaft 8 Ecken), Standfläche und Wandung gesteindelt, teilweise mit transparenten Farben (blau, grün, rot) bemalt
H 30,2, Du 12,4, Do 14,1
Inv.: ÖMAK, W.I. 1597
(inventarisiert am 1. 6. 1915, erworben um 37,50 Kronen von Meyr's Neffe)

145
VASE
Meyr's Neffe, Adolf
Cut crystal glass (stem 8-sided), base and side with strawberry diamond cutting, partly painted with transparent colours (blue, green, red)
H 30.2, Db 12.4, Dt 14.1
Inv.: ÖMAK, W.I. 1597
(inventoried 01/06/15; acquired for 37,50 crowns from Meyr's Neffe)

146
VASE
Meyr's Neffe, Adolf
Schliff (Schaft 8 Ecken), Standfläche und Wandung gesteindelt, teilweise mit transparenten Farben (blau, grün, rot) bemalt
H 29,2, Du 12, Do 15,2
Inv.: ÖMAK, W.I. 1596
(inventarisiert am 1. 6. 1915, erworben um 30 Kronen von Meyr's Neffe)

146
VASE
Meyr's Neffe, Adolf
Cut crystal glass (stem 8-sided), base and side with strawberry diamond cutting, partly painted with transparent colours (blue, green, red)
H 29.2, Db 12, Dt 15.2
Inv.: ÖMAK, W.I. 1596
(inventoried 01/06/15; acquired for 30 crowns from Meyr's Neffe)

146

147

147
VASE
auf drei Füßchen
Gerner, Haida
Werknummer 4819
Kantenschliff
H 17,3, Do 3,9, Du 5,4
Ausst.: ÖMKI 1915
Inv.: ÖMAK, W.I. 1694
(inventarisiert am
1. 4. 1916, erworben um
9 Kronen von Gerner,
Haida)

147
VASE
on three feet
Gerner, Haida
Serial number 4819
Cut crystal glass,
cut edges
H 17.3, Dt 3.9, Db 5.4
Exhibition(s): ÖMKI 1915
Inv.: ÖMAK, W.I. 1694
(inventoried 01/04/16;
acquired for 9 crowns
from Gerner, Haida)

148
VASE
Meltzer, Langenau
Serial number 2245
Cut crystal glass (8 sides),
cut edges
H 30.7, Dt 9, Db 9, Dm 11
Exhibition(s): ÖMKI 1915
Inv.: ÖMAK, W.I. 1699
(inventoried 01/04/16;
acquired for 25.20 crowns
from Meltzer, Langenau)

148
VASE
Meltzer, Langenau
Werknummer 2245
Schliff (8 Ecken),
Kantenschliff
H 30,7, Do 9, Du 9, Dg 11
Ausst.: ÖMKI 1915
Inv.: ÖMAK, W.I. 1699
(inventarisiert am
1. 4. 1916, erworben um
25,20 Kronen von Meltzer,
Langenau)

149
VASE
Meyr's Neffe, Adolf
Cut crystal glass,
star in bottom (24 sides),
cut shoulder
H 15, Dm 13.8, Dt 12.8,
Db 8
Inv.: ÖMAK, W.I. 1618
(inventoried 01/06/15;
acquired for 2.64 crowns
from Meyr's Neffe)

150
JAR ("CAKESDOSE")
Meyr's Neffe, Adolf
Optical glass,
cut: star in bottom
(24-sided), shoulder
with strawberry diamond
cutting, frosted lip
(lid probably missing)
H 15.1, Dt 10.3, Db 9.3
Inv.: ÖMAK, W.I. 1617
(inventoried 01/06/15;
acquired for 3.36 crowns
from Meyr's Neffe)

148

149

149
VASE
Meyr's Neffe, Adolf
Schliff: Bodenstern (24teilig) und Schulter
H 15, Dg 13,8, Do 12,8, Du 8

Inv.: ÖMAK, W.I. 1618 (inventarisiert am 1. 6. 1915, erworben um 2,64 Kronen von Meyr's Neffe)

150

150
DOSE („CAKESDOSE")
Meyr's Neffe, Adolf
Optisches Glas, Schliff: Bodenstern (24teilig), Schulter gesteindelt, mattierter Mundrand (vermutlich fehlt der Deckel)
H 15,1, Do 10,3, Du 9,3
Inv.: ÖMAK, W.I. 1617
(inventarisiert am 1. 6. 1915, erworben um 3,36 Kronen von Meyr's Neffe)

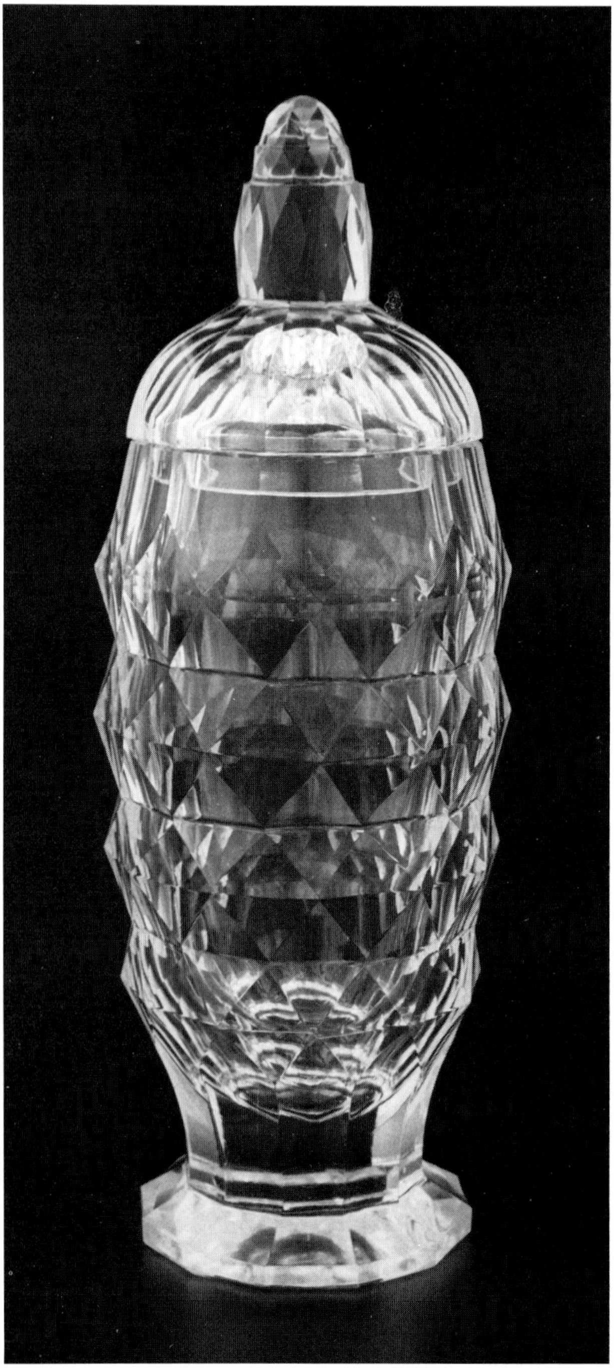

151
DECKELPOKAL
Entwurf:
Fachschule Haida
Ausführung:
Oertel, Haida
Werknummer 2720
(Oertel)
Schliff facettiert
(12seitig)
H 21,6, Dg 8,1
Ausst.: ÖMKI 1915
Inv.: ÖMAK, W.I. 1660
(inventarisiert am
1. 4. 1916, erworben um
24 Kronen von Oertel,
Haida)

151
LIDDED GOBLET
Design: Haida school of
glassmaking
Manufacturer: Oertel, Haida
Serial number 2720
(Oertel)
Bevel-cut glass
(12 sides)
H 21.6, Dm 8.1
Exhibition(s): ÖMKI 1915
Inv.: ÖMAK, W.I. 1660
(inventoried 01/04/16;
acquired for 24 crowns
from Oertel, Haida)

151

152
VASE
Meyr's Neffe, Adolf
Schliff (facettiert, „Diamantschliff")
H 27,6, Do und Du 9, Dg 12,6
Inv.: ÖMAK, W.I. 1103 (inventarisiert am 15. 7. 1912, erworben um 53 Kronen von Meyr's Neffe)

152
VASE
Meyr's Neffe, Adolf
Cut crystal glass (Diamond cutting)
H 27.6, Dt und Db 9, Dm 12.6
Inv.: ÖMAK, W.I. 1103 (inventoried 15/07/12; acquired for 53 crowns from Meyr's Neffe)

152

153

153
VASE
Gebr. Zahn, Haida
Werknummer 6208 (Zahn)
Schliff,vertikal 20teilig,
24teiliger Bodenstern
H 21,2, Do 15,5, Du 9,5
Klebeetikett:
Hochglanz, 62 H
Ausst.: ÖMKI 1915
(Foto ÖMAK Inv. VS 173 A)
Lit.:
KKH XVIII/1915, S. 431
Inv.: ÖMAK, W.I. 1708
(inventarisiert am
1. 4. 1916, erworben um
14 Kronen von Gebr. Zahn,
Haida)

153
VASE
Gebr. Zahn, Haida
Serial number 6208 (Zahn)
Cut crystal glass
(20 sides), star in
bottom (24-sided)
H 21.2, Dt 15.5, Db 9.5
Label with "Hochglanz,
62 H"
Exhibition(s): ÖMKI 1915
(photograph ÖMAK,
VS 173 A)
Lit.:
KKH XVIII/1915, p. 431
Inv.: ÖMAK, W.I. 1708
(inventoried 01/04/16;
acquired for 14 crowns
from Gebr. Zahn, Haida)

153

154

154
JARDINIERE
Harrach, Neuwelt
Werknummer 32167
Oval, Rautenschliff
H 11,7, 15 × 27
(größte Ausdehnung)
Zwei Klebeetiketten:
rechteckige Marke mit
No 32167, ovaler
Prägedruck
Ausst.: ÖMKI 1915
Inv.: ÖMAK, W.I. 1702
(inventarisiert am
1. 4. 1916, erworben um
50 Kronen von Harrach,
Neuwelt)

154
JARDINIERE
Harrach, Neuwelt
Serial number 32167
Shape: oval,
lozenge cutting
H 11.7, 15 × 27
(max. extent)
Two labels: square mark
with no. 32167, oval
stamp
Exhibition(s): ÖMKI 1915
Inv.: ÖMAK, W.I. 1702
(inventoried 01/04/16;
acquired for 50 crowns
from Harrach, Neuwelt)

154

155

155
SCHALE
Meltzer/Langenau
Schliff im „Kristallstil“
Ausst.: ÖMKI 1915
Inv.: ÖMAK, VS 175 C
(zeitgenössisches Foto)

155
BOWL
Meltzer/Langenau
Cut in “crystal style”
Exhibition(s): ÖMKI 1915
Inv.: ÖMAK, VS 175 C
(contemporary photograph)

156

157

156
BLUMENKORB
Meyr's Neffe, Adolf
Schliff im „Kristallstil"
Ausst.: ÖMKI 1903/04
Inv.: ÖMAK, VS 175 C
(zeitgenössisches Foto)

156
FLOWER BASKET
Meyr's Neffe, Adolf
Cut in "crystal style"
Exhibition(s): ÖMKI 1903/04
Inv.: ÖMAK, VS 175 C
(contemporary photograph)

157
SCHÜSSEL
Harrach/Neuwelt
Schliff im „Kristallstil"
Ausst.: ÖMKI 1915
Inv.: ÖMAK, VS 179 A
(zeitgenössisches Foto)

157
BOWL
Harrach/Neuwelt
Cut in "crystal style"
Exhibition(s): ÖMKI 1915
Inv.: ÖMAK, VS 179 A
(contemporary photograph)

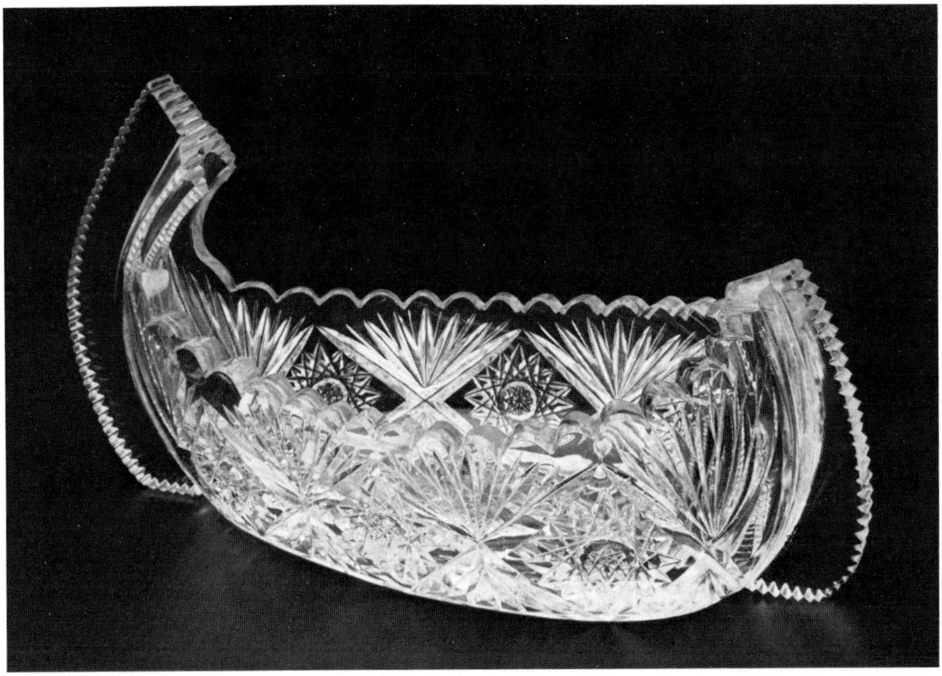

158

158
JARDINIERE
in „Schiff-Form“
Harrach/Neuwelt
Werknummer 31468
Bleiglas, Tiefschliff
im „Kristallstil“
H 14, L 27
Ausst.: ÖMKI 1915
Lit.:
KKH XVIII/1915, S. 433
Inv.: ÖMAK, W.I. 1702a
(inventarisiert am
1. 4. 1916, erworben um
50 Kronen von Harrach,
Neuwelt)

158
JARDINIERE
“ship-shaped”
Harrach/Neuwelt
Serial number 31468
Lead glass, deep cut in
“crystal style”
H 14, L 27
Exhibition(s): ÖMKI 1915
Lit.:
KKH XVIII/1915, p. 433
Inv.: ÖMAK, W.I. 1702a
(inventoried 01/04/16;
acquired for 50 crowns
from Harrach, Neuwelt)

159

159
AUFSATZ
Zahn, Haida
Werknummer 6211 (Zahn)
Schliff im „Kristallstil"
H 22, Do 24, Du 13,7
Firmenetikett: GZ FEIN KRISTALL HOCHGLANZ
Ausst.: ÖMKI 1915
Inv.: ÖMAK, W.I. 1709
(inventarisiert am 1. 4. 1916, erworben um 36 Kronen von Zahn)

159
CENTREPIECE
Zahn, Haida
Serial number 6211 (Zahn)
Cut in "crystal style"
H 22, Dt 24, Db 13.7
Label with "GZ FEIN KRISTALL HOCHGLANZ"
Exhibition(s): ÖMKI 1915
Inv.: ÖMAK, W.I. 1709
(inventoried 01/04/16; acquired for 36 crowns from Zahn, Haida)

159

160

160
SCHALE
Gebr. Zahn, Haida
Werknummer 6215 (Zahn)
Schliff im „Kristallstil“
H 10, Do 21,5, Du 17,8
Ausst.: ÖMKI 1915
Inv.: ÖMAK, W.I. 1710
(inventarisiert am
1. 4. 1916, erworben um
18 Kronen von Gebr. Zahn,
Haida)

160
BOWL
Gebr. Zahn, Haida
Serial number 6215 (Zahn)
Cut in "crystal style"
H 10, Dt 21.5, Db 17.8
Exhibition(s): ÖMKI 1915
Inv.: ÖMAK, W.I. 1710
(inventoried 01/04/16;
acquired for 18 crowns
from Gebr. Zahn, Haida)

161
SCHALE
in „Schiff-Form“
Bleiglas, „Tiefschliff“
Gebr. Zahn, Haida
(in der zeitgenössischen
Literatur irrtümlich als
Harrach, Neuwelt,
bezeichnet)
Ausst.: ÖMKI 1915
Lit.:
KKH XVIII/1915, S. 433
Eisler 1916, S. 163
DK XXIV/1916, S. 55
Inv.: ÖMAK, VS 175 C
(zeitgenössisches Foto)

161
BOWL
"ship-shaped"
Lead glass, deep cut in
"crystal style"
Gebr. Zahn, Haida
(erroneously attributed
to Harrach, Neuwelt, in
contemporary magazines)
Exhibition(s): ÖMKI 1915
Lit.:
KKH XVIII/1915, p. 433
Eisler 1916, p. 163
DK XXIV/1916, p. 55
Inv.: ÖMAK, VS 175 C
(contemporary photograph)

160

161

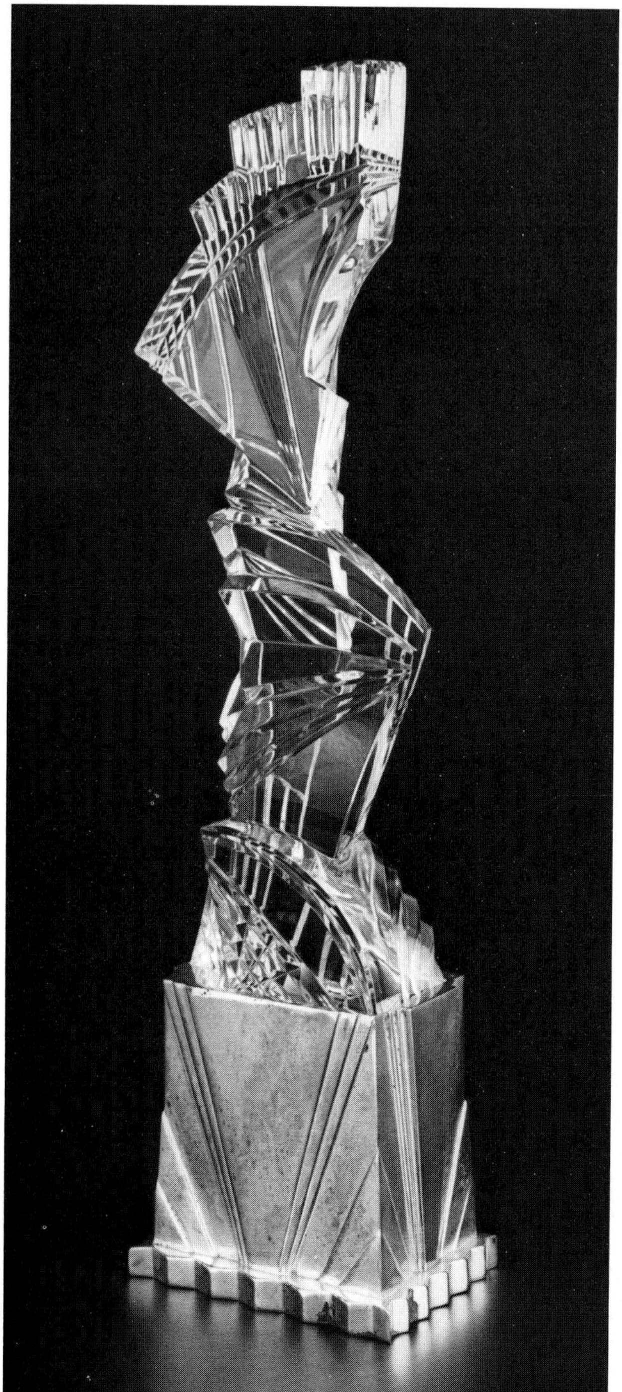

162
GLASPLASTIK
„kubistische Säule"
Packfongsockel
Entwurf: O. E. Wagner
(Schmidt: „nach Angaben
von Prof. Franz
Cizek, 1924")
Verleger: Lobmeyr, Wien
H 42,8
Lit.: Robert Schmidt,
100 Jahre österreichische
Glaskunst, Wien 1925,
Taf. 35
Inv.: ÖMAK, Gl 2426
(inventarisiert am
30. 12. 1925, erworben von
Lobmeyr; keine Preis-
angabe)

162
GLASS SCULPTURE
"cubist column" (inventory)
Cut crystal glass,
pakfong base
Design: O. E. Wagner
(Schmidt: "to instructions
by Prof. Franz Cizek,
1924")
Commissioned by:
Lobmeyr, Vienna
H 42.8
Lit.: Robert Schmidt,
100 Jahre österreichische
Glaskunst, Vienna 1925,
plate 35
Inv.: ÖMAK, Gl 2426
(inventoried 30/12/25;
acquired from Lobmeyr;
no prices given)

162

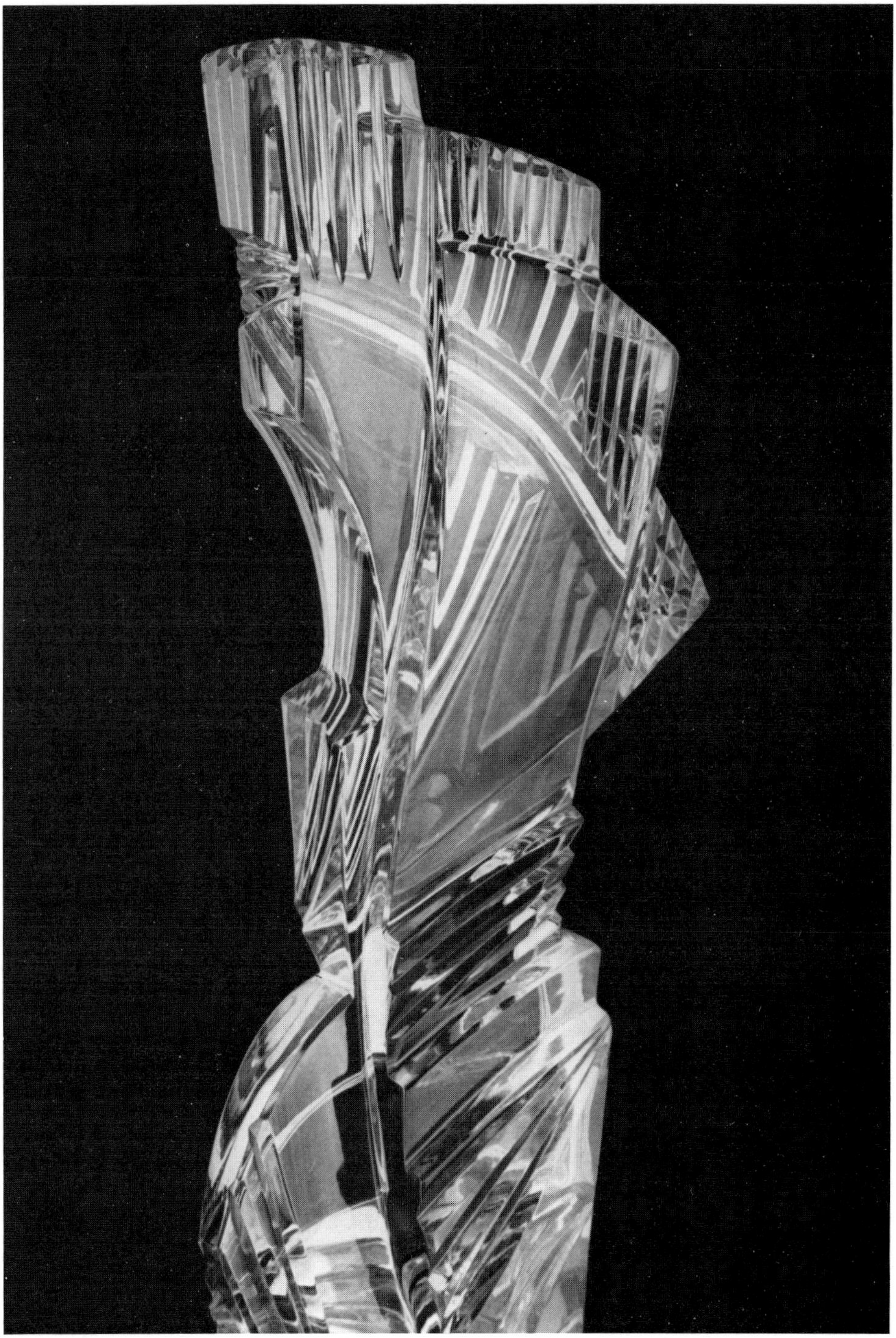

162

163

163
VASE
Goldberg, Haida
Werknummer 835
Farbglas („Kunckel-Glas“, rubin), Schliff (14 Ecken)
H 16,7, Do 13,5, Du 10,1
Eingeritzt: 835
Ausst.: ÖMKI 1915
Inv. ÖMAK, W.I. 1723
(inventarisiert am 1. 4. 1916, erworben um 40 Kronen von Goldberg)

163
VASE
Goldberg, Haida
Serial number 835
Coloured glass ("Kunckel" glass, ruby), cut (14 sides)
H 16.7, Dt 13.5, Db 10.1
Scratched: 835
Exhibition(s): ÖMKI 1915
Inv. ÖMAK, W.I. 1723
(inventoried 01/04/16; acquired for 40 crowns from Goldberg)

164
VASE
Fachschule Haida
Farbglas (Vollrubin, gekugelt)
H 25,8, Do 8,7, Du 8,6
Ausst.: ÖMAK 1973
Lit.: Neuwirth 1973, Nr. 49, S. 152, 153
Inv.: ÖMAK, W.I. 1240
(inventarisiert am 7.1.1914, erworben um 32,40 Kronen von der Fachschule Haida)

164
VASE
Haida school of glassmaking
Coloured glass (ruby glass, cut)
H 25.8, Dt 8.7, Db 8.6
Exhibition(s): ÖMAK 1973

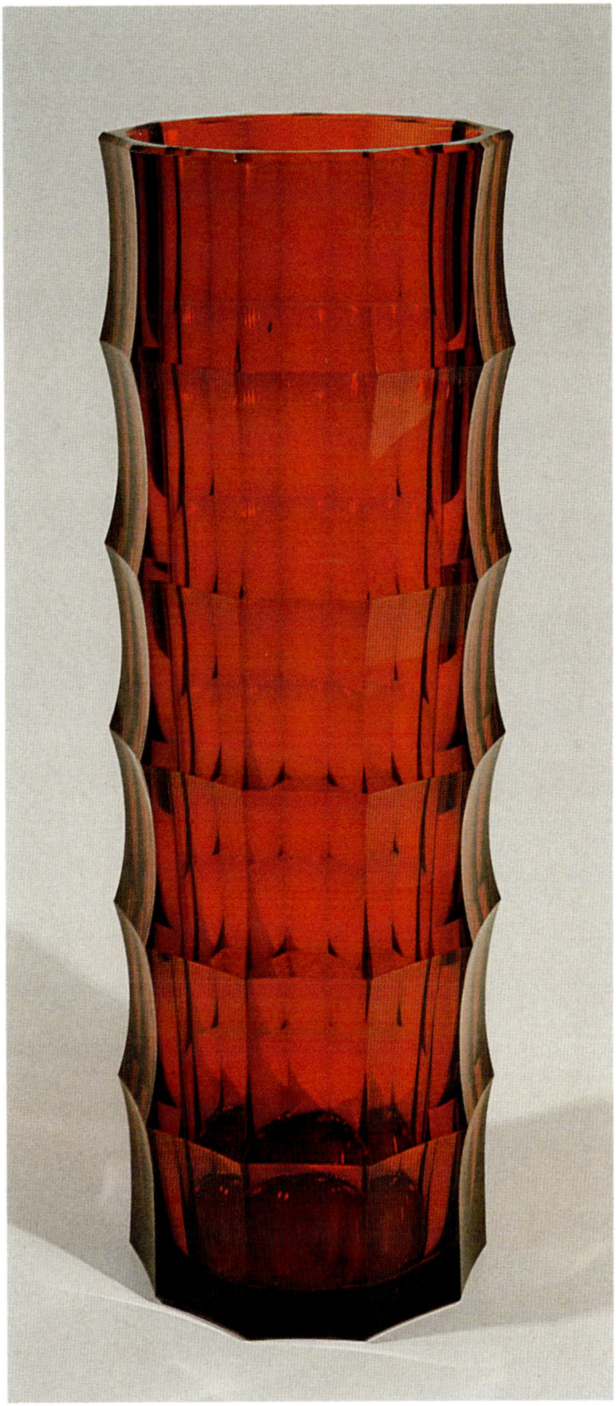

164

165

Lit.: Neuwirth 1973,
no. 49, pp. 152, 153
Inv.: ÖMAK, W.I. 1240
(inventoried 07/01/14;
acquired for 32.40 crowns
from Haida school of
glassmaking)

165
VASE
Mühlhaus, Haida
Farbglas (rubin),
Schliff (10 Ecken)
H 11,3, Do 6,1, Du 5,5
Inv.: ÖMAK, W.I. 1111
(inventarisiert am
15. 7. 1912, erworben um
3 Kronen von Mühlhaus,
Haida)

165
VASE
Mühlhaus, Haida
Coloured glass (ruby),
cut (10 sides)
H 11.3, Dt 6.1, Db 5.5
Inv.: ÖMAK, W.I. 1111
(inventoried 15/07/12;
acquired for 3 crowns
from Mühlhaus, Haida)

166
VASE
Mühlhaus, Haida
Farbglas (rubin),
Schliff (10 Ecken)
H 29,5, Do 6,3, Du 8,6
Inv.: ÖMAK, W.I. 1107
(inventarisiert am
15. 7. 1912, erworben um
19,50 Kronen von
Mühlhaus, Haida)

166
VASE
Mühlhaus, Haida
Coloured glass (ruby),
cut (10 sides)
H 29.5, Dt 6.3, Db 8.6
Inv.: ÖMAK, W.I. 1107
(inventoried 15/07/12;
acquired for 19.50 crowns
from Mühlhaus, Haida)

166

167
VASE
Goldberg, Haida
Werknummer 833
„Kunckel-Glas“, rubin,
Schliff (14 Ecken)
H 26,8, Do 18 cm,
Du 12,8 cm
Klebeetikett:
KUNCKEL-GLAS
1650 A.D. 1732
Ausst.: ÖMKI 1915
Lit.:
KKH XVIII/1915, S. 457
DKD 37/1915-16, S. 165
DK XXIV/1916, S. 61
Inv.: ÖMAK, W.I. 1722
(inventarisiert am
1. 4. 1916, erworben um
60 Kronen von Goldberg,
Haida)

167

167
VASE
Goldberg, Haida
Serial number 833
"Kunckel" glass, ruby,
cut (14 sides)
H 26.8, Dt 18, Db 12.8
Label with
"KUNCKEL-GLAS
1650 A.D. 1732"
Exhibition(s): ÖMKI 1915
Lit.:
KKH XVIII/1915, p. 457
DKD 37/1915-16, p. 165
DK XXIV/1916, p. 61
Inv.: ÖMAK, W.I. 1722
(inventoried 01/04/16;
acquired for 60 crowns
from Goldberg, Haida)

168
VASE
Goldberg, Haida
Werknummer 836
„Kunckel-Glas“, rubin,
Schliff (12 Ecken)
H 17,9, Do 7,2, Du 6,7
Eingeritzt: 836
Ausst.: ÖMKI 1915
Inv.: ÖMAK, W.I. 1724
(inventarisiert am
1. 4. 1916, erworben um
20 Kronen von Goldberg,
Haida)

169
VASE
Goldberg, Haida
Werknummer 896
Farbglas („Kunckel-Glas“,
rubin), Schliff (14 Ecken)
H 23,8, Do 16, Du 13,8
Ausst.: ÖMKI 1915
Inv.: ÖMAK, W.I. 1726
(inventarisiert am
1. 4. 1916, erworben um
40 Kronen von Goldberg,
Haida)

168
VASE
Goldberg, Haida
Serial number 836
"Kunckel" glass, ruby,
cut (12 sides)
H 17.9, Dt 7.2, Db 6.7
Scratched: 836
Exhibition(s): ÖMKI 1915
Inv.: ÖMAK, W.I. 1724
(inventoried 01/04/16;
acquired for 20 crowns
from Goldberg, Haida)

169
VASE
Goldberg, Haida
Serial number 896
Coloured glass ("Kunckel"
glass, ruby), cut (14 sides)
H 23.8, Dt 16, Db 13.8
Exhibition(s): ÖMKI 1915
Inv.: ÖMAK, W.I. 1726
(inventoried 01/04/16;
acquired for 40 crowns
from Goldberg, Haida)

167

168

169

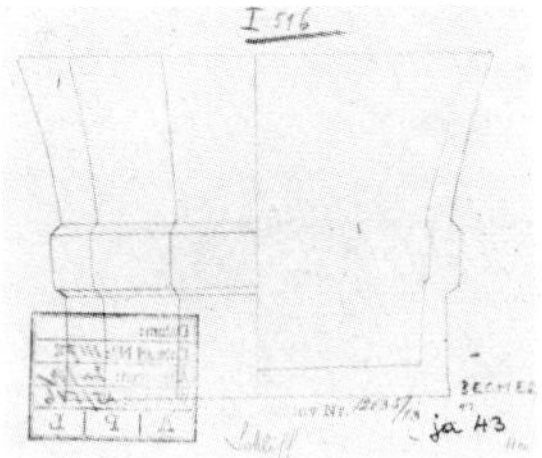

171

170
BONBONNIERE
Wiener Werkstätte
Werknummer A I 614
(später do 51)
Werkzeichnung nach
einem Entwurf von
Josef Hoffmann
Bez.: „I 614, zu schmal, richtige Form, Briefe vom 19/VIII 2, do 51, R 8.-, BONBONIERE, do 51, Archivstempel der Wiener Werkstätte (703/1, J. HOFFMANN 1915)"
H 16
Inv.: ÖMAK, K.I. 12039/27

171
VASE
Wiener Werkstätte
Werknummer A I 516
Werkzeichnung (Pause)
nach einem Entwurf
von Josef Hoffmann
Bez.: I 516, „BECHER", ja 43, HO, Schliff
H 12
Inv.: ÖMAK, K.I. 12035/13

171
VASE
Wiener Werkstätte
Serial number A I 516
Working drawing (copy) after a design of Josef Hoffmann
Description: "I 516, BECHER, ja 43, HO, Schliff"
H 12
Inv.: ÖMAK, K.I. 12035/13

170
CHOCOLATE DISH
Wiener Werkstätte
Serial number A I 614
(later do 51)
Working drawing after a design of Josef Hoffmann
Description: "I 614, too narrow, correct shape, letters of 19/VIII 2, do 51, R 8.-, BONBONNIERE, do 51", archive stamp of the Wiener Werkstätte (703/1, J. HOFFMANN 1915)
H 16
Inv.: ÖMAK, K.I. 12039/27

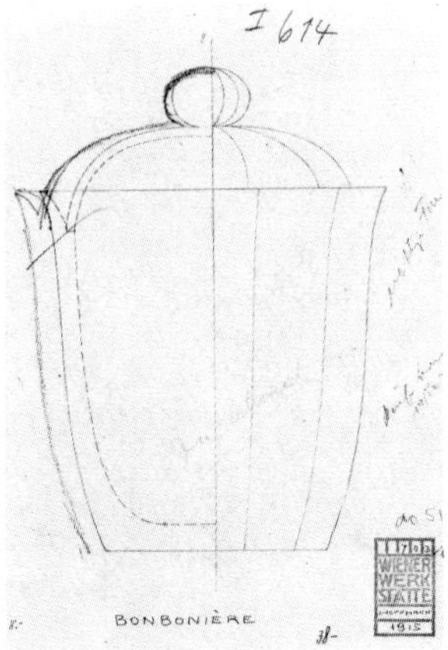

170

172
BONBONNIERE
Wiener Werkstätte
Werknummer A I 614
bzw. A I 755 (später do 51)
Entwurf: Josef Hoffmann
Ausführung in Kristall: Meyr's Neffe, Adolf und Oertel, Haida (1917-1918)
Ausführung in Farbglas (violett, blau, dunkelgrün und gelb, Werknummer A I 755): Meyr's Neffe, Adolf und Oertel, Haida (1917-1919) und später Farbglas (violett), Schliff (12 Ecken)
H 17,2, D Mundrand 12, Du 7
Ausst.: ÖMAK 1967, Kat. Nr. 321
Inv.: ÖMAK, Gl 3112 (1952 nachträglich inventarisiert)

172
CHOCOLATE JAR
Wiener Werkstätte
Serial number A I 614 and A I 755 (later do 51)
Design: Josef Hoffmann
Manufactured in crystal glass by Meyr's Neffe, Adolf, and Oertel, Haida (1917-1918), manufactured in coloured glass (violet, blue, dark green, yellow)
Serial number A I 755)
Meyr's Neffe, Adolf and Oertel, Haida (1917-1919) and later by unknown glass manufacturers
Coloured glass (violet), cut (12 sides)
H 17.2, D (lip) 12, Db 7
Exhibition(s):
ÖMAK 1967, no. 321
Inv.: ÖMAK, Gl 3112 (inventoried only 1952)

172

173
SCHALE
Wiener Werkstätte
Werknummer A I 542, später ja 41
Entwurf: Josef Hoffmann
Ausführung:
Meyr's Neffe, Adolf, und Oertel, Haida (1915-1927)
Farbglas (violett), Schliff (12 Ecken), runder Fuß
H 10,8, Do 14,3, Du 8,8
Ausst.:
ÖMAK 1967, Kat. Nr. 320
Lit.: WWMB 61, S. 542
WW Karteikarte ja 41
Inv.: ÖMAK, Gl 3110 (1952 nachträglich inventarisiert; Werkzeichnung ÖMAK, K.I. 12035/2)

173
BOWL
Wiener Werkstätte
Serial number A I 542, later ja 41
Design: Josef Hoffmann

173

Manufacturer:
Meyr's Neffe, Adolf, and Oertel, Haida (1915-1927)
Coloured glass (violet), cut (12 sides), round foot
H 10.8, Dt 14.3, Db 8.8
Exhibition(s):
ÖMAK 1967, no. 320
Lit.: WWMB 61, p. 542
WW filing card ja 41
Inv.: ÖMAK, Gl 3110 (inventoried only 1952; working drawing ÖMAK, K.I. 12035/2)

174

174
SCHALE
Wiener Werkstätte
Werknummer A I 516
bzw. ja 43
Entwurf: Josef Hoffmann,
um 1914/15
Ausführung:
Meyr's Neffe, Adolf und
Oertel, Haida (1915-1926)
Farbglas (violett),
Schliff (12 Ecken)
H 12,2, Do 17,2, Du 14,1
Ausst.:
ÖMAK 1967, Kat. Nr. 319
Lit.: WWMB 61, S. 516 und
WW Karteikarte ja 43
Inv.: ÖMAK, Gl 3111
(1952 nachträglich
inventarisiert)

174
BOWL
Wiener Werkstätte
Serial number A I 516
and ja 43
Design: Josef Hoffmann,
around 1914/15
Manufacturer:
Meyr's Neffe, Adolf and
Oertel, Haida (1915-1926)
Coloured glass (violet),
cut (12 sides)
H 12.2, Dt 17.2, Db 14.1
Exhibition(s):
ÖMAK 1967, no. 319
Lit.: WWMB 61, p. 516 and
WW filing card ja 43
Inv.: ÖMAK, Gl 3111
(inventoried only 1952)

175

175
VASE
Farbglas (violett),
Schliff (20 Ecken)
H 16,5, Dg 20,8, D Fuß 12
Inv.: ÖMAK, Gl 3342
(1976 erworben)

175
VASE
Coloured glass (violet),
cut (20 sides)
H 16.5, Dm 20.8, D foot 12
Inv.: ÖMAK, Gl 3342
(acquired 1976)

175

176

176
DECKELDOSE
Wiener Werkstätte
Werknummer se 1032
(Marmeladedose)
Entwurf:
Josef Hoffmann, um 1921
Ausführung: Moser,
Karlsbad (1923-1925)
Farbglas (dunkelviolett),
Schliff (16 Ecken)
H 13, D Mundrand 14,5
Bez. auf der Standfläche:
WW-Monogramm,
MOSER KARLSBAD
CZECHOSLOVAKIA
Lit.: WW Karteikarte
se 1032/M
Inv.: ÖMAK, Gl 3439
(1983 erworben; Werkzeichnung: ÖMAK K.I. 11940/3)

176
JAM BOWL
Wiener Werkstätte
Serial number se 1032
Design:
Josef Hoffmann, about 1921
Manufacturer: Moser,
Karlsbad (1923-1925)
Coloured glass (dark violet)
cut (16 sides)
H 13, D (lip) 14.5
Marked on base:
WW monogram,
MOSER KARLSBAD
CZECHOSLOVAKIA
Lit.: WW filing card
se 1032/M
Inv.: ÖMAK, Gl 3439
(acquired 1983;
working drawing:
ÖMAK K.I. 11940/3)

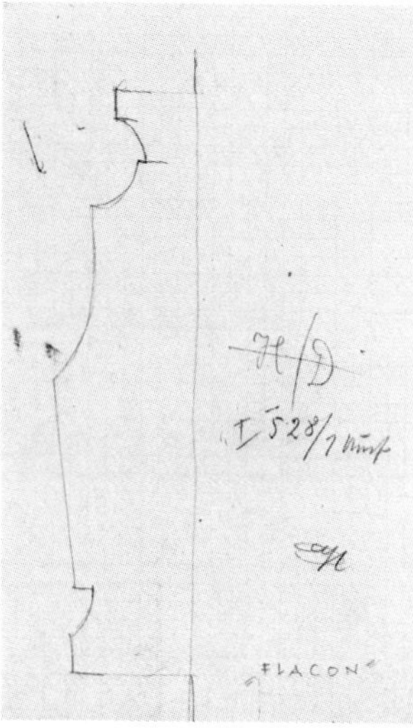

177

178

178
FLAKON
Wiener Werkstätte
Werknummer A I 528
Entwurf: Josef Hoffmann
Ausführung: Meyr's Neffe (1915 in Kristall), vermutlich andere Glashütte später in Farbglas
Farbglas (dunkelgrün), Schliff (17 Ecken)
H 18,7, Du 8,5
D Mundrand 6,8,
Bez.:
WW-Monogramm (Fuß)
Lit.: WWMB 61, S. 528
Inv.: ÖMAK, Gl 3308
(erworben 1971)

178

177
FLAKON
Entwurf von
Josef Hoffmann
Werknummer A I 528/1
Sign.: JH-Monogramm
Bez.: H/D, I 528/1 Ausf, „FLACON“
H 19,2
Inv.: ÖMAK, K.I. 12063/7

177
BOTTLE
Design by Josef Hoffmann
Serial number A I 528/1
Signed: monogram JH
Description: "H/D, I 528/1 Ausf, FLACON"
H 19.2
Inv.: ÖMAK, K.I. 12063/7

178
BOTTLE
Wiener Werkstätte
Serial number A I 528
Design: Josef Hoffmann
Manufacturer: Meyr's Neffe (1915 in crystal), probably other glass works later in coloured glass
Coloured glass (dark green), cut (17 sides)
H 18.7, Db 8.5 D (lip) 6.8,
Marked:
WW monogram (foot)
Lit.: WWMB 61, p. 528
Inv.: ÖMAK, Gl 3308
(acquired 1971)

179
VASE
Meyr's Neffe
Farbglas (dunkelgrün), Schliff (8 Ecken)
H 26,1, Do 11, Du 10,5
Inv.: ÖMAK, W.I. 1601
(inventarisiert am 1. 6. 1915, erworben um 12,50 Kronen von Meyr's Neffe)

180
VASE
Meyr's Neffe
Farbglas (hellgrün), Schliff (8 Ecken)
H 26,1, Do 11, Du 10,8
Inv.: ÖMAK, W.I. 1600
(inventarisiert am 1. 6. 1915, erworben um 12,50 Kronen von Meyr's Neffe)

179 180

179
VASE
Meyr's Neffe, Adolf
Coloured glass (dark green),
cut (8 sides)
H 26.1, Dt 11, Db 10.5
Inv.: ÖMAK, W.I. 1601
(inventoried 01/06/15;
acquired for 12.50 crowns
from Meyr's Neffe)

180
VASE
Meyr's Neffe, Adolf
Coloured glass (pale green),
cut (8 sides)
H 26.1, Dt 11, Db 10.8
Inv.: ÖMAK, W.I. 1600
(inventoried 01/06/15;
acquired for 12.50 crowns
from Meyr's Neffe)

186

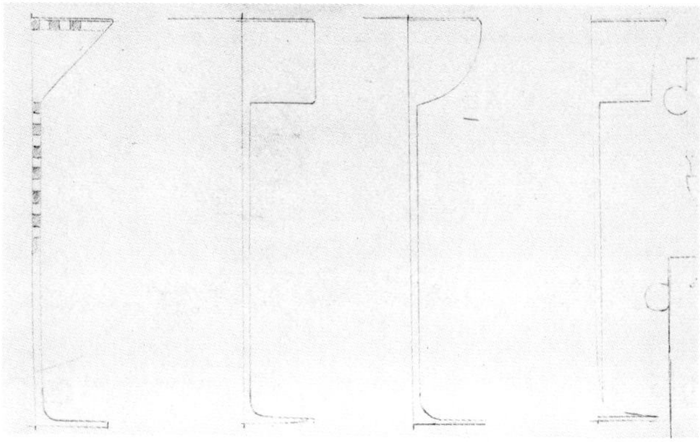

181

181
VIER GLÄSER
Werkzeichnungen
Entwurf: Otto Prutscher
Verleger: Bakalowits, Wien
H 22-22,2
Inv.: ÖMAK, B.I. 32066 c

181
FOUR GLASSES
Working drawings
Design: Otto Prutscher
Commissioned by:
Bakalowits, Vienna
H 22-22.2
Inv.: ÖMAK, B.I. 32066 c

184
SIX GLASSES
Design: Otto Prutscher
Manufacturer: probably
Meyr's Neffe, Adolf
Lit.:
DKD 25/1909-10, p. 376
Studio Year Book 1912,
p. 223
Cat. Expozice užitého
umění, Moravská galerie v
Brně, Brno 1975, no. 150,
p. 218 (three glasses:
left-hand glass, right-hand
glass, third glass from left)
Kat. Kunsthandwerk im
Grassimuseum, Leipzig
1981, 3. part, Fig. 28
(right-hand glass)
Barbara Mundt, Nostalgie
warum? Berlin 1982, no. 4,
p. 20 (second glass from
left)
České Sklo ze Sbírek
Západočeského Muzea v
Plzni, Květen-Srpen 1984,
unpaged, (second glass
from left)
Inv.: ÖMAK, Archiv WW
(Contemporary
photograph)

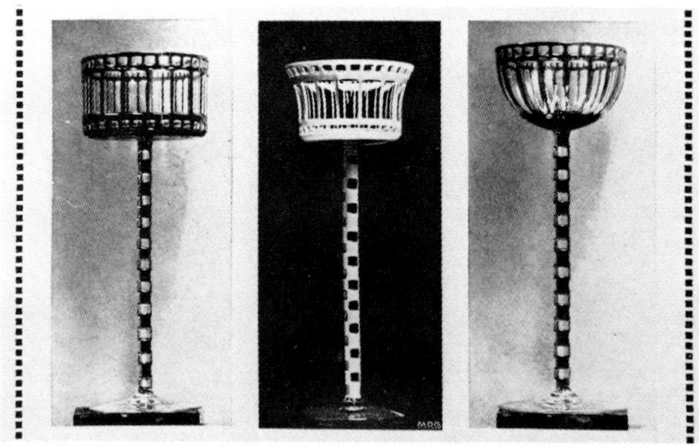

182

182
DREI GLÄSER
Entwurf: Otto Prutscher
Verleger: Bakalowits, Wien
Reproduktion aus:
DKD 20/1907, S. 340

182
THREE GLASSES
Design: Otto Prutscher
Commissioned by:
Bakalowits, Vienna
Reproduced from:
DKD 20/1907, p. 340

183

183
GLÄSER
Entwurf: Otto Prutscher
Verleger: Bakalowits, Wien
Ausst.:
Kunstschau Wien 1908
Reproduktion aus:
DK XVI/1908, S. 542

183
GLASSES
Design: Otto Prutscher
Commissioned by:
Bakalowits, Vienna
Exhibition(s):
Vienna art show 1908
Reproduced from:
DK XVI/1908, p. 542

185
GOBLET
Design: Otto Prutscher
Manufacturer: probably
Meyr's Neffe, Adolf
Crystal, cased, cut
H 21, Dt 8.7, Db 8.1
Exhibition(s):
ÖMKI 1910/11
Lit.:
DKD 20/1907, p. 340
DKD 25/1909-10, p. 376
Studio Year Book 1912,
p. 223
Kat. Expozice užitého
umění, Moravská galerie v
Brně, Brno 1975,
no. 150, p. 218
Inv.: Joanneum, AKGW,
no. 12685
(acquired 04/01/10 for
14.80 crowns from ÖMKI)

186
GOBLET
Design: Otto Prutscher
Manufacturer:
Meyr's Neffe, Adolf
Crystal, cased, cut,
silver-yellow, green
enamel spots, foot with
cut star
H 20.5, Dt 7.3, Db 7.9
Exhibition(s):
ÖMKI 1915. – ÖMAK 1973
Lit.:
Neuwirth 1973, no. 172,
p. 308
Inv.: ÖMAK, W.I. 1693
(inventoried 01/04/16;
acquired for 14 crowns
from Meyr's Neffe)

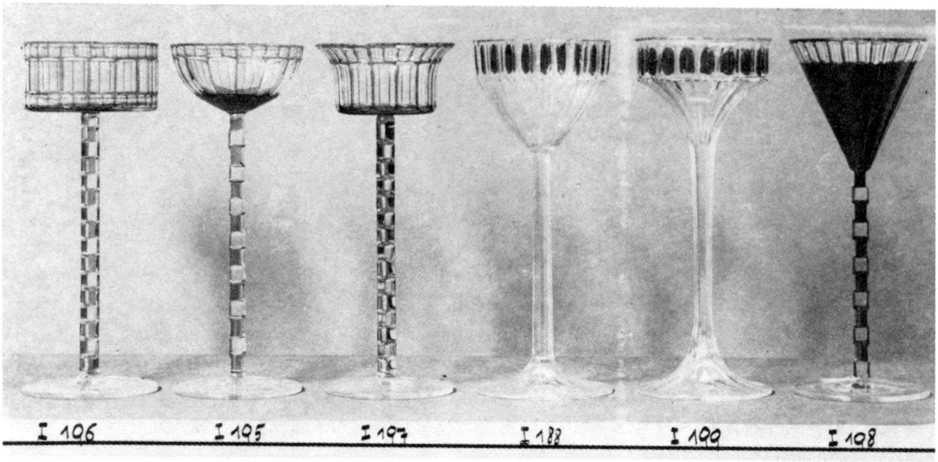

184

184
SECHS GLÄSER
Entwurf: Otto Prutscher
Ausführung: vermutlich Meyr's Neffe, Adolf
Lit.:
DKD 25/1909-10, S. 376
Studio Year Book 1912, S. 223
Kat. Expozice užitého umění, Moravská galerie v Brně, Brno 1975, Nr. 150, S. 218 (3 Gläser: ganz links, ganz rechts, drittes von links)
Kat. Kunsthandwerk im Grassimuseum, Leipzig 1981, 3. Heft, Abb. 28 (Glas ganz rechts)
Barbara Mundt, Nostalgie warum? Berlin 1982, Nr. 4, S. 20 (2. Glas von links)
České Sklo ze Sbírek Západočeského Muzea v Plzni, Květen-Srpen 1984, unpag. Abb. (zweites Glas von links)
Zeitgenössisches Foto
Inv.: ÖMAK, Archiv WW

185
KELCHGLAS
Entwurf: Otto Prutscher
Ausführung: wohl Meyr's Neffe, Adolf
Kristall, Überfang, geschliffen
H 21, Do 8,7, Du 8,1
Ausst.: ÖMKI 1910/11
Lit.:
DKD 20/1907, S. 340
DKD 25/1909-10, S. 376
Studio Year Book 1912, S. 223
Kat. Expozice užitého umění, Moravská galerie v Brně, Brno 1975, Nr. 150, S. 218
Inv.: Joanneum, AKGW, Nr. 12685 (erworben am 4. 1. 1910 um 14,80 Kronen vom ÖMKI)

186
KELCHGLAS
Entwurf: Otto Prutscher
Ausführung: Meyr's Neffe, Adolf
Kristall, Überfang, geschliffen, Silbergelb, grüne Emailpunkte, Fuß mit Strahlenschliff
H 20,5, Do 7,3, Du 7,9
Ausst.:
ÖMKI 1915. – ÖMAK 1973
Lit.:
Neuwirth 1973, Nr. 172, S. 308
Inv.: ÖMAK, W.I. 1693 (inventarisiert am 1. 4. 1916, erworben um 14 Kronen von Meyr's Neffe)

185 186

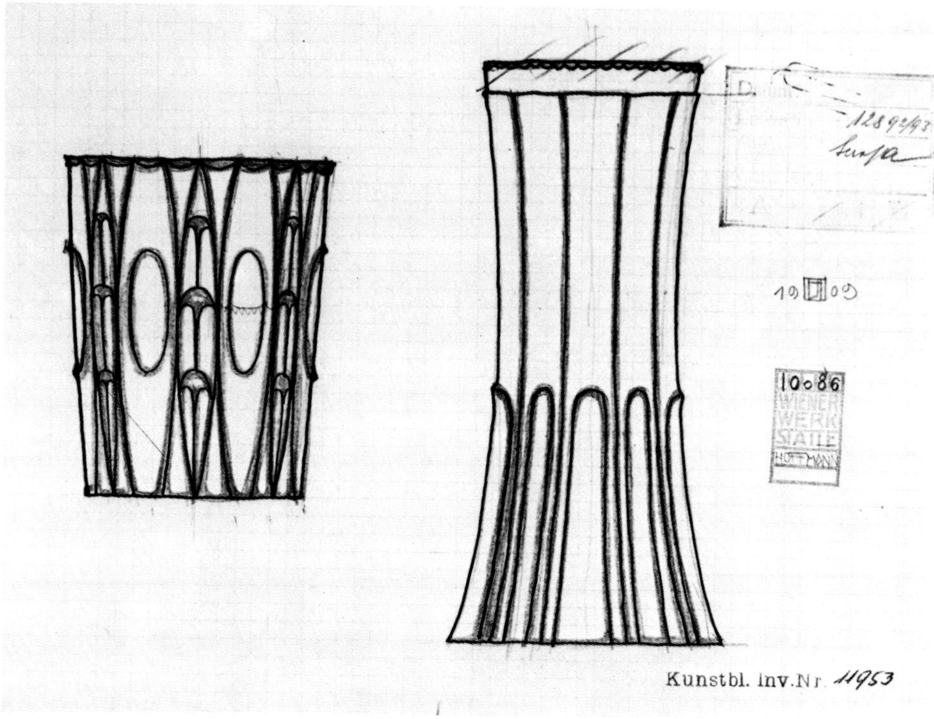

187

187
ZWEI GLÄSER
Entwurf Josef Hoffmann
Sign. und dat.: 19 JH 09
Archivstempel der
Wiener Werkstätte
H 9,5 bzw. 15,5
(korrigierte Höhe)
Lit.: WWMB 61, S. 303,
rechtes Glas
(„außen blau überfangen
mit Schliff"; Rechnung
Meyr's Neffe 1910)
Inv.: ÖMAK, K.I. 11953

187
TWO GLASSES
Design by Josef Hoffmann
Signed and dated: 19 JH 09
Archive stamp of the
Wiener Werkstätte
H 9.5 and 15.5
(corrected height)
Lit.: WWMB 61, p. 303,
right-hand glass ("cut
blue overlay", invoices of
Meyr's Neffe 1910)
Inv.: ÖMAK, K.I. 11953

188

188
VIER GLÄSER
Kristall, Überfang,
Schliff
Lit.:
WWMB 61, S. 316, 310, 323: Vase rechts, Likörflasche links, Krug (Monogramm von Otto Prutscher, Rechnungen Meyr's Neffe 1910-1911, Krug 1910-1912; Vase blau oder rosa überfangen, Likörflasche blau bzw. grün, Krug mit blauen Fäden)
Zeitgenössisches Foto
Inv.: ÖMAK, Archiv WW

188
FOUR GLASSES
Crystal, casing, cut
Lit.:
WWMB 61, pp. 316, 310, 323: right-hand vase, left-hand bottle, jar (monogram of Otto Prutscher, invoices of Meyr's Neffe 1910-1911, jar 1910-1912; vase with blue or pink casing, liqueur bottle blue or green casing, jar with blue seam cutting
Inv.: ÖMAK, Archiv WW
(contemporary photograph)

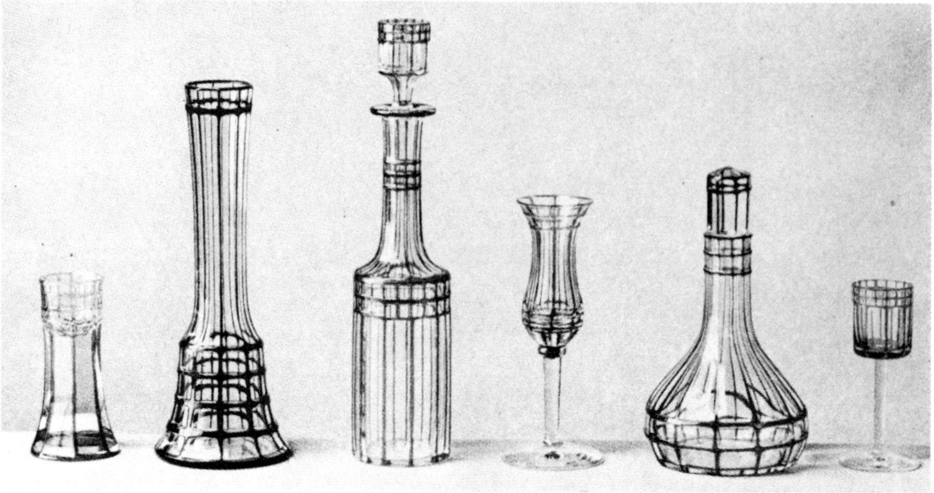

189

189
SECHS GLÄSER
Meyr's Neffe, Adolf
Kristall, Überfang,
Schliff
Reproduktion aus:
DK 13.Jg./1910, S. 452
(„Gläser, Vase und
Fläschchen, außen blau
überfangen mit
Linienschliff")

189
SIX GLASSES
Meyr's Neffe, Adolf
Crystal, casing, cut
Reproduced from:
DK, 13th year/1910, p. 452
("Glasses, vase and
bottle, blue casing with
cutting")

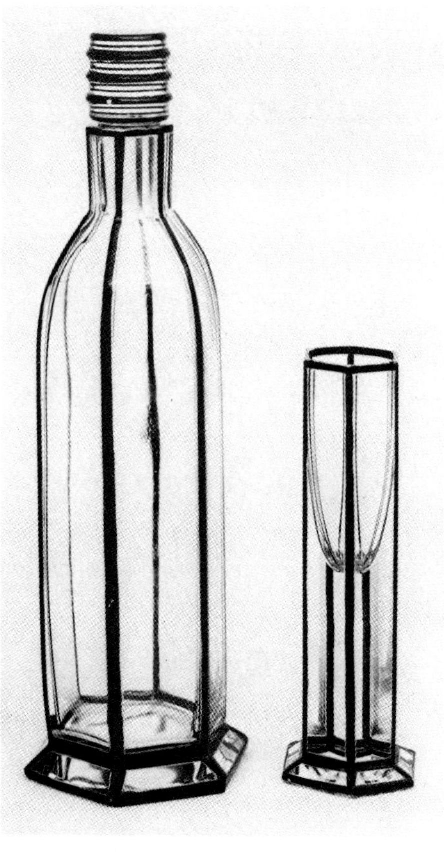

190

190
LIKÖRFLASCHE
UND LIKÖRGLAS
Kristall, Überfang,
geschliffen
Verleger: Bakalowits, Wien
Ausst.: ÖMKI 1911/12,
Nr. 42
Inv.: ÖMAK, VS 175 A
(zeitgenössisches Foto)

191
DOSE
Verleger: Bakalowits, Wien
Kristall, Überfang,
geschliffen (Wandung
14 Ecken)
H 7,9 (Deckel fehlt),
Do 7,2, Du 8
Ausst.: ÖMAK 1973
Lit.:
Neuwirth 1973, Nr. 23,
S. 122, 123
Inv.: ÖMAK, W.I. 894
(inventarisiert am
21. 2. 1911, erworben um
9 Kronen von Bakalowits)

191
JAR
Commissioned by:
Bakalowits, Vienna
Crystal, casing, cut
(14 sides)
H 7.9 (missing lid),
Dt 7.2, Db 8
Exhibition(s): ÖMAK 1973
Lit.:
Neuwirth 1973, no. 23,
pp. 122, 123
Inv.: ÖMAK, W.I. 894
(inventoried 21/02/11;
acquired for 9 crowns
from Bakalowits)

191

192

190
LIQUEUR DECANTER
AND GLASS
Crystal, casing, cut
Commissioned by:
Bakalowits, Vienna
Exhibition(s):
ÖMKI 1911/12, no. 42
Inv.: ÖMAK, VS 175 A
(contemporary photograph)

192
DREI GLÄSER
Meyr's Neffe, Adolf
Kristall, Überfang,
Schliff
Reproduktion aus:
DK 13.Jg./1910, S. 452
(„Honigdose, schwarz überfangen mit Linienschliff,
Dosen mit farbiger
Verzierung, geschliffen")

192
THREE JARS
Meyr's Neffe, Adolf
Crystal, casing, cut
Reproduced from:
DK, 13th year/1910, p. 452
("honey jar, black casing,
cutting of strips; jars
with colour decoration,
cutting")

193

193
SECHS GLÄSER
Kristall, Überfang, Schliff
Entwurf: Otto Prutscher
Ausführung: Meyr's Neffe, Adolf
Lit.:
Studio Year Book 1912, S. 223 (die drei links abgebildeten Vasen)
WWMB 61, S. 305, 306, 311, 334: 3. Vase von links, 2. Vase von links, Becher (3. Glas von rechts), Whiskyglas (2. Glas von rechts) (Monogramm von Otto Prutscher, Rechnungen Meyr's Neffe 1910, Whiskyglas auch 1911; Vasen und Becher blau überfangen, Whiskyglas mit blauen Fäden)
Inv.: ÖMAK, Archiv WW (Zeitgenössisches Foto)

193
SIX GLASSES
Crystal, casing, cut
Design: Otto Prutscher
Manufacturer:
Meyr's Neffe, Adolf
Lit.:
Studio Year Book 1912, p. 223 (three vases illustrated on the left)
WWMB 61, pp. 305, 306, 311, 334: third vase from left, second vase from left, beaker (third glass from right), whisky glass (second glass from right) (monogram of Otto Prutscher, invoices of Meyr's Neffe 1910, whisky glass 1910 and 1911)
Vase and beaker with blue casing, whisky glass with blue threads
Inv.: ÖMAK, Archiv WW (contemporary photograph)

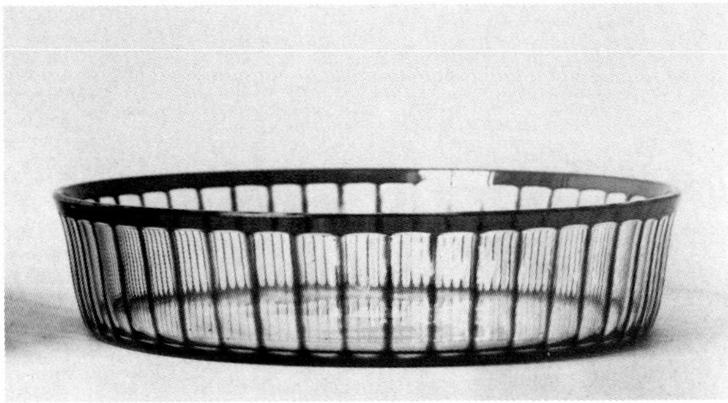

194

194
SCHALE
Kristall, Überfang,
geschliffen
Inv.: ÖMAK, Archiv WW
(zeitgenössisches Foto)

194
DISH
Crystal, casing, cut
Inv.: ÖMAK, Archiv WW
(contemporary photograph)

195

195
SCHALE
Kristall, Überfang,
geschliffen
Lit.:
Studio Year Book 1912,
S. 223
Inv.: ÖMAK, Archiv WW
(zeitgenössisches Foto)

195
DISH
Crystal, casing, cut
Lit.:
Studio Year Book 1912,
p. 223
Inv.: ÖMAK, Archiv WW
(contemporary photograph)

196

196
DECKELDOSE
UND STEHLAMPE
Kristall, Überfang,
geschliffen
Verleger: Bakalowits, Wien
Ausst.: ÖMKI 1910/11
Lit.:
KKH XIII/1910, S. 663
(Stehlampe, Entwurf
O. Prutscher)
Inv.: ÖMAK, VS 177 A
(zeitgenössisches Foto)

196
JAR AND TABLE LAMP
Crystal, casing, cut
Commissioned by:
Bakalowits, Vienna
Exhibition(s):
ÖMKI 1910/11
Lit.:
KKH XIII/1910, p. 663
(table lamp, design
O. Prutscher)
Inv.: ÖMAK, VS 177 A
(contemporary photograph)

197

197
JARDINIERE
Entwurf: Josef Rosipal
(Artěl, Prag)
Werknummer 3 R (Artěl)
Kristall, Überfang,
geschliffen
H 11,6, Du 16
Ausst.: ÖMKI 1915
(Foto ÖMAK VS 173 A)
Lit.:
KKH XVIII/1915, S. 453
DK XXIV/1916, S. 60
Inv.: ÖMAK, W.I. 1515
(inventarisiert am
24. 3. 1915, erworben um
20 Kronen von Artěl, Prag)

197
JARDINIERE
Design: Josef Rosipal
(Artěl, Prague)
Serial number 3 R (Artěl)
Crystal, casing, cut
H 11.6, Db 16
Exhibition(s): ÖMKI 1915
(photograph ÖMAK,
VS 173 A)
Lit.:
KKH XVIII/1915, p. 453
DK XXIV/1916, p. 60
Inv.: ÖMAK, W.I. 1515
(inventoried 24/03/15;
acquired for 20 crowns
from Artěl, Prague)

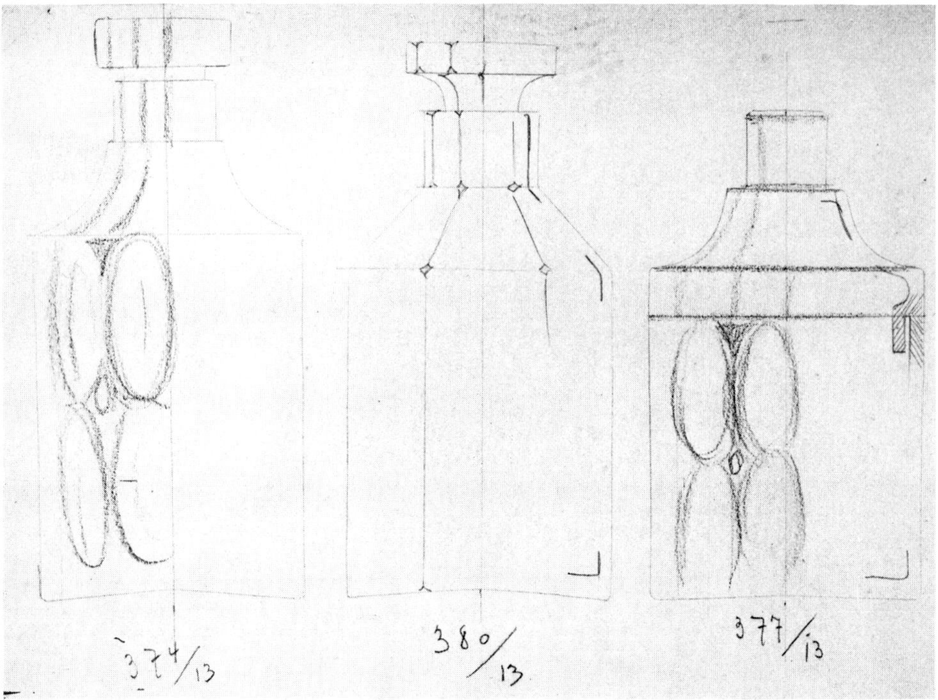

198

198
DECKELDOSEN
Werkzeichnung
Entwurf:
Josef Emanuel Margold
Verleger: Bakalowits, Wien
Werknummern:
374/13 (H 17,6)
380/13 (H 16,8)
377/13 (H 14,9)
Inv.: ÖMAK, B.I. 32066 c

198
BOTTLES FROM
A TOILET SET
Working drawing
Design:
Josef Emanuel Margold
Commissioned by:
Bakalowits, Vienna
Serial numbers:
374/13 (H 17,6)
380/13 (H 16,8)
377/13 (H 14,9)
Inv.: ÖMAK, B.I. 32066 c

199
FLAKON AUS EINER
TOILETTEGARNITUR
Entwurf:
Josef Emanuel Margold
Verleger: Bakalowits, Wien
Kristall, Überfang,
geschliffen (8teilige
Gliederung der Wandung)
H 14,5, D Mundrand 8,5,
Du 8,3
Ausst.: ÖMKI 1913/14,
Nr. 27. – ÖMAK 1973
Lit.:
KKH 16/1913, S. 619
Neuwirth 1973, Nr. 24,
S. 122, 123
Inv.: ÖMAK, W.I. 1231
(inventarisiert am
7. 1. 1914, erworben um
18 Kronen von Bakalowits,
Wien)

199
BOTTLE FROM A
TOILET SET
Design:
Josef Emanuel Margold
Commissioned by:
Bakalowits, Vienna
Crystal, casing,
8-part cutting
H 14.5, D (lip) 8.5,
Db 8.3
Exhibition(s):
ÖMKI 1913/14, no. 27
ÖMAK 1973
Lit.:
KKH 16/1913, p. 619
Neuwirth 1973, no. 24,
pp. 122, 123
Inv.: ÖMAK, W.I. 1231
(inventoried 07/01/14;
acquired for 18 crowns
from Bakalowits, Vienna)

199

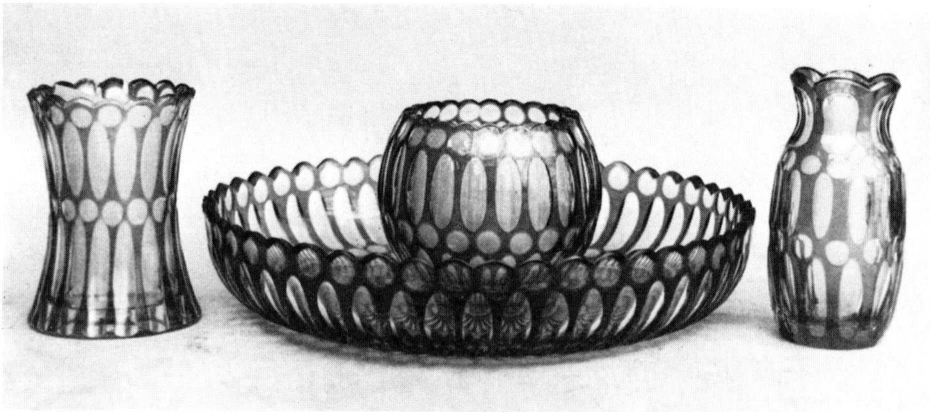

200

200
VASEN UND SCHALEN
Mühlhaus/Haida
Kristall, Überfang,
geschliffen
Ausst.: ÖMKI 1912, Nr. 583
Inv.: ÖMAK, VS 180 B
(zeitgenössisches Foto)

200
VASES AND DISHES
Mühlhaus, Haida
Crystal, casing, cut
Exhibition(s):
ÖMKI 1912, no. 583
Inv.: ÖMAK, VS 180 B
(contemporary photograph)

201
VASE
Mühlhaus/Haida
Kristall, Überfang,
geschliffen (Hals 6teilig,
Wandung 12teilig)
H 12, Do 5,2, Du 4,6,
Dg 6,3
Ausst.: ÖMKI 1912, Nr. 583
ÖMAK 1973
Lit.:
Neuwirth 1973, Nr. 176,
S. 314, 315
Inv.: ÖMAK, W.I. 1109
(inventarisiert am
15. 7. 1912, erworben um
3,80 Kronen von Mühlhaus)

201
VASE
Mühlhaus, Haida
Crystal, casing, cut
(neck 6 sides, body
12 sides)
H 12, Dt 5.2, Db 4.6,
Dm 6.3
Exhibition(s):
ÖMKI 1912, no. 583
ÖMAK 1973
Lit.:
Neuwirth 1973, no. 176,
pp. 314, 315
Inv.: ÖMAK, W.I. 1109
(inventoried 15/07/12;
acquired for 3.80 crowns
from Mühlhaus)

201

202

202
SCHALE
Mühlhaus/Haida
Kristall, Überfang,
geschliffen
H 5,3, Do 26,4
Ausst.:
ÖMKI 1912, Nr. 583
ÖMAK 1973
Lit.:
KKH XV/1912, S. 367
Neuwirth 1973, Nr. 178,
S. 314, 315
Inv.: ÖMAK, W.I. 1110
(inventarisiert am
15. 7. 1912, erworben um
16,50 Kronen von Mühlhaus)

203
DECKELPOKAL
Fachschule Haida
Kristallglas, blau
überfangen, geschliffen
Ausst.:
ÖMKI 1911/12, Nr. 289
Inv.: ÖMAK, VS 176 A
(zeitgenössisches Foto)

202
DISH
Mühlhaus, Haida
Crystal, casing, cut
H 5.3, Dt 26.4
Exhibition(s):
ÖMKI 1912, no. 583
ÖMAK 1973
Lit.:
KKH XV/1912, p. 367
Neuwirth 1973, no. 178,
pp. 314, 315
Inv.: ÖMAK, W.I. 1110
(inventoried 15/07/12;
acquired for 16.50 crowns
from Mühlhaus)

203
LIDDED GOBLET
Haida school
of glassmaking
Crystal, blue casing, cut
Exhibition(s):
ÖMKI 1911/12, no. 289
Inv.: ÖMAK, VS 176 A
(contemporary photograph)

204
VASE
Mühlhaus/Haida
Crystal, ruby casing,
cut (16 sides)
H 21.8, Dt 7.1, Db 7.4
Exhibition(s):
ÖMKI 1912, no. 582
ÖMAK 1973
Lit.:
Neuwirth 1973, no. 177,
pp. 314, 315
Inv.: ÖMAK, W.I. 1112
(inventoried 15/07/12;
acquired for 8.30 crowns
from Mühlhaus, Haida)

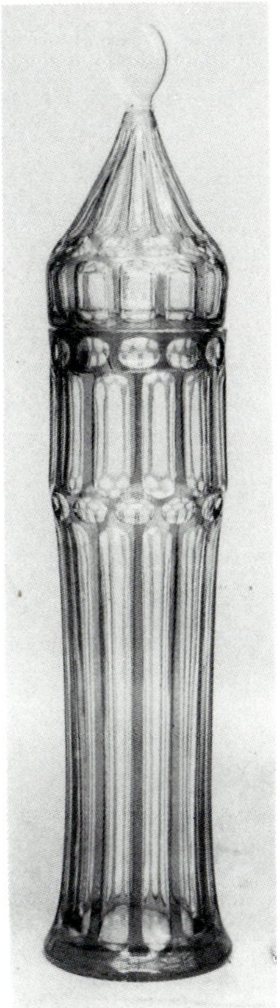

203

204
VASE
Mühlhaus/Haida
Kristall, Überfang (rubin), geschliffen (16teilig)
H 21,8, Do 7,1, Du 7,4
Ausst.:
ÖMKI 1912, Nr. 582
ÖMAK 1973
Lit.:
Neuwirth 1973, Nr. 177, S. 314, 315
Inv.: ÖMAK, W.I. 1112 (inventarisiert am 15. 7. 1912, erworben um 8,30 Kronen von Mühlhaus, Haida)

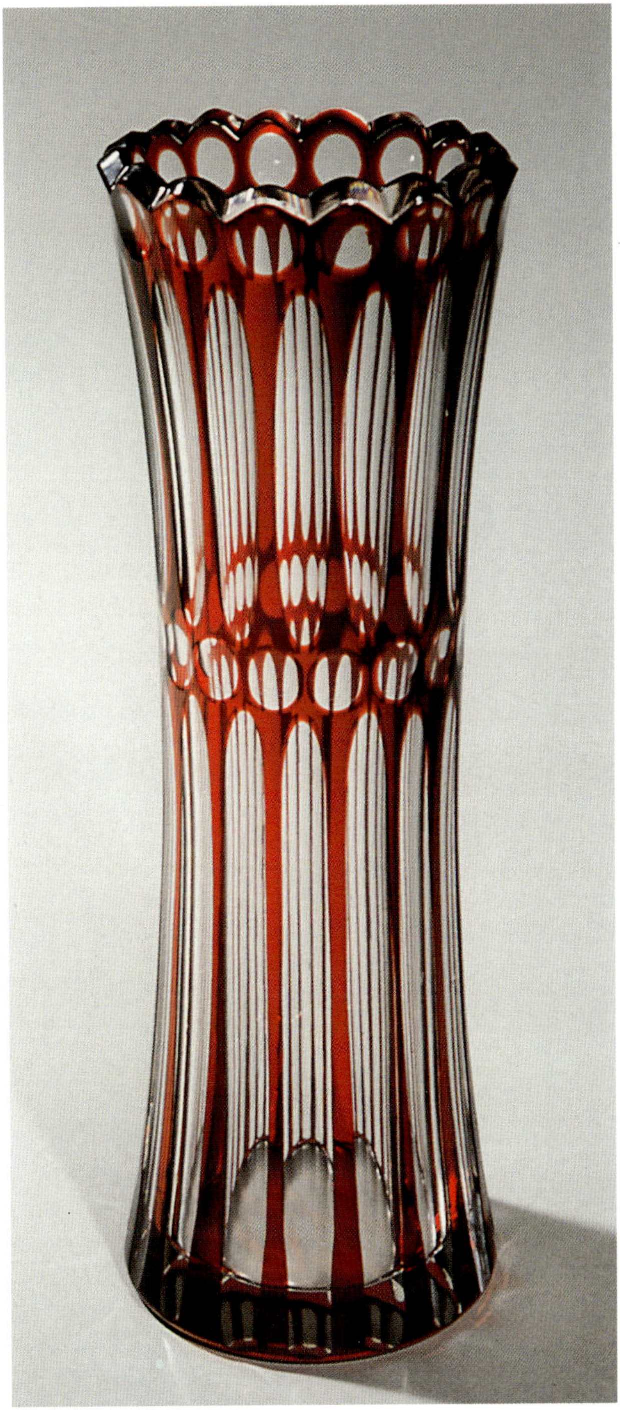

204

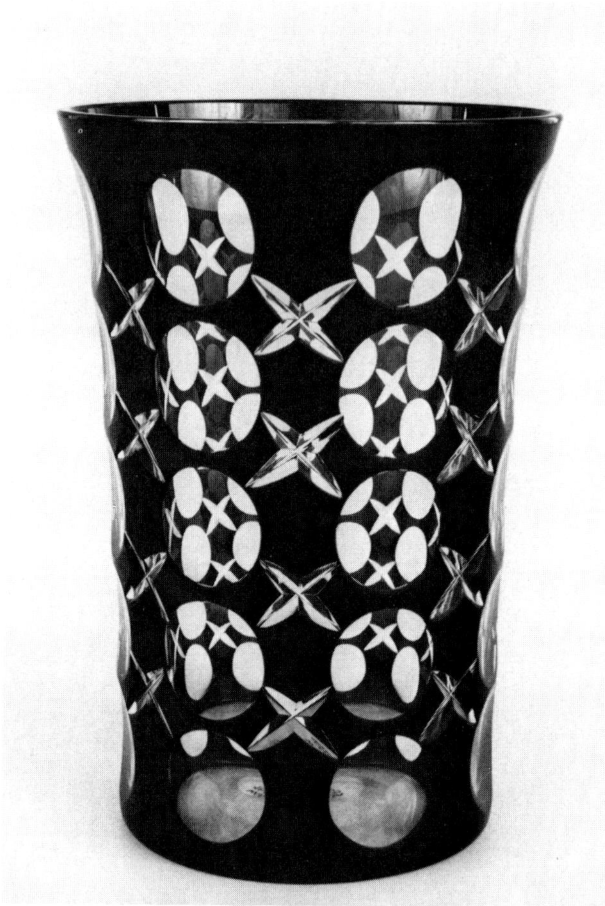

205

206

205
TRAUBENWASCHER
Verleger: Bakalowits, Wien
Kristall, Überfang (fast schwarzes Rot), geschliffen
H 17, Do 12, Du 9,3
Ausst.: ÖMKI 1915
(Foto ÖMAK VS 179 A)
Lit.:
KKH XVIII/1915, S. 456
Inv.: ÖMAK, W.I. 1685
(inventarisiert am 1. 4. 1916, erworben um 14 Kronen von Bakalowits)

205
GRAPE BOWL
Commissioned by:
Bakalowits, Vienna
Crystal, casing (almost black red), cut
H 17, Dt 12, Db 9.3
Exhibition(s): ÖMKI 1915
(photograph ÖMAK, VS 179 A)
Lit.:
KKH XVIII/1915, p. 456
Inv.: ÖMAK, W.I. 1685
(inventoried 01/04/16; acquired for 14 crowns from Bakalowits)

206
TRAUBENWASCHER
Werkskizze
Bez.: 38 39 40 41 / 15
Verleger: Bakalowits, Wien
H 17
Inv.: ÖMAK, B.I. 32066 c

206
GRAPE BOWL
Working sketch
Description:
38 39 40 41 / 15
Commissioned by:
Bakalowits, Vienna
H 17
Inv.: ÖMAK, B.I. 32066 c

207

207
TELLER
Verleger: Bakalowits, Wien
Kristall, Überfang (fast schwarzes Rot), geschliffen
H 2,9, Do 25
Ausst.: ÖMKI 1915
(Foto ÖMAK VS 179 A)
Lit.:
KKH XVIII/1915, S. 455
Inv.: ÖMAK, W.I. 1682 (inventarisiert am 1. 4. 1916, erworben um 38 Kronen von Bakalowits)

207
PLATE
Commissioned by: Bakalowits, Vienna
Crystal, casing (almost black red), cut
H 2.9, Dt 25
Exhibition(s): ÖMKI 1915 (photograph ÖMAK, VS 179 A)
Lit.:
KKH XVIII/1915, p. 455
Inv.: ÖMAK, W.I. 1682 (inventoried 01/04/16; acquired for 38 crowns from Bakalowits)

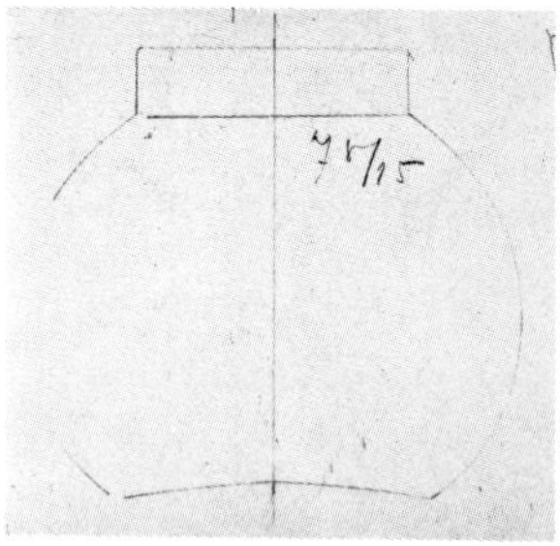

208

208
BLUMENKUGEL
Werkzeichnung
Werknummer 78/15
Verleger: Bakalowits, Wien
H 14
Inv.: ÖMAK, B.I. 32066 c

208
SPHERICAL VASE
Working drawing
Serial number 78/15
Commissioned by:
Bakalowits, Vienna
H 14
Inv.: ÖMAK, B.I. 32066 c

209

209
BLUMENKUGEL
Verleger: Bakalowits, Wien
Kristall, Überfang (fast schwarzes Rot), geschliffen
H 13,5, Do 9,7, Du 11, Dg 15,2
Ausst.: ÖMKI 1915
Inv.: ÖMAK, W.I. 1684 (inventarisiert am 1. 4. 1916, erworben um 25 Kronen von Bakalowits)

209
SPHERICAL VASE
Commissioned by:
Bakalowits, Vienna
Crystal, casing (almost black red), cut
H 13.5, Dt 9.7, Db 11, Dm 15.2
Exhibition(s): ÖMKI 1915
Inv.: ÖMAK, W.I. 1684 (inventoried 01/04/16; acquired for 25 crowns from Bakalowits)

210

210
OVALE JARDINIERE
Verleger: Bakalowits, Wien
Kristall, Überfang (fast schwarzes Rot), geschliffen
H 10,7, oben 12,2 × 17,9, größte Ausdehnung 18,3 × 24,2
Ausst.: ÖMKI 1915
Inv.: ÖMAK, W.I. 1683 (inventarisiert am 1. 4. 1916, erworben um 56 Kronen von Bakalowits)

210
OVAL JARDINIERE
Commissioned by: Bakalowits, Vienna
Crystal, casing (almost black red), cut
H 10.7, 12.2 × 17.9 (top), 18,3 × 24,2 (max. extent)
Exhibition(s): ÖMKI 1915
Inv.: ÖMAK, W.I. 1683 (inventoried 01/04/16; acquired for 56 crowns from Bakalowits)

211
FLASCHE
Verleger: Bakalowits, Wien
Kristall, Überfang (blau), Schliff (Wandung 4 Ecken; Schulter, Hals und Stöpsel 8 Ecken)
H 26,5, unten 6,9 × 6,9
Ausst.: ÖMKI 1915
(Foto ÖMAK VS 175 A)
Lit.:
KKH XVIII/1915, S. 456
Inv.: ÖMAK, W.I. 1690 (inventarisiert am 1. 4. 1916, erworben um 25 Kronen von Bakalowits)

211
BOTTLE
Commissioned by: Bakalowits, Vienna
Crystal, blue casing, cut (body 4 sides; shoulder, neck and stopper 8 sides)
H 26.5, 6.9 × 6.9 (bottom)
Exhibition(s): ÖMKI 1915 (photograph ÖMAK, VS 175 A)
Lit.:
KKH XVIII/1915, p. 456
Inv.: ÖMAK, W.I. 1690 (inventoried 01/04/16; acquired for 25 crowns from Bakalowits)

212
DECKELDOSE
Meltzer, Langenau
Werknummer 2287
Kristall, Überfang (violett), Schliff (16teilig)
H 14,8, Du 4,9, Dg 9,3
Ausst.: Berlin 1916
Lit.: DKD 38/1916, S. 278
Inv.: ÖMAK, W.I. 1700 (inventarisiert am 1. 4. 1916, erworben um 17,20 Kronen von Meltzer, Langenau)

212
COVERED JAR
Meltzer, Langenau
Serial number 2287
Crystal, casing (violet), cut (16 sides)
H 14.8, Db 4.9, Dm 9.3
Exhibition(s): Berlin 1916
Lit.: DKD 38/1916, p. 278
Inv.: ÖMAK, W.I. 1700 (inventoried 01/04/16; acquired for 17.20 crowns from Meltzer, Langenau)

211

212

212

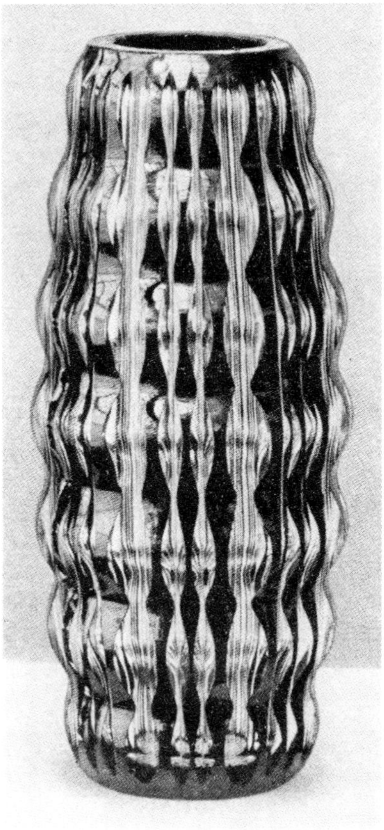

213

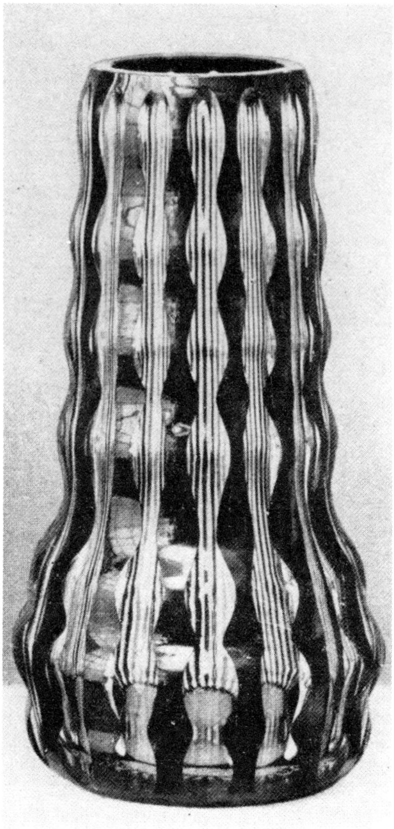

214

213
VASE
Meltzer, Langenau
Kristall, Überfang,
geschliffen
Ausst.: Berlin 1916
Reproduktion aus:
DKD 38/1916, S. 278

213
VASE
Meltzer, Langenau
Crystal, casing, cut
Exhibition(s): Berlin 1916
Reproduced from:
DKD 38/1916, p. 278

214
VASE
Meltzer, Langenau
Kristall, Überfang,
geschliffen
Ausst.: Berlin 1916
Reproduktion aus:
DKD 38/1916, S. 278

214
VASE
Meltzer, Langenau
Crystal, casing, cut
Exhibition(s): Berlin 1916
Reproduced from:
DKD 38/1916, p. 278

215

215
AUFSATZ
Entwurf: Fachschule Haida
Ausführung:
Meltzer, Langenau
Kristall, Überfang (grün), geschliffen
H 12,1, Do 21,2,
Dg 23,2, Du 12,7
Ausst.: ÖMKI 1915
(Foto ÖMAK VS 174 A)
Lit.:
KKH XVIII/1915, S. 453
Wiener Privatbesitz

215
CENTREPIECE
Design: Haida school of glassmaking
Manufacturer:
Meltzer, Langenau
Crystal, green casing, cut
H 12.1, Dt 21.2,
Dm 23.2, Db 12.7
Exhibition(s): ÖMKI 1915
(photograph ÖMAK, VS 174 A)
Lit.:
KKH XVIII/1915, p. 453
On loan (private collection in Vienna)

216

216
DREI GLÄSER
Fachschule Haida
Kristall, Überfang,
geschliffen
Reproduktion aus:
DKD 34/1914, S. 377

216
THREE GLASSES
Haida school of glassmaking
Crystal, casing, cut
Reproduced from:
DKD 34/1914, p. 377

218
DREI GLÄSER
Entwurf: Fachschule Haida
Ausführung:
Meltzer, Langenau
Kristall, Überfang,
geschliffen
Ausst.: ÖMKI 1915
(Glas Mitte; Foto
ÖMAK VS 175 A)
Lit.: KKH XVIII/1915,
S. 452 (Glas Mitte)
Reproduktion aus:
DK XXIV/1916, S. 62 (Glas
Mitte)
Pazaurek 1925, S. 137

218
THREE GLASSES
Design: Haida school of
glassmaking
Manufacturer:
Meltzer, Langenau
Crystal, casing, cut
Exhibition(s):
ÖMKI 1915 (middle glass)
(photograph ÖMAK,
VS 175 A)
Lit.: KKH XVIII/1915,
p. 452 (middle glass)
Reproduced from:
DK XXIV/1916, p. 62
(middle glass)
Pazaurek 1925, p. 137

217
DECKELPOKAL
Meltzer, Langenau
Kristall, Überfang,
geschliffen
Ausst.: Berlin 1916
Reproduktion aus:
DKD 38/1916, S. 278

217
LIDDED GOBLET
Meltzer, Langenau
Crystal, casing, cut
Exhibition(s): Berlin 1916
Reproduced from:
DKD 38/1916, p. 278

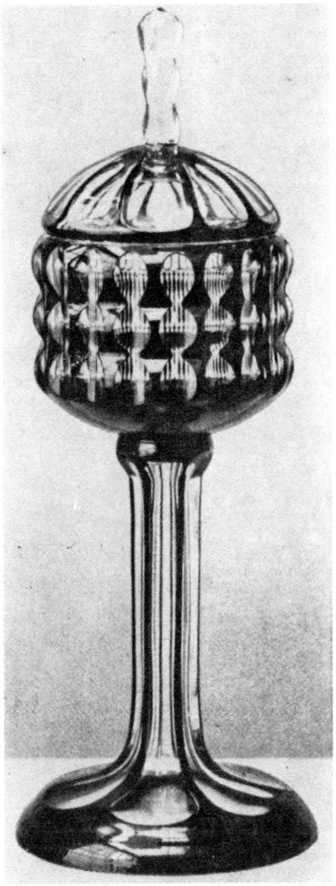

217

218

219

219
VASE
Entwurf: vermutlich
Fachschule Haida
Ausführung:
Meltzer, Langenau
Werknummer 2293
(Meltzer)
Kristall, Überfang (rot), geschliffen (12teilig)
H 25,6, Dg 9, Do 7,3, Du 7,7
Ausst.: ÖMKI 1915
Lit.: DKD 34/1914, S. 377 (dort als Fachschule Haida bezeichnet)
Inv.: ÖMAK, W.I. 1701 (inventarisiert am 1. 4. 1916, erworben um 27,50 Kronen von Meltzer, Langenau)

219
VASE
Design: probably Haida school of glassmaking
Manufacturer:
Meltzer, Langenau
Serial number 2293
(Meltzer)
Crystal, red casing, cut (12 sides)
H 25.6, Dm 9, Dt 7.3, Db 7.7
Exhibition(s): ÖMKI 1915
Lit.: DKD 34/1914, p. 377 (described there as Haida school of glassmaking)
Inv.: ÖMAK, W.I. 1701 (inventoried 01/04/16; acquired for 27.50 crowns from Meltzer, Langenau)

219

220

220
SCHALE
Entwurf: Josef Rosipal
(Artěl, Prag)
Werknummer 5 R (Artěl)
Kristall, Überfang (blau), geschliffen
H 4,2, Do 14, Du 3,8
Ausst.: ÖMAK 1973
Lit.:
Neuwirth 1973, Nr. 19, S. 116
Inv.: ÖMAK, W.I. 1519 (inventarisiert am 24. 3. 1915, erworben um 4,50 Kronen von Artěl, Prag)

220
DISH
Design: Josef Rosipal
(Artěl, Prague)
Serial number 5 R (Artěl)
Crystal, blue casing, cut
H 4.2, Dt 14, Db 3.8
Exhibition(s): ÖMAK 1973
Lit.:
Neuwirth 1973, no. 19, p. 116
Inv.: ÖMAK, W.I. 1519 (inventoried 24/03/15; acquired for 4.50 crowns from Artěl, Prague)

222

221

221
SCHALE
Entwurf: Artěl, Prag
Kristall, Überfang (blau), geschliffen
H 4,7, Do 33,5
Inv.: ÖMAK, W.I. 1534
(inventarisiert am 24. 3. 1915, erworben um 29 Kronen von Artěl, Prag)

221
DISH
Design: Artěl, Prague
Crystal, blue casing, cut
H 4.7, Dt 33.5
Inv.: ÖMAK, W.I. 1534
(inventoried 24/03/15; acquired for 29 crowns from Artěl, Prague)

222
VASE
Entwurf: Josef Rosipal (Artěl, Prag)
Werknummer 2 R (Artěl)
Kristall, Überfang (blau), geschliffen
Klebeetikett: K 17.-
H 35, Do 4, Du 8,7
Ausst.: ÖMAK 1973
Lit.:
Neuwirth 1973, Nr. 15, S. 114, 115
Inv.: ÖMAK, W.I. 1518
(inventarisiert am 24. 3. 1915, erworben um 17 Kronen von Artěl, Prag)

222
VASE
Design: Josef Rosipal (Artěl, Prague)
Serial number 2 R (Artěl)
Crystal, blue casing, cut
Label with "K 17.-"
H 35, Dt 4, Db 8.7
Exhibition(s): ÖMAK 1973
Lit.:
Neuwirth 1973, no. 15, pp. 114, 115
Inv.: ÖMAK, W.I. 1518
(inventoried 24/03/15; acquired for 17 crowns from Artěl, Prague)

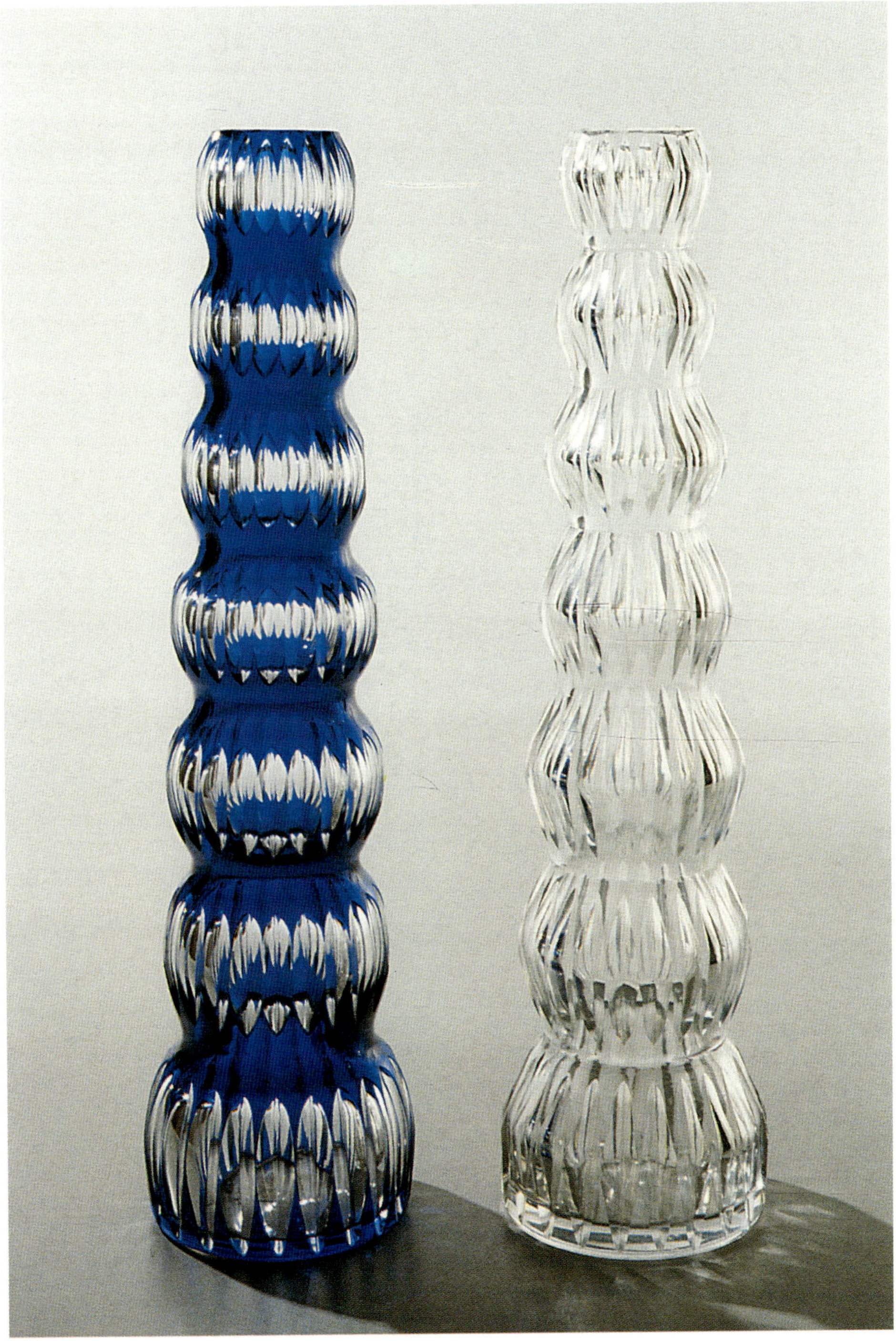

222 95

223

223
VASE
Entwurf: Josef Rosipal
(Artěl, Prag)
Werknummer 1 R (Artěl)
Kristall, Überfang (rot), geschliffen
H 24,6, Do 8,3, Du 8,9
Ausst.: ÖMAK 1973
Lit.: Neuwirth 1973, Kat.Nr. 10, S. 110
Inv.: ÖMAK, W.I. 1516 (inventarisiert am 24. 3. 1915, erworben um 7 Kronen von Artěl, Prag)

224
BIERSERVICE
Henkelkrug und sechs Gläser
Entwurf: Josef Rosipal
(Artěl, Prag)
Werknummer 38 R (Artěl)
Kristall, Überfang (rot), geschliffen (Krug 5teilig, Gläser 6teilig)
Krug: H 32,2, Du 13,7
Gläser: H 20,7-20,9, Do 6,2-6,3, Du 6,9-7,2
Ausst.: ÖMAK 1973
Lit.:
Neuwirth 1973, Nr. 14, S. 114
Inv.: ÖMAK, W.I. 1510/1-7 (inventarisiert am 24. 3. 1915, erworben um 50 Kronen von Artěl, Prag)

224

223
VASE
Design: Josef Rosipal
(Artěl, Prague)
Serial number 1 R (Artěl)
Crystal, red casing, cut
H 24.6, Dt 8.3, Db 8.9
Exhibition(s): ÖMAK 1973
Lit.: Neuwirth 1973,
Kat.no. 10, p. 110
Inv.: ÖMAK, W.I. 1516
(inventoried 24/03/15;
acquired for 7 crowns
from Artěl, Prague)

224
BEER SERVICE
Handled jug and six
glasses
Design: Josef Rosipal
(Artěl, Prague)
Serial number 38 R (Artěl)
Crystal, red casing,
cut (jug 5 sides,
glasses 6 sides)
Jug: H 32.2, Db 13.7
Glasses: H 20.7-20.9,
Dt 6.2-6.3,
Db 6.9-7.2
Exhibition(s): ÖMAK 1973
Lit.:
Neuwirth 1973, no. 14,
p. 114
Inv.: ÖMAK, W.I. 1510/1-7
(inventoried 24/03/15;
acquired for 50 crowns
from Artěl, Prague)

225
AUFSATZ
Entwurf: Josef Rosipal
(Artěl, Prag)
Werknummer 26 R (Artěl)
Kristall, Überfang (rot),
geschliffen (6fache
Motivwiederholung)
H 30,5, Do 14,8, Du 4,2
Inv.: ÖMAK, W.I. 1526
(inventarisiert am
24. 3. 1915, erworben um
70 Kronen von Artěl, Prag)

225
CENTREPIECE
Design: Josef Rosipal
(Artěl, Prague)
Serial number 26 R (Artěl)
Crystal, red casing,
cut (motif repeated
6 times)
H 30.5, Dt 14.8, Db 4.2
Inv.: ÖMAK, W.I. 1526
(inventoried 24/03/15;
acquired for 70 crowns
from Artěl, Prague)

225

226
SCHALE
Entwurf: Josef Rosipal
(Artěl, Prag)
Werknummer 21 R (Artěl)
Kristall, Überfang (rot),
geschliffen (3fache
Motivwiederholung),
16teiliger Bodenstern
H 5,2, Do 14,8, Du 4,2
Ausst.: ÖMAK 1973
Lit.:
Neuwirth 1973, Nr. 6,
S. 110
Inv.: ÖMAK, W.I. 1520
(inventarisiert am
24. 3. 1915, erworben um
9 Kronen von Artěl, Prag)

226
DISH
Design: Josef Rosipal
(Artěl, Prague)
Serial number 21 R (Artěl)
Crystal, red casing,
cut (motif repeated 3 times),
star in bottom (16 facets)
H 5.2, Dt 14.8, Db 4.2
Exhibition(s): ÖMAK 1973
Lit.:
Neuwirth 1973, no. 6,
p. 110
Inv.: ÖMAK, W.I. 1520
(inventoried 24/03/15;
acquired for 9 crowns
from Artěl, Prague)

227
CHAMPAGNE GLASS
Design: Josef Rosipal
(Artěl, Prague)
Serial number 28 R (Artěl)
Crystal, red casing, cut
(motif repeated 8 times)
H 17.7, Dt 10.8, Db 5.9
Exhibition(s): ÖMAK 1973
Lit.:
Neuwirth 1973, no. 7,
p. 110
Inv.: ÖMAK, W.I. 1521
(inventoried 24/03/15;
acquired for 10 crowns
from Artěl, Prague)

228
LIQUEUR SERVICE
Decanter and six glasses
Design: Josef Rosipal
(Artěl, Prague)
Serial number 37 R (Artěl)
Crystal, red casing,
cut (decanter 6 motifs,
glasses 5 motifs)
Decanter: H 32.6, Dt 2.7,
Db 11.8
Glasses: H 12.2-12.4,
Dt 2.7-3, Db 2.8-3
Exhibition(s): ÖMAK 1973
Lit.:
Neuwirth 1973, no. 13,
pp. 112, 113
Victoria and Albert
Museum, Bohemian Glass,
London 1965, Abb. 35
Inv.: ÖMAK, W.I. 1525/1-7
(inventoried 24/03/15;
acquired for 28 crowns
from Artěl, Prague)

226

227

227
CHAMPAGNERGLAS
Entwurf: Josef Rosipal
(Artěl, Prag)
Werknummer 28 R (Artěl)
Kristall, Überfang (rot), geschliffen (8fache Motivwiederholung)
H 17,7, Do 10,8, Du 5,9
Ausst.: ÖMAK 1973
Lit.:
Neuwirth 1973, Nr. 7, S. 110
Inv.: ÖMAK, W.I. 1521 (inventarisiert am 24. 3. 1915, erworben um 10 Kronen von Artěl, Prag)

228
LIKÖRSERVICE
Flasche und fünf Gläser
Entwurf: Josef Rosipal
(Artěl, Prag)
Werknummer 37 R (Artěl)
Kristall, Überfang (rot), geschliffen
(Flasche 6 Motive, Gläser 5 Motive)
Flasche: H 32,6, Do 2,7, Du 11,8
Gläser: H 12,2-12,4, Do 2,7-3, Du 2,8-3
Ausst.: ÖMAK 1973
Lit.:
Neuwirth 1973, Nr. 13, S. 112, 113
Victoria and Albert Museum, Bohemian Glass, London 1965, Abb. 35
Inv.: ÖMAK, W.I. 1525/1-7 (inventarisiert am 24. 3. 1915, erworben um 28 Kronen von Artěl, Prag)

228

229

230

229
BOWLEGARNITUR
Bowle und drei Gläser
(Löffel und drei Gläser
fehlen: Kriegsverlust)
Entwurf: Josef Rosipal
(Artěl, Prag)
Werknummer 36 R (Artěl)
Kristall, Überfang (rot),
geschliffen
(Bowle 10 Motive,
Gläser 6 Motive)
Bowle mit Deckel: H 40,3,
D Mundrand 31,2,
D Deckel 31,4, D Fuß 18,5
Gläser: H 15,7, Do 7,2,
Du 5,2-5,3
Etikett:
Rosipal / D 36 R /
K 145 / 47
Ausst.: ÖMAK 1973
Lit.:
Neuwirth 1973, Nr. 11,
S. 112
Inv.: ÖMAK, W.I.1523/1,3-5
(inventarisiert am
24. 3. 1915, erworben um
100 Kronen von Artěl,
Prag)

229

229
PUNCH SET
Bowl and three glasses
Spoon and three glasses
missing (war loss)
Design: Josef Rosipal
(Artěl, Prague)
Serial number 36 R (Artěl)
Crystal, red casing,
cut (bowl 10 motifs,
glasses 6 motifs)
Bowl with lid: H 40.3,
D (lip) 31.2, D (lid) 31.4,
D (foot) 18.5
Glasses: H 15.7, Dt 7.2,
Db 5.2-5.3
Label with "Rosipal /
D 36 R / K 145 / 47"
Exhibition(s): ÖMAK 1973
Lit.:
Neuwirth 1973, no. 11,
p. 112
Inv.: ÖMAK, W.I.1523/1,3-5
(inventoried 24/03/15;
acquired for 100 crowns
from Artěl, Prague)

230
BIERSERVICE
Krug und sechs Gläser
Entwurf: Josef Rosipal
(Artěl, Prag)
Werknummer 39 R (Artěl)
Kristall, Überfang (rot),
geschliffen
(Krug 5 Motive,
Gläser 6 Motive)
Krug: H 32,6, Du 13,5,
D Mundrand 9,6,
Gläser: H 19,6-19,7,
Do 5,8, Du 6,3-6,5
Ausst.: ÖMKI 1915
(Foto ÖMAK, VS 173 A)
ÖMAK 1973
Lit.:
DK XXIV/1916, S. 60
Neuwirth 1973, Nr. 12,
S. 112, 113
Inv.: ÖMAK, W.I. 1527/1-7
(inventarisiert am
24. 3. 1915, erworben um
90 Kronen von Artěl, Prag)

230
BEER SERVICE
Jug and six glasses
Design: Josef Rosipal
(Artěl, Prague)
Serial number 39 R (Artěl)
Crystal, red casing,
cut (jug 5 motifs, glasses
6 motifs)
Jug: H 32.6, Db 13.5,
D (lip) 9.6,
Glasses: H 19.6-19.7,
Dt 5.8, Db 6.3-6.5
Exhibition(s): ÖMKI 1915
(photograph ÖMAK,
VS 173 A)
ÖMAK 1973
Lit.:
DK XXIV/1916, p. 60
Neuwirth 1973, no. 12,
pp. 112, 113
Inv.: ÖMAK, W.I. 1527/1-7
(inventoried 24/03/15;
acquired for 90 crowns
from Artěl, Prague)

231

231
GIESSGEFÄSS
Entwurf: Josef Rosipal
(Artěl, Prag)
Kristall, Überfang (rot), geschliffen (8 Motive)
H 5,7 (Griff beschädigt)
Inv.: ÖMAK, Gl 3484
(1985 nachträglich inventarisiert)

231
SPOUTED VESSEL
Design: Josef Rosipal
(Artěl, Prague)
Crystal, red casing, cut (8 motifs)
H 5.7 (handle damaged)
Inv.: ÖMAK, Gl 3484
(inventoried only 1985)

232

232
VASE
Fachschule Steinschönau
Kristall, Überfang (rot),
geschliffen (Dekor 5teilig)
H 19,5, Do und unten 7,5
Bez.: Monogramm FK
(= vermutlich Franz
Krause), K.K.F.-S.ST.
Klebeetikett:
K. K. FACHSCHULE
STEINSCHÖNAU 1682
Inv.: ÖMAK, Gl 2726
(1933 nachträglich
inventarisiert)

232
VASE
Steinschönau school of
glassmaking
Crystal, red casing,
cut (5 part decoration)
H 19.5, Dt and Db 7.5
Marked: monogram FK
(= probably Franz
Krause), K.K.F.-S.ST.
Label with
"K. K. FACHSCHULE
STEINSCHÖNAU 1682"
Inv.: ÖMAK, Gl 2726
(inventoried only 1933)

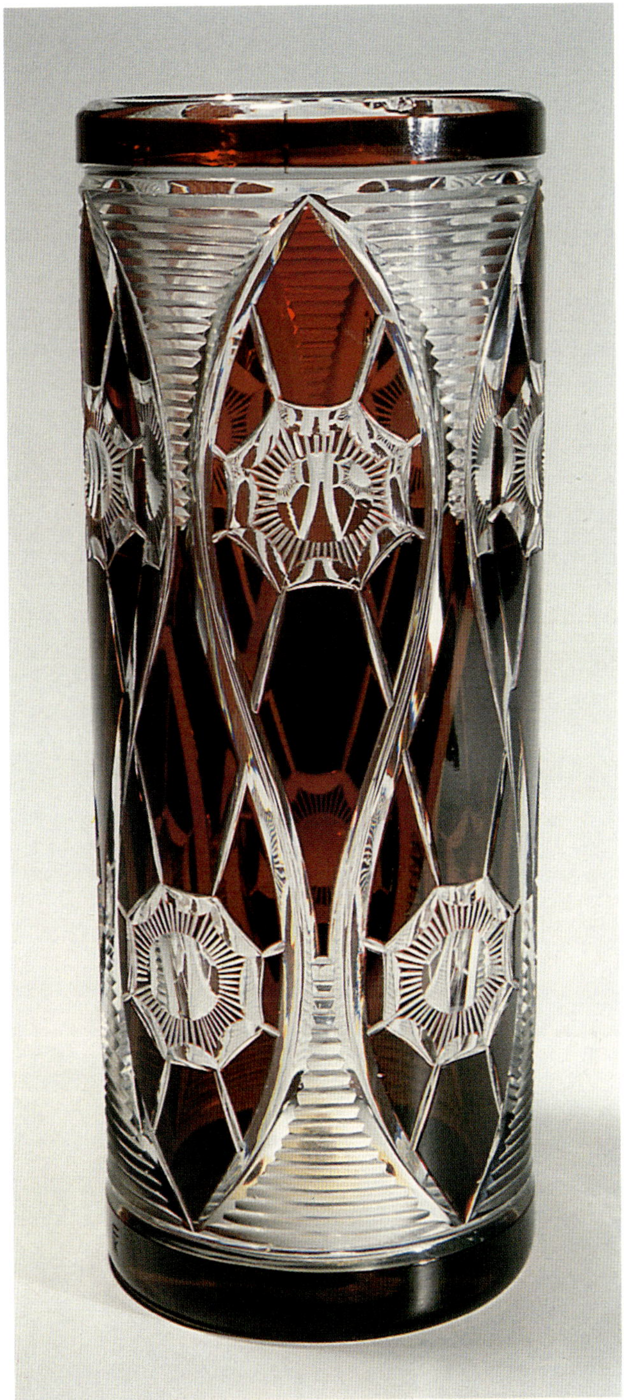

232

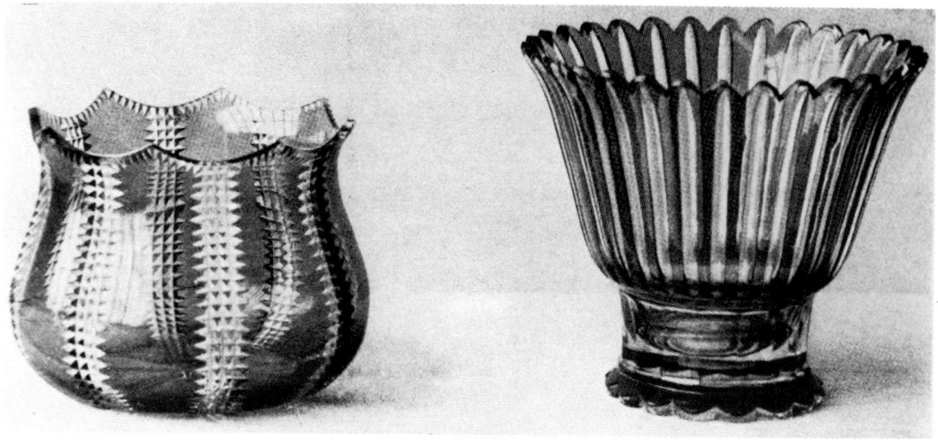

233

233
ZWEI GLÄSER
Edelglaswerke Stockerau,
Leopold Forstner
Kristall, Überfang
(rosa Goldrubin),
geschliffen
Reproduktion aus:
Pazaurek 1925, S. 168

233
TWO GLASSES
Edelglaswerke Stockerau,
Leopold Forstner
Crystal, casing (pink
gold ruby), cut
Reproduced from:
Pazaurek 1925, p. 168

234

234
ZWEI GLÄSER
Edelglaswerke Stockerau,
Leopold Forstner
Kristall, Überfang
(Kupferrubin), geschliffen
Reproduktion aus:
Pazaurek 1925, S. 168

234
TWO GLASSES
Edelglaswerke Stockerau,
Leopold Forstner
Crystal, casing (copper
ruby), cut
Reproduced from:
Pazaurek 1925, p. 168

235

235
SCHALE
Entwurf: Fachschule Haida
Ausführung: Oertel, Haida
Kristall, Überfang (rot), geschliffen
H 7,9, Do 16,2, Du 10,3
Ausst.: ÖMKI 1915
Inv.: ÖMAK, W.I. 1657 (inventarisiert am 1. 4. 1916, erworben um 19 Kronen von Oertel)

235
DISH
Design: Haida school of glassmaking
Manufacturer: Oertel, Haida
Crystal, red casing, cut
H 7.9, Dt 16.2, Db 10.3
Exhibition(s): ÖMKI 1915
Inv.: ÖMAK, W.I. 1657 (inventoried 01/04/16; acquired for 19 crowns from Oertel)

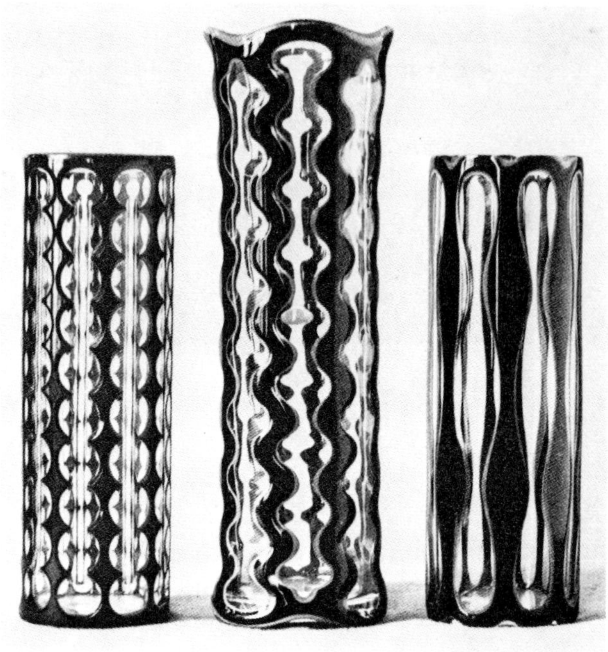

236

236
DREI VASEN
Entwurf: Fachschule Haida
Ausführung: Oertel, Haida
Kristall, zweifarbig
überfangen, geschliffen
Reproduktion aus:
DK 16.Jg./1913, S. 571

236
THREE VASES
Design: Haida school of
glassmaking
Manufacturer: Oertel, Haida
Crystal, cased in two
colours, cut
Reproduced from:
DK, 16th year/1913, p. 571

237
AUFSATZ
Entwurf: Fachschule Haida
Ausführung: Oertel, Haida
Vermutlich Werknummer
1010 (Oertel)
Kristall, Überfang
(violett), geschliffen
(8teiliger Dekor)
Dieselbe Form mit Silber-
gelb (ÖMAK, W.I. 1651) und
Malerei (ÖMAK, W.I. 1737)
H 21,6, Do 18,6, Du 13,6
Ausst.:
Berlin 1916. – ÖMAK 1973
Lit.: DKD 38/1916, S. 280
Neuwirth 1973, Nr. 185,
S. 322, 323
Inv.: ÖMAK, W.I. 1741
(inventarisiert am
11. 5. 1916, Geschenk von
Oertel, Haida)

237
CENTREPIECE
Design: Haida school of
glassmaking
Manufacturer: Oertel, Haida
Probably serial
number 1010 (Oertel)
Crystal, casing (violet),
cut (8 part decoration)
The same shape with
silver-yellow (ÖMAK,
W.I. 1651) and painting
(ÖMAK, W.I. 1737) in
the ÖMAK collection
H 21.6, Dt 18.6, Db 13.6
Exhibition(s):
Berlin 1916. – ÖMAK 1973
Lit.: DKD 38/1916, p. 280
Neuwirth 1973, no. 185,
pp. 322, 323
Inv.: ÖMAK, W.I. 1741
(inventoried 11/05/16;
donated by Oertel, Haida)

237

238

238
FLAKON
mit Stöpsel
Carl Goldberg, Haida
Kristall, Überfang (violett), geschliffen
H 26,5, D Fuß 7,1
Ausst.: ÖMKI 1915
Inv.: Joanneum, AKGW, Nr. 16641
(erworben am 12. 8. 1915 um 12 Kronen vom ÖMKI)

238
BOTTLE WITH STOPPER
Carl Goldberg, Haida
Crystal, casing (violet), cut
H 26.5, D (foot) 7.1
Exhibition(s): ÖMKI 1915
Inv: Joanneum, AKGW, no. 16641
(acquired 12/08/15 for 12 crowns from ÖMKI)

238

239

239
KARAFFE UND SCHALE
S. Reich & Co., Haida
Kristall, Überfang,
geschliffen
Reproduktion aus:
DKD 38/1916, S. 279

239
CARAFE AND DISH
S. Reich & Co., Haida
Crystal, casing, cut
Reproduced from:
DKD 38/1916, p. 279

240

240
DECKELDOSE
Goldberg, Haida
Werknummer 803 (Goldberg)
Kristall, Überfang (grün), geschliffen
H 5,2, D 10
Ausst.: ÖMKI 1915
Inv.: ÖMAK, W.I. 1721
(inventarisiert am 1. 4. 1916, erworben um 16 Kronen von Goldberg, Haida)

240
COVERED BOWL
Goldberg, Haida
Serial number 803
Crystal, green casing, cut
H 5.2, D 10
Exhibition(s): ÖMKI 1915
Inv.: ÖMAK, W.I. 1721
(inventoried 01/04/16; acquired for 16 crowns from Goldberg, Haida)

241

242

241
DECKELDOSE
Wiener Werkstätte
Werknummer A I 816/179
Ausführung:
Oertel, Haida (1919)
Kristall, Überfang (rot),
geschliffen (12 Ecken)
H 17,4, Dg 12,9
Eingeschnitten: WW
Ausst.: ÖMAK 1967, Nr. 340
Lit.: WWMB 62, S. 816
Inv.: ÖMAK, Gl 3305
(1971 erworben)

241
LIDDED BOWL
Wiener Werkstätte
Serial number A I 816/179
Manufacturer:
Oertel, Haida (1919)
Crystal, red casing,
cut (12 sides)
H 17.4, Dm 12.9
Engraved: WW
Exhibition(s):
ÖMAK 1967, no. 340
Lit.: WWMB 62, p. 816
Inv.: ÖMAK, Gl 3305
(acquired 1971)

241

244
VASES AND BOX
Design: Haida school of glassmaking
Manufacturer: Oertel, Haida
Crystal, double casing, cut
Lit.: Eisler 1916, p. 164
(box)
Reproduced from:
DK 17th year/1914, p. 377

242
DECKELDOSE
Wiener Werkstätte
Werknummer A I 816/282
Ausführung:
Oertel, Haida (1919)
Kristall, Überfang (rot),
geschliffen (Wandung Mitte 14 Ecken, sonst gerieft)
H 18,5, Dg 12,6
Ausst.: ÖMAK 1967, Nr. 339
Lit.: WWMB 62, S. 816
Inv.: ÖMAK, Gl 3304
(1971 erworben)

242
LIDDED BOWL
Wiener Werkstätte
Serial number A I 816/282
Manufacturer:
Oertel, Haida (1919)
Crystal, red casing,
cut (14 facets in middle of side, otherwise grooved)
H 18.5, Dm 12.6
Exhibition(s):
ÖMAK 1967, no. 339
Lit.: WWMB 62, p. 816
Inv.: ÖMAK, Gl 3304
(acquired 1971)

245
TWO LIDDED VASES
Design: Julius Jelínek
Manufacturer:
Harrach, Neuwelt
Crystal, casings, cut
Exhibition(s):
ÖMKI 1913/14, no. 312 (lidded goblet, copper ruby with chinese yellow), 311 (lidded goblet, black with Japanese red)
Lit.:
DK, 17th year/1914, p. 380
Inv.: ÖMAK, VS 196 A
(contemporary photograph)

243
VASE
Wiener Werkstätte
Unterfang (rot),
Kristall, Überfang (weiß),
Schliff (Kuppa 24 Ecken, vier weiße Blattmotive)
H 24,3, Do 17, Du 11,1
Etikett mit WW-Monogramm
Inv.: ÖMAK, Gl 3307
(1971 inventarisiert)

243
VASE
Wiener Werkstätte
Red basis, covered by a crystal and white casing, cut (bowl 24 sides, four white leaf motifs)
H 24.3, Dt 17, Db 11.1
Label with WW monogram
Inv.: ÖMAK, Gl 3307
(inventoried 1971)

243

246
VASE
Design: Haida school of glassmaking
Manufacturer: Oertel, Haida
Crystal, casing (red, black), decorative cut seam
H 15.8, Dt 14, Db 15.7
Exhibition(s): ÖMAK 1973
Lit.:
DK, 17th year/1914, p. 377
Eisler 1916, p. 165
Neuwirth 1973, no. 179, pp. 316, 317
Inv.: ÖMAK, W.I. 1272
(inventoried 07/01/14; acquired for 56 crowns from Oertel, Haida)

243

244

245

244
VASEN UND DOSE
Entwurf: Fachschule Haida
Ausführung: Oertel, Haida
Kristall, doppelter Überfang, geschliffen
Lit.: Eisler 1916, S. 164 (Deckeldose)
Reproduktion aus:
DK 17. Jg./1914, S. 377

245
ZWEI DECKELVASEN
Entwurf: Julius Jelínek
Ausführung:
Harrach, Neuwelt
Kristall, Überfang, geschliffen
Ausst.:
ÖMKI 1913/14, Nr. 312 (Pokal mit Deckel, Kupferrubin mit Chinagelb), 311 (Pokal mit Deckel, Schwarz mit Japanrot)
Lit.:
DK 17.Jg./1914, S. 380
Inv.: ÖMAK VS 196 A (zeitgenössisches Foto)

246
VASE
Entwurf: Fachschule Haida
Ausführung: Oertel, Haida
Kristall, Überfang (rot, schwarz), Ziersaumschliff
H 15,8, Do 14, Du 15,7
Ausst.: ÖMAK 1973
Lit.:
DK 17. Jg./1914, S. 377
Eisler 1916, S. 165
Neuwirth 1973, Nr. 179, S. 316, 317
Inv.: ÖMAK, W.I. 1272 (inventarisiert am 7. 1. 1914, erworben um 56 Kronen von Oertel, Haida)

246

247

247
DECKELPOKAL
Entwurf: Julius Jelínek
Ausführung:
Harrach, Neuwelt
Kristall, Überfang
(rot, schwarz),
Ziersaumschliff
H 33,8, D Deckel 11,1,
D Mundrand 9,8, Du 9,9,
D Wandung 10,7
Etikett: Harrach
Ausst.:
ÖMKI 1913/14, Nr. 311
ÖMAK 1973
Lit.:
DK 17. Jg./1914, S. 380
KKH 16/1913, S. 620
Neuwirth 1973, Nr. 73,
S. 190, 191
Inv.: ÖMAK, W.I. 1247
(inventarisiert am
7. 1. 1914, erworben um
70 Kronen von Harrach,
Neuwelt)

247
LIDDED VASE
Design: Julius Jelínek
Manufacturer:
Harrach, Neuwelt
Crystal, casing,
decorative cut seam
H 33.8, D (lid) 11.1,
D (lip) 9.8, Db 9.9,
D (body) 10.7
Label: "Harrach"
Exhibition(s):
ÖMKI 1913/14, no. 311
ÖMAK 1973
Lit.:
DK, 17th year/1914, p. 380
KKH 16/1913, p. 620
Neuwirth 1973, no. 73,
pp. 190, 191
Inv.: ÖMAK, W.I. 1247
(inventoried 07/01/14;
acquired for 70 crowns
from Harrach, Neuwelt)

247

248

248
VASE
Entwurf: Julius Jelínek
Ausführung: Harrach, Neuwelt
Kristall, Überfang (blau, grün), geschliffen (Ziersaum)
H 20,6, Do 6, Du 7,8, D Mitte 10
Ausst.:
ÖMKI 1913/14, Nr. 316 (Schwarzbraun mit Spezialblau-Email)
Lit.:
Kat. Tschechische Kunst 1878-1914, Darmstadt 1984-1985, Nr. 632 (Vase verwandter Form, ebenfalls doppelter Überfang in Blau und Grün, H 38, mit Etikett Comte Harrach Neuwelt Austria, 1910 vom Krajské muzeum Hradec Králové erworben)
Kat. Česká Secese, užité umění, Prag 1981, S. 68
Inv.: Joanneum, AKGW, Nr. 15500 (erworben am 23. 11. 1913 um 60 Kronen vom ÖMKI)

248
VASE
Design: Julius Jelínek
Manufacturer: Harrach, Neuwelt
Crystal, casing (blue, green), cut (decorative seam)
H 20.6, Dt 6, Db 7.8, D (body) 10
Exhibition(s):
ÖMKI 1913/14, no. 316 (blackish brown with special blue enamel)
Lit.:
Cat. Tschechische Kunst 1878-1914, Darmstadt 1984-1985, no. 632 (vase of similar shape with

248

249

double casing in blue
and green, H 38, with
label "Comte Harrach
Neuwelt, Austria",
acquired 1910 from
Krajské muzeum Hradec
Králové)
Kat. Česká Secese, užité
umění, Prague 1981, p. 68
Inv.: Joanneum,
AKGW, no. 15500
(acquired 23/11/13 for
60 crowns from ÖMKI)

249
VASEN UND DOSE
Entwurf: Fachschule Haida
Ausführung: Oertel, Haida
Kristall, Überfang
(zweifach),
Ziersaumschliff
Reproduktion aus:
DK 17.Jg./1914, S. 381

249
VASES AND BOX
Design: Haida school of
glassmaking
Manufacturer: Oertel, Haida
Crystal, casing (double),
decorative cut seam
Reproduced from:
DK, 17th year/1914, p. 381

250
DECKELDOSE
Entwurf: Fachschule Haida
Ausführung: Oertel, Haida
Kristall, Überfang
(blau, schwarz),
Ziersaumschliff (Deckel
und Wandung 10teilig)
H 15,8, Du 10,
D Deckel 9,9,
D Mundrand 8,9
Lit.:
DK 17. Jg./1914, S. 381
Eisler 1916, S. 250
Inv.: ÖMAK, W.I. 1273
(inventarisiert am
7. 1. 1914, erworben um
57 Kronen von Oertel,
Haida)

250

251

251
GLÄSER
Entwurf: Fachschule Haida
Ausführung: Oertel, Haida
Kristall, Überfang,
geschliffen
Reproduktion aus:
DKD 32/1913, S. 216

251
GLASSES
Design: Haida school of
glassmaking
Manufacturer: Oertel, Haida
Crystal, casing, cut
Reproduced from:
DKD 32/1913, p. 216

250
JAR
Design: Haida school of
glassmaking
Manufacturer: Oertel, Haida
Crystal, casing (blue,
black), decorative
cut seam
Lid and body 10 sides
H 15.8, Db 10,
D (lid) 9.9, D (lip) 8.9
Lit.:
DK, 17th year/1914, p. 381
Eisler 1916, p. 250
Inv.: ÖMAK, W.I. 1273
(inventoried 07/01/14;
acquired for 57 crowns
from Oertel, Haida)

252
VASE
Fachschule Haida
Kristall, Überfang (blau, schwarz), Ziersaumschliff (6teiliger Dekor)
H 15,9, Do 5,9, Du 5,9
Lit.: DKD 32/1913, S. 216
Eisler 1916, S. 165
Inv.: ÖMAK, W.I. 1238
(inventarisiert am 7. 1. 1914, erworben um 10,20 Kronen von der Fachschule Haida)

252
VASE
Haida school of glassmaking
Crystal, casing (blue, black), decorative cut seam (6-part decoration)
H 15.9, Dt 5.9, Db 5.9
Lit.: DKD 32/1913, p. 216
Eisler 1916, p. 165
Inv.: ÖMAK, W.I. 1238
(inventoried 07/01/14; acquired for 10.20 crowns from Haida school of glassmaking)

252

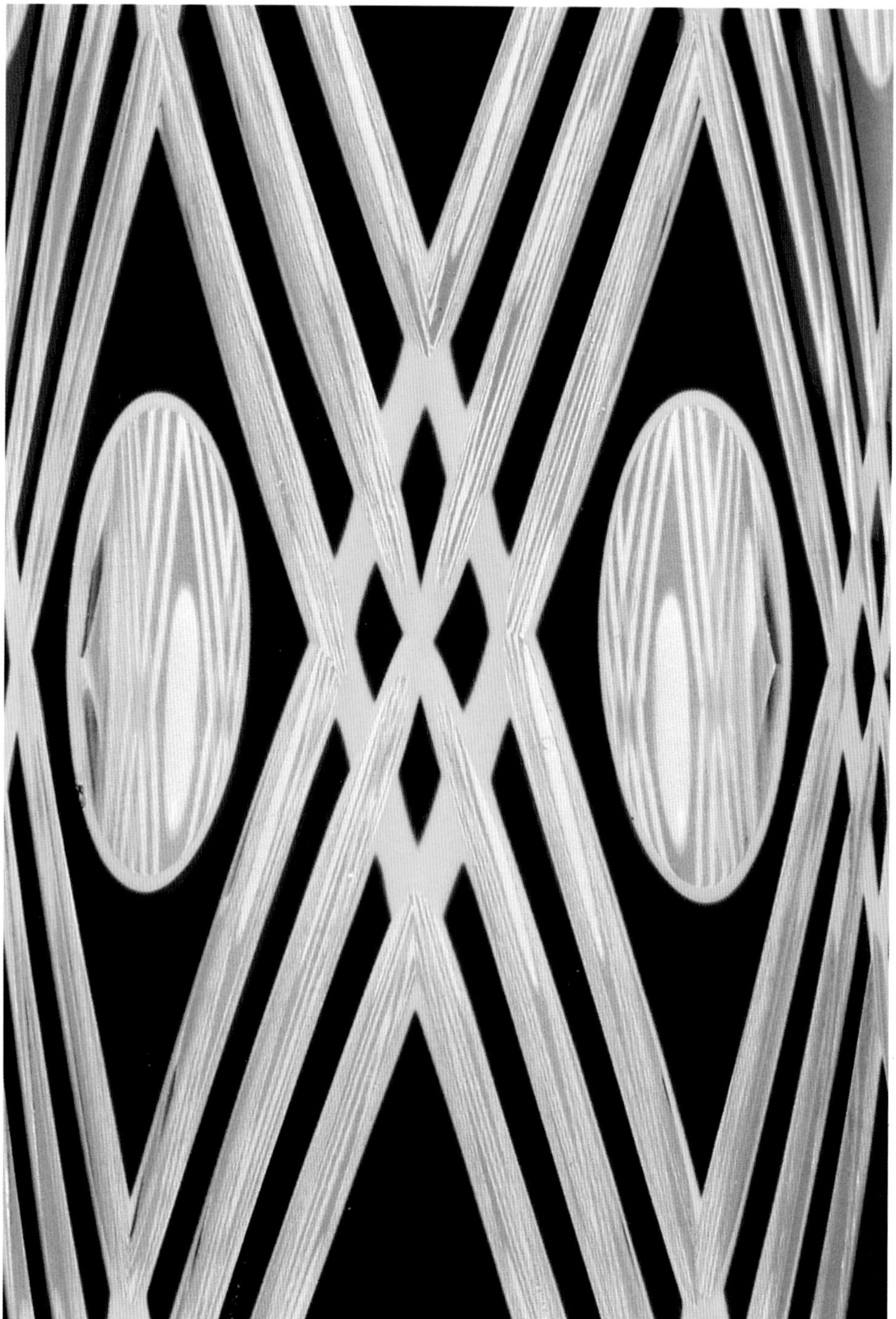

253

253
VASE
Entwurf: Fachschule Haida
Ausführung: Oertel, Haida
Kristall, Überfang (gelb, schwarz), geschliffen
H 26,5, Do und unten 8,7
Firmenetikett von Oertel, Haida
Ausst.:
ÖMKI 1913/14, Nr. 852
Lit.:
DKD 32/1913, S. 216
Inv.: Joanneum, AKGW, Nr. 15499
(erworben am 23. 11. 1913 um 50 Kronen vom ÖMKI)

253

253
VASE
Design: Haida school of glassmaking
Manufacturer: Oertel, Haida
Crystal, casing (yellow, black), decorative cut seam
H 26.5, Dt and Db 8.7
Company label of Oertel, Haida
Exhibition(s):
ÖMKI 1913/14, no. 852
Lit.:
DKD 32/1913, p. 216
Inv.: Joanneum, AKGW, no. 15499
(acquired 23/11/13 for 50 crowns from ÖMKI)

253

254

254
VASE
Entwurf: Fachschule Haida
Ausführung: Oertel, Haida
Werknummer 2654
Kristall, Überfang (weiß, blau), Ziersaumschliff
H 20,6, Do 6,6, Du 6,9
Ausst.: ÖMKI 1915
Inv.: ÖMAK, W.I. 1656 (inventarisiert am 1. 4. 1916, erworben um 18 Kronen von Oertel, Haida)

254
VASE
Design: Haida school of glassmaking
Manufacturer: Oertel, Haida
Serial number 2654
Crystal, casing (white, blue), decorative cut seam
H 20.6, Dt 6.6, Db 6.9
Exhibition(s): ÖMKI 1915
Inv.: ÖMAK, W.I. 1656 (inventoried 01/04/16; acquired for 18 crowns from Oertel, Haida)

254

255

255
VASE
Entwurf: Fachschule Haida
Ausführung: Oertel, Haida
Werknummer (Oertel): 2683
Kristall, Überfang (Kuppa: blau, weiß, schwarz), Schliff (8teiliger Dekor)
H 24,7, Do 9, D Fuß 9,7
Ausst.: ÖMKI 1915
(Foto ÖMAK VS 174 A)
Lit.:
KKH XVIII/1915, S. 448
DK XXIV/1916, S. 60
Inv.: ÖMAK, W.I. 1658
(inventarisiert am 1. 4. 1916, erworben um 36 Kronen von Oertel)

255
VASE
Design: Haida school of glassmaking
Manufacturer: Oertel, Haida
Serial number 2683 (Oertel)
Crystal, casing (bowl: blue, white, black), cutting (8-part decoration)
H 24.7, Dt 9, D foot 9.7
Exhibition(s): ÖMKI 1915
(photograph ÖMAK, VS 174 A)
Lit.:
KKH XVIII/1915, p. 448
DK XXIV/1916, p. 60
Inv.: ÖMAK, W.I. 1658
(inventoried 01/04/16; acquired for 36 crowns from Oertel)

256
VASE
Entwurf: Fachschule Haida
Ausführung: Oertel, Haida
Werknummer (Oertel): 2648
Kristall, Überfang (Kuppa: blau, weiß, schwarz), Schliff (8teiliger Dekor)
H 24,6, Do 9,1, D Fuß 9,7
Ausst.: ÖMKI 1915
Inv.: ÖMAK, W.I. 1654 (inventarisiert am 1. 4. 1916, erworben um 42 Kronen von Oertel)

256
VASE
Design: Haida school of glassmaking
Manufacturer: Oertel, Haida
Serial number 2648 (Oertel)
Crystal, casing (bowl: blue, white, black), cutting (8-part decoration)
H 24.6, Dt 9.1, D foot 9.7
Exhibition(s): ÖMKI 1915
Inv.: ÖMAK, W.I. 1654 (inventoried 01/04/16; acquired for 42 crowns from Oertel)

256

257

257
VASE
Kristall, Überfang (blau, schwarz), Schliff
H 23,8, Do 4, D Fuß 7,1
Inv.: ÖMAK, Gl 3459
(1984 erworben)

257
VASE
Crystal, casing (blue, black), cutting
H 23.8, Dt 4, D foot 7.1
Inv.: ÖMAK, Gl 3459
(acquired 1984)

258
VASE
Entwurf: Fachschule Haida
Ausführung: Oertel, Haida
Werknummer (Oertel): 2651
Kristall, Überfang (blau, schwarz), Schliff
H 21,3, Do 7,4, D Fuß 9, Dg 8,3
Ausst.: ÖMKI 1915
Inv.: ÖMAK, W.I. 1655 (inventarisiert am 1. 4. 1916, erworben um 40 Kronen von Oertel, Haida)

258
VASE
Design: Haida school of glassmaking
Manufacturer: Oertel, Haida
Serial number 2651 (Oertel)
Crystal, casing (blue, black), cut
H 21.3, Dt 7.4, D foot 9, Dm 8.3
Exhibition(s): ÖMKI 1915
Inv.: ÖMAK, W.I. 1655 (inventoried 01/04/16; acquired for 40 crowns from Oertel, Haida)

258

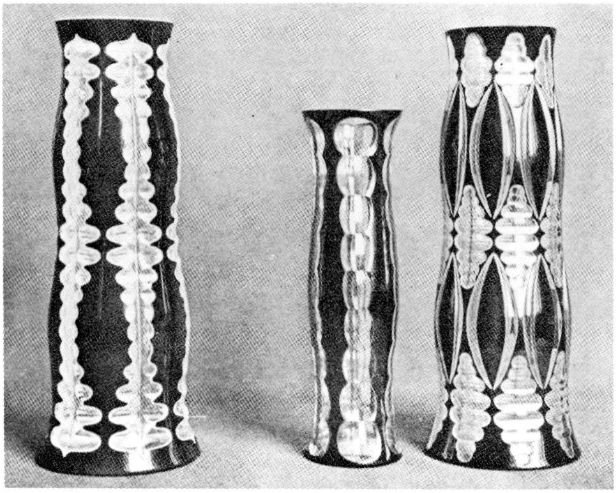

259

259
VASEN
Entwurf: Fachschule Haida
Ausführung: Oertel, Haida
Kristall, Überfang
(zweifach), geschliffen
Reproduktion aus:
DK 16.Jg./1913, S. 569

259
VASES
Design: Haida school of glassmaking
Manufacturer: Oertel, Haida
Crystal, casing (double), cut
Reproduced from:
DK, 16th year/1913, p. 569

260

260
VASEN UND DOSE
Fachschule Haida
Kristall, Überfang, geschliffen
Ausst.: ÖMKI 1913/14, Nr. 169, 159, 168
Lit.:
KKH XVI/1913, S. 616, 617
(Vase rechts, Dose Mitte)
Inv.: ÖMAK, VS 180 B
(zeitgenössisches Foto)

260
VASES AND LIDDED JAR
Haida school of glassmaking
Crystal, casing, cut
Exhibition(s):
ÖMKI 1913/14, nos. 169, 159, 168
Lit.:
KKH XVI/1913, pp. 616, 617
(right-handed vase, middle box)
Inv.: ÖMAK, VS 180 B
(contemporary photograph)

261
VASE
Entwurf: Fachschule Haida
Ausführung: Oertel, Haida
Kristall, Überfang (blau, schwarz), Ziersaumschliff (6teiliger Dekor)
H 34,2, Do 9,5, Du 12,8
Ausst.: ÖMKI 1913/14
Lit.:
DK 16.Jg./1913, S. 569
Eisler 1916, S. 29
Inv.: ÖMAK, W.I. 1274 (inventarisiert am 7. 1. 1914, erworben um 95 Kronen von Oertel, Haida)

261
VASE
Design: Haida school of glassmaking
Manufacturer: Oertel, Haida
Crystal, casing (blue, black), decorative cut seam (6-part decoration)
H 34.2, Dt 9.5, Db 12.8
Exhibition(s):
ÖMKI 1913/14
Lit.:
DK, 16th year/1913, p. 569
Eisler 1916, p. 29
Inv.: ÖMAK, W.I. 1274 (inventoried 07/01/14; acquired for 95 crowns from Oertel, Haida)

261

263
DISH
Black and white
casing, cut
Design: Prof. A. Walter
(Steinschönau school of
glassmaking)
Manufacturer:
Steinschönau school of
glassmaking
Exhibition(s): Köln 1914
Reproduced from:
DKD 35/1914-1915, p. 166

264
DISH
Black and white
casing, cut
Design: Prof. A. Walter
(Steinschönau school of
glassmaking)
Manufacturer:
Steinschönau school of
glassmaking
Exhibition(s): Köln 1914
Reproduced from:
DKD 35/1914-1915, p. 166

262

262
VASE
Franz Krause (Fachschule
Steinschönau)
Kristall, Überfang
(schwarz, gelb),
geschliffen
Ausst.:
ÖMKI 1913/14, Nr. 191
Lit.: KKH XVI/1913, S. 616
Inv.: ÖMAK, VS 180 B
(zeitgenössisches Foto)

262
VASE
Franz Krause (Steinschönau
school of glassmaking)
Crystal, casing (black,
yellow), cut
Exhibition(s):
ÖMKI 1913/14, no. 191
Lit.: KKH XVI/1913, p. 616
Inv.: ÖMAK, VS 180 B
(contemporary photograph)

263
SCHALE
Schwarz und weiß überfangen, geschliffen
Entwurf: Prof. A. Walter (Fachschule Steinschönau)
Ausführung: Fachschule Steinschönau
Ausst.: Köln 1914
Reproduktion aus: DKD 35/1914-1915, S. 166

263

264
SCHALE
Schwarz und weiß überfangen, geschliffen
Entwurf: Prof. A. Walter (Fachschule Steinschönau)
Ausführung: Fachschule Steinschönau
Ausst.: Köln 1914
Reproduktion aus: DKD 35/1914-1915, S. 166

264

267
VASE
Design: Prof. A. Walter
Manufacturer: Steinschönau school of glassmaking
Crystal, bowl with casing in black and white, foot with casing in white and black, cut
H 13, Dt 11.1, Db 10.9
Exhibition(s): ÖMKI 1913/14, 193
Exhibition(s): ÖMAK 1973
Lit.: Neuwirth 1973, no. 72, pp. 186-187
Inv.: ÖMAK, W.I. 1242 (inventoried 07/01/14; acquired for 35 crowns from Steinschönau school of glassmaking)

265
VASE
Design: Adolf Beckert
Manufacturer: Steinschönau school of glassmaking
Crystal, casing (white and black), cut
Exhibition(s): ÖMKI 1913/14, no. 195 ("Vase, crystal, casing in black and enamel white, modern cutting. Design by Adolf Beckert, 23 crowns")
Lit.: KKH XVI/1913, p. 618
Inv.: ÖMAK, VS 180 B (contemporary photograph)

266
VASE
Design: Prof. Max
Manufacturer: Steinschönau school of glassmaking
Crystal, casing (black and white), cut, painted
Exhibition(s): ÖMKI 1913/14, no. 200 ("Decorative vase, crystal, with foot, casing in white and black, cutting and painting. Design by Prof. Max. Not for sale")
Lit.: KKH XVI/1913, p. 618
Eisler 1916, p. 166
Inv.: ÖMAK, VS 180 B (contemporary photograph)

265 266

265
VASE
Entwurf: Adolf Beckert
Ausführung:
Fachschule Steinschönau
Kernkristall, Überfang
(weiß und schwarz),
geschliffen
Ausst.:
ÖMKI 1913/14, Nr. 195
(„Schale, Kristall,
schwarz=emailweiß überfangen, modern gekugelt.
Nach Entwurf von Fachschullehrer Adolf Beckert,
23 Kronen")
Lit.: KKH XVI/1913, S. 618
Inv.: ÖMAK, VS 180 B
(zeitgenössisches Foto)

266
VASE
Entwurf: Prof. Max
Ausführung:
Fachschule Steinschönau
Kernkristall, Überfang
(weiß und schwarz),
geschliffen, bemalt
Ausst.:
ÖMKI 1913/14, Nr. 200
(„Ziervase. Kristall,
mit Fuß, weiß=schwarz
überfangen, mit Schliff
und Malerei. Nach Entwurf
von Prof. Max.
Unverkäuflich")
Lit.: KKH XVI/1913, S. 618
Eisler 1916, S. 166
Inv.: ÖMAK, VS 180 B
(zeitgenössisches Foto)

267
VASE
Entwurf: Prof. A. Walter
Ausführung:
Fachschule Steinschönau
Kernkristall,
Schale schwarz und weiß
überfangen, Fuß weiß und
schwarz überfangen,
geschliffen
H 13, Do 11,1, u 10,9
Ausst.:
ÖMKI 1913/14, 193
ÖMAK 1973
Lit.:
Neuwirth 1973, Nr. 72,
S. 186-187
Inv.: ÖMAK, W.I. 1242
(inventarisiert am
7. 1. 1914, erworben um
35 Kronen von der
Fachschule Steinschönau)

267

268

268
VIER GLÄSER
Entwurf: Fachschule Haida
Ausführung: Oertel, Haida
Kristall, Überfang,
Ziersaumschliff
Reproduktion aus:
DK 16.Jg./1913, S. 571

268
FOUR GLASSES
Design: Haida school of glassmaking
Manufacturer: Oertel, Haida
Crystal, casing,
decorative cut seam
Reproduced from:
DK, 16th year/1913, p. 571

269

269
JARDINIERE,
ZWEI DOSEN
Schappel, Haida
Kristall, Überfang,
Ziersaumschliff
Ausst.: ÖMKI 1913/14,
Nr. 985, 984, 986
Lit.: Eisler 1916, S. 164
Inv.: ÖMAK, VS 174 B
(zeitgenössisches Foto)

269
JARDINIERE, TWO JARS
Schappel, Haida
Crystal, casing,
decorative cut seam
Exhibition(s):
ÖMKI 1913/14, nos. 985,
984, 986
Lit.: Eisler 1916, p. 164
Inv.: ÖMAK, VS 174 B
(contemporary photograph)

270
VASE
Entwurf: Julius Jelínek
Ausführung: Harrach, Neuwelt
Kernkristall, Überfang (weiß und schwarz), geschliffen
12fache Motivwiederholung auf der Wandung (vertikal)
H 30,5, Dg 11,5
Ausst.: ÖMAK 1973
Lit.: Neuwirth 1973, S. 294-295
Inv.: ÖMAK, W.I. 1246 (inventarisiert am 7. 1. 1914, erworben um 50 Kronen von Harrach)

270
VASE
Design: Julius Jelínek
Manufacturer: Harrach, Neuwelt
Crystal, casing (white and black), cut (motifs repeated 12 times)
H 30.5, Dm 11.5
Exhibition(s): ÖMAK 1973
Lit.: Neuwirth 1973, pp. 294-295
Inv.: ÖMAK, W.I. 1246 (inventoried 07/01/14; acquired for 50 crowns from Harrach)

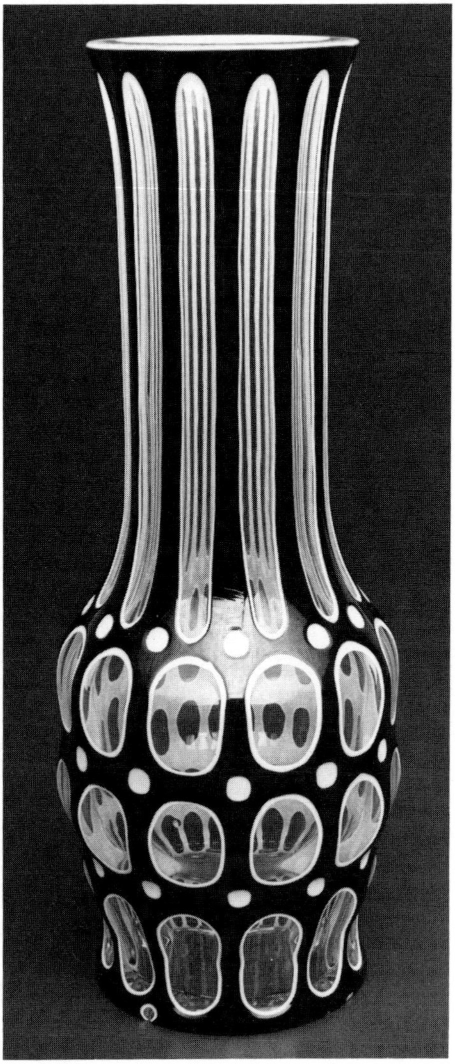

270

271
DECKELPOKAL
Entwurf: Fachschule Haida
Ausführung: Oertel, Haida
Kernkristall, Überfang
(weiß und schwarz),
geschliffen (6fache
Wiederholung des Motivs,
vertikal)
H 33, Dg (Fuß) 9,6
Ausst.:
ÖMKI 1913/14, Nr. 838
Lit.:
KKH XVI/1913, S. 621
(Knauf ohne Schliff)
Eisler 1916, S. 165
(Variante mit geringfügigen Änderungen)
Inv.: ÖMAK, W.I. 1271
(inventarisiert am
7. 1. 1914 (erworben um
65 Kronen von Oertel,
Haida)

272
DECKELVASE
Entwurf: Fachschule Haida
Ausführung: Oertel, Haida
Kernkristall, Überfang
(weiß und schwarz),
geschliffen (6fache
Wiederholung des Motivs,
vertikal)
H 33,5, Dg (Fuß) 9,6,
D Mundrand 8,5
Ausst.:
ÖMKI 1913/14, Nr. 838
Lit.:
KKH XVI/1913, S. 621
(Knauf ohne Schliff)
Eisler 1916, S. 165
(Variante mit geringfügigen Änderungen)
Inv.: Joanneum,
AKGW, Nr. 15498
(erworben am 23. 11. 1913
um 30 Kronen vom ÖMKI)

271
LIDDED GOBLET
Design: Haida school of
glassmaking
Manufacturer: Oertel, Haida
Crystal, casing (white and
black), cut (motif repeated
6 times)
H 33, Dm (foot) 9.6
Exhibition(s):
ÖMKI 1913/14, no. 838
Lit.:
KKH XVI/1913, p. 621
(knob without cutting)
Eisler 1916, p. 165
(similar model with slight
alterations)
Inv.: ÖMAK, W.I. 1271
(inventoried 07/01/14;
acquired for 65 crowns
from Oertel, Haida)

272
LIDDED VASE
Design: Haida school of
glassmaking
Manufacturer: Oertel, Haida
Crystal, casing (white and
black), cut (motif
repeated 6 times)
H 33.5, Dm (foot) 9.6,
D (lip) 8.5
Exhibition(s):
ÖMKI 1913/14, no. 838
Lit.:
KKH XVI/1913, p. 621
(knob uncut)
Eisler 1916, p. 165
(similar model with slight
alterations)
Inv.: Joanneum,
AKGW, no. 15498
(acquired 23/11/13 for
30 crowns from ÖMKI)

271

272

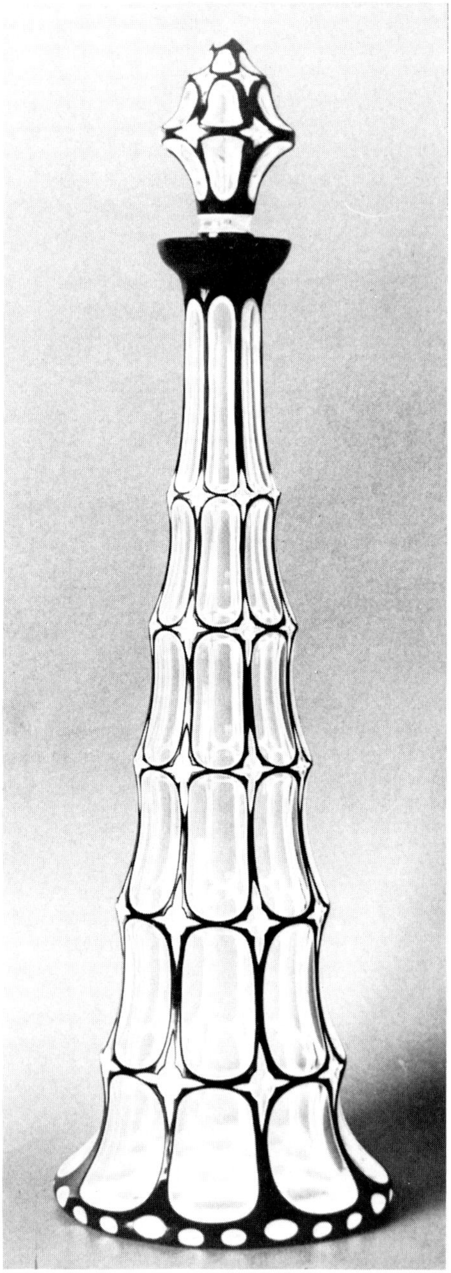

273

273
FLASCHE MIT STÖPSEL
Karl Goldberg, Haida
Kernkristall, Überfang,
geschliffen
Ausst.: ÖMKI 1915
Lit.:
KKH XVIII/1915, S. 447
Inv.: ÖMAK, VS 175 A
(zeitgenössisches Foto)

273
BOTTLE WITH STOPPER
Karl Goldberg, Haida
Crystal, casing, cut
Exhibition: ÖMKI 1915
Lit.:
KKH XVIII/1915, p. 447
Inv.: ÖMAK, VS 175 A
(contemporary photograph)

275
DECKELPOKAL
Tschernich & Co., Haida
Kernkristall, Überfang
(weiß und schwarz),
geschliffen
Ausst.: ÖMKI 1915
Lit.:
KKH XVIII/1915, S. 448
Inv.: ÖMAK, VS 178 A
(zeitgenössisches Foto)

274

275

274
SCHALE
Tschernich & Co., Haida
Kernkristall, Überfang
(weiß und schwarz),
geschliffen
Ausst.: ÖMKI 1915
Inv.: ÖMAK, VS 178 A
(zeitgenössisches Foto)

274
DISH
Tschernich & Co., Haida
Crystal, casing (white
and black), cut
Exhibition: ÖMKI 1915
Inv.: ÖMAK, VS 178 A
(contemporary photograph)

275
LIDDED GOBLET
Tschernich & Co., Haida
Crystal, casing (white
and black), cut
Exhibition(s): ÖMKI 1915
Lit.:
KKH XVIII/1915, p. 448
Inv.: ÖMAK, VS 178 A
(contemporary photograph)

Kunstschale

aus feinem Kristall, gelb und weiß überfangen, mit hochfeinem Schliff.

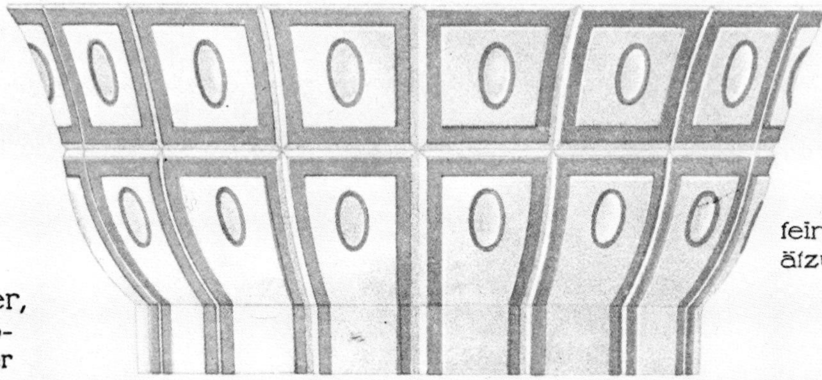

·cher,
Gelb-
feiner

feines
ätzung
(

Nr. 87.
65.— per Stück.

276

Kunstschale,

feinstes Kristall, orange und schwarz überfangen, feinster Schliff.
Entwurf: Architekt Emanuel Margold, Darmstadt, Künstlerkolonie.

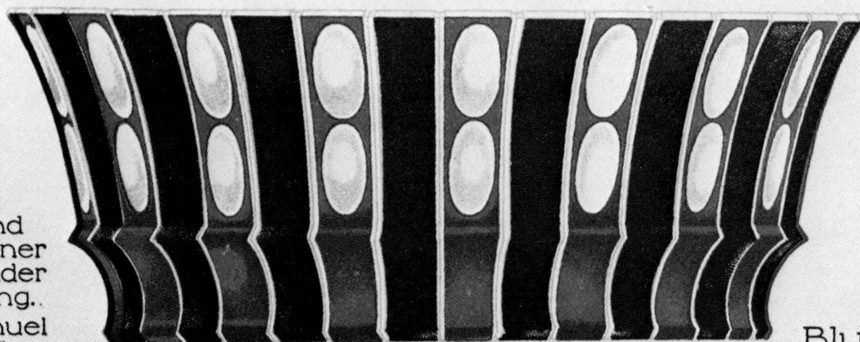

und
einer
hilder
ung..
anuel
sfler-

Nr. 64.
64.— per Stück.

Blum
feinstes Kristall
Schildern und

277

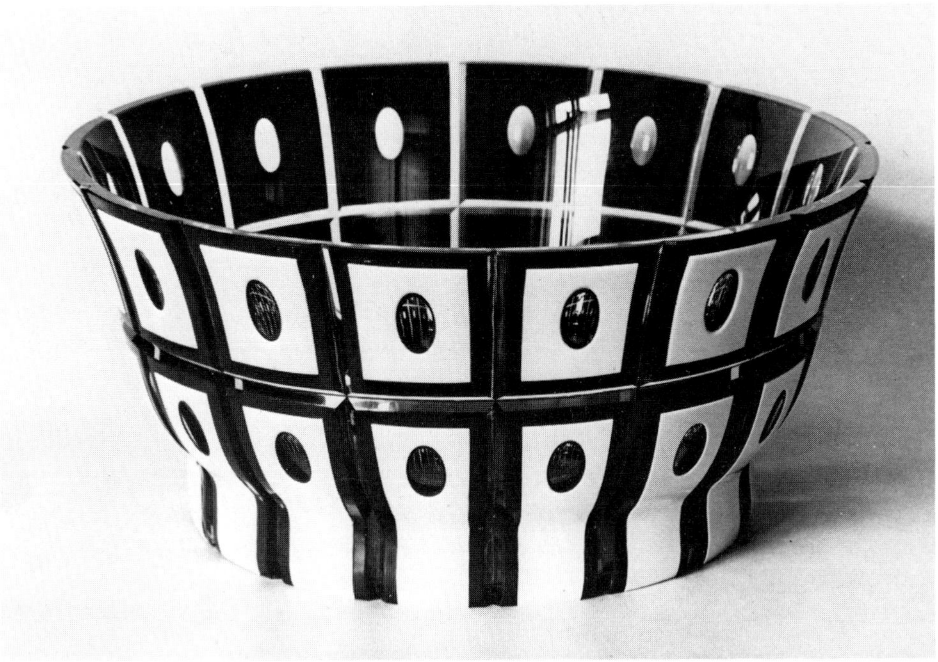

278

276
SCHALE
Entwurf: E. J. Margold
Ausführung:
Carl Schappel, Haida
Kristall, Überfang (gelb und weiß), geschliffen
Reproduktion aus:
Kat. Schappel, Kunstgläser

276
DISH
Design: E. J. Margold
Manufacturer:
Carl Schappel, Haida
Crystal, casing (yellow and white), cut
Reproduced from:
Kat. Schappel, Kunstgläser

277
SCHALE
Entwurf: E. J. Margold
Ausführung:
Carl Schappel, Haida
Kristall, Überfang (orange und schwarz), geschliffen
Reproduktion aus:
Kat. Schappel, Kunstgläser

277
DISH
Design: E. J. Margold
Manufacturer:
Carl Schappel, Haida
Crystal, casing (orange and black), cut
Reproduced from:
Kat. Schappel, Kunstgläser

278
SCHALE
Entwurf: E. J. Margold
Ausführung:
Carl Schappel, Haida
Kernkristall, Überfang (schwarz und weiß), geschliffen
Ausst.: ÖMKI 1915
Lit.:
KKH XVIII/1915, S. 449
DK XXIV/1916, S. 62
Inv.: ÖMAK, VS 174 A
(zeitgenössisches Foto)

278
BOWL
Design: E. J. Margold
Manufacturer:
Carl Schappel, Haida
Crystal, casing (black and white), cut
Exhibition(s): ÖMKI 1915
Lit.:
KKH XVIII/1915, p. 449
DK XXIV/1916, p. 62
Inv.: ÖMAK, VS 174 A
(contemporary photograph)

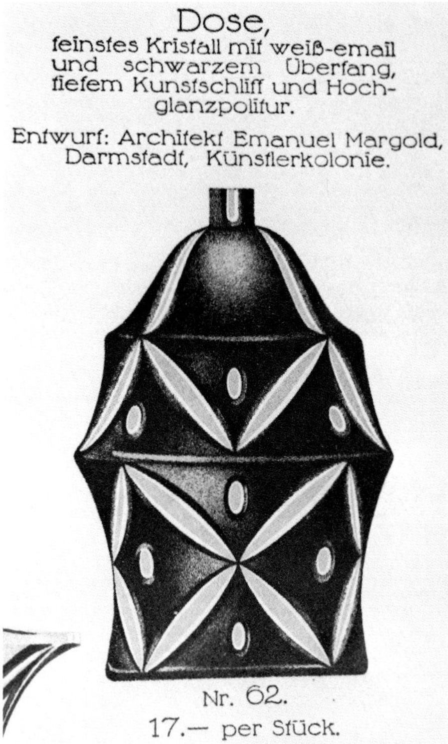

279

279
DOSE
Entwurf: J. E. Margold
Ausführung:
Schappel, Haida
Kristall, Überfang (weiß,
schwarz), geschliffen
Reproduktion aus:
Kat. Schappel, Kunstgläser

279
JAR
Design: J. E. Margold
Manufacturer:
Schappel, Haida
Crystal, casing (white,
black), cut
Reproduced from:
Kat. Schappel, Kunstgläser

280
PREISLISTE
der Borussia-Gläser
von Carl Schappel, Haida
Reproduktion aus:
Kat. Schappel, Borussia

280
PRICE LIST
of the Borussia glasses
by Carl Schappel, Haida
Reproduced from:
Kat. Schappel, Borussia

Boruſſia-Gläſer

aus Kernkriſtall, ſchwarz und weiß überfangen, mit Zierſaumſchliffen

Nr.		per Stück
5254	Likörflaſche	23.—
	Likörbecher hierzu ..	4.50
5255	Kompottſchale	37.—
5256/5	Vaſe	6.70
5256/7	Vaſe	12.—
5256/9	Vaſe	16.75
5822	Vaſe	14.50
6203	Vaſe	7.70
6204	Römer	16.75
6385	Vaſe	30.—
6386	Vaſe	43.—
6387	Vaſe	57.—
6388	Vaſe	30.—
6389	Vaſe	26.50
6390	Vaſe	39.—
6391	Vaſe mit erhabenen Walzenſchliff	75.—
6437	Vaſe	30.—
6438	Vaſe	17.20
6440	Zierpokal	18.—
6441	Zierpokal	45.—
6442	Vaſe	13.50
6443	Blumenkugel	24.60
6459	Vaſe mit erhabenen Walzenſchliff	76.—
6460	Jardinière	29.—
6461	Jardinière	29.—
6462	Jardinière	25.—
6463	Zierpokal	34.60
6464	Zierrömer	17.30
6465	Rumflakon	9.40
6466	Zuckerdoſe	19.20
6467	Zuckerſtreuer	13.20
6468	Milchkännchen	13.40
6469	Sahnenkännchen ..	11.50
6470	Rumflakon	10.50

Nr.		per Stück
6471	Zuckerdoſe	23.40
6472	Zuckerſtreuer	14.70
6473	Milchkännchen	15.40
6474	Sahnenkännchen ..	14.—
6510	Jardinière	46.—
6511	Vaſe	17.20
6717	Vaſe	45.—
6718	Vaſe	33.—
6719	Vaſe	36.—
6720	Vaſe	32.—
6721	Vaſe	25.60
6722	Vaſe	7.60
6723	Pokal	34.—
6724	Pokal	39.—
6725	Tabakdoſe	32.60
6726	Jardinière	25.—
6744	Vaſe	6.20
6745	Fingerſchale	10.—
6746	Jardinière	26.—
6747	Zuckerdoſe	17.50
6748	Tabakdoſe	33.50
6749	Pokal	40.—
6750	Cakesdoſe	53.—
6751	Vaſe	25.—
6752	Jardinière	10.70
6753	Vaſe	27.—
6754	Traubenſpüler	27.—
6755	Vaſe	22.50
6756	Weinflaſche	40.—
6757	Weinbecher	8.50
6758	Likörflaſche	28.—
6759	Jardinière	11 20
6783	Kompottſchale	62.50
6784	Vaſe	30.—
6785	Bonbonnière	17.70

280

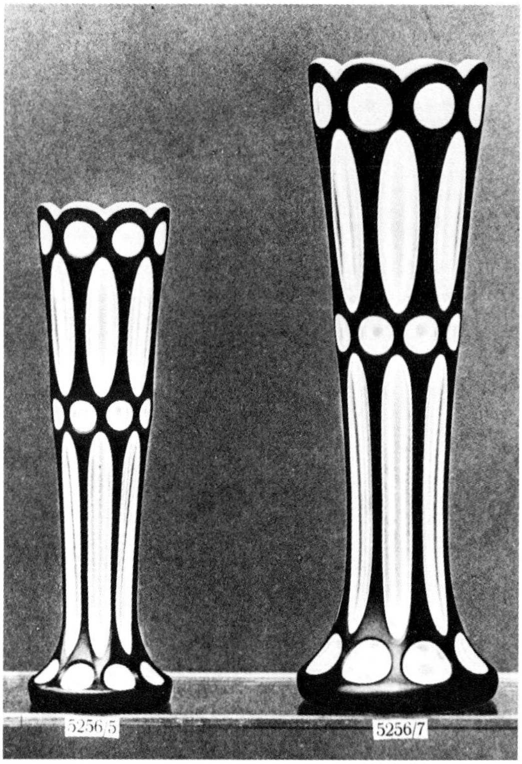

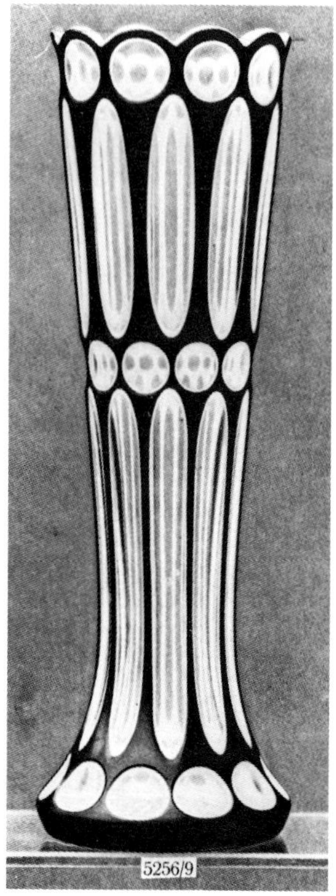

281 282 283

281-283
VASEN
Modelle Nr. 5256/5,
5256/7 und Nr. 5256/9
Reproduktion aus:
Kat. Schappel, Borussia

281-283
VASES
Model nos. 5256/5,
5256/7 and 5256/9
Reproduced from:
Kat. Schappel, Borussia

284
VASE
Carl Schappel, Haida
Modell Nr. 5256/9
Kernkristall, Überfang
(weiß und schwarz),
geschliffen
(10fache Motivwiederholung
auf der Wandung, vertikal)
geschliffener 16teiliger
Bodenstern
H 26,9, D (Fuß) 9
Ausst.: ÖMKI 1913/14,
Nr. 994 (K 15)
ÖMAK 1973
Lit.:
Kat. Schappel, Borussia,
Nr. 5256/9 (K 16,75)
Neuwirth 1973, Nr. 193,
S. 331
Inv.: ÖMAK, W.I. 1314
(inventarisiert am
4. 3. 1914, Geschenk von
Schappel)

284
VASE
Carl Schappel, Haida
Model no. 5256/9
Crystal, casing (white
and black), cut
(motif repeated 10 times),
cut 16-facet star in bottom
H 26.9, D (foot) 9
Exhibition(s):
ÖMKI 1913/14, no. 994
(K 15). – ÖMAK 1973
Lit.:
Kat. Schappel, Borussia,
no. 5256/9 (K 16.75)
Neuwirth 1973, no. 193,
p. 331
Inv.: ÖMAK, W.I. 1314
(inventoried 04/03/14;
donated by Schappel)

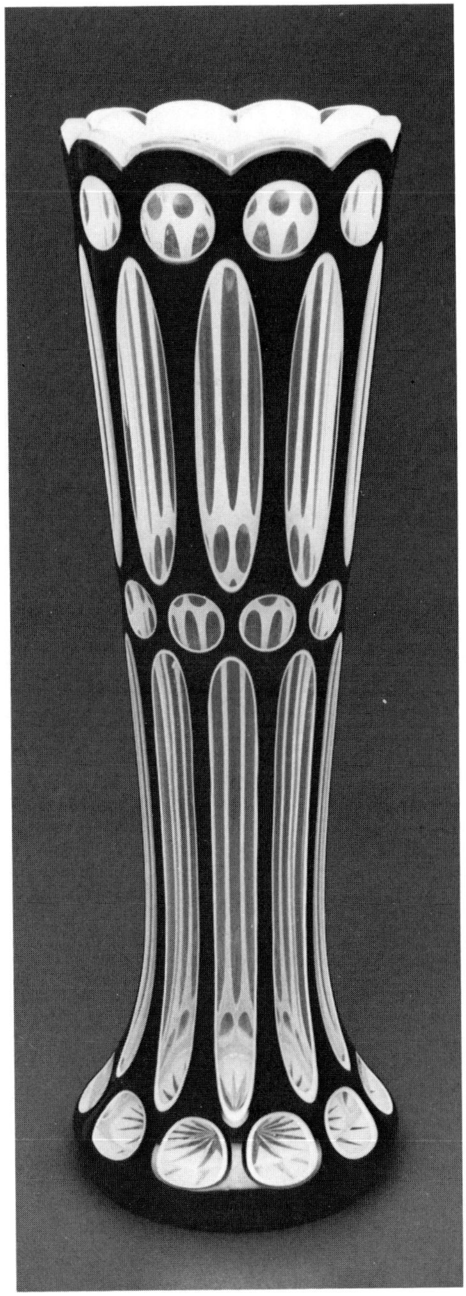

284

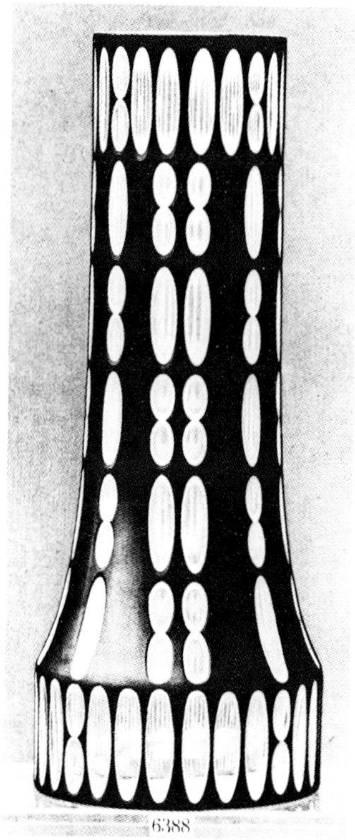

285

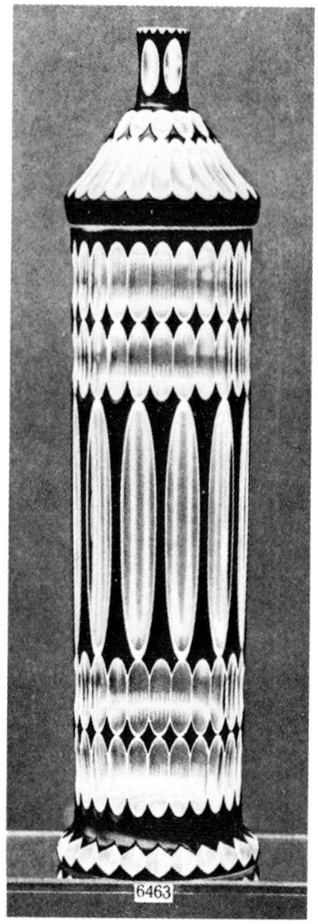

286

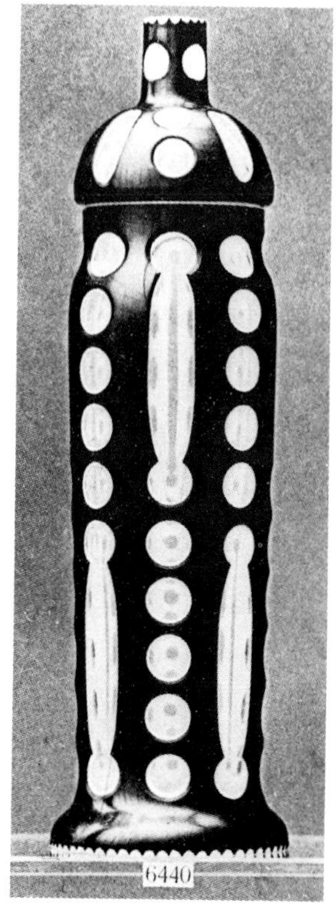

287

285
VASE
Vase Nr. 6388
Reproduktion aus:
Kat. Schappel, Borussia

286
ZIERPOKAL
Pokal Nr. 6463
Reproduktion aus:
Kat. Schappel, Borussia

287
ZIERPOKAL
Pokal Nr. 6440
Reproduktion aus:
Kat. Schappel, Borussia

285
VASE
Vase no. 6388
Reproduced from:
Kat. Schappel, Borussia

286
DECORATIVE CUP
Cup no. 6463
Reproduced from:
Kat. Schappel, Borussia

287
DECORATIVE CUP
Cup no. 6440
Reproduced from:
Kat. Schappel, Borussia

288
JARDINIERE
Jardinière no. 6759
Reproduced from:
Kat. Schappel, Borussia

289
CUP
Cup no. 6724
Reproduced from:
Kat. Schappel, Borussia

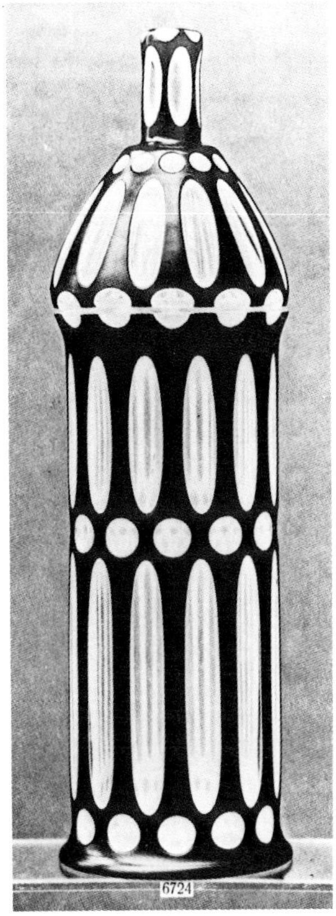

289

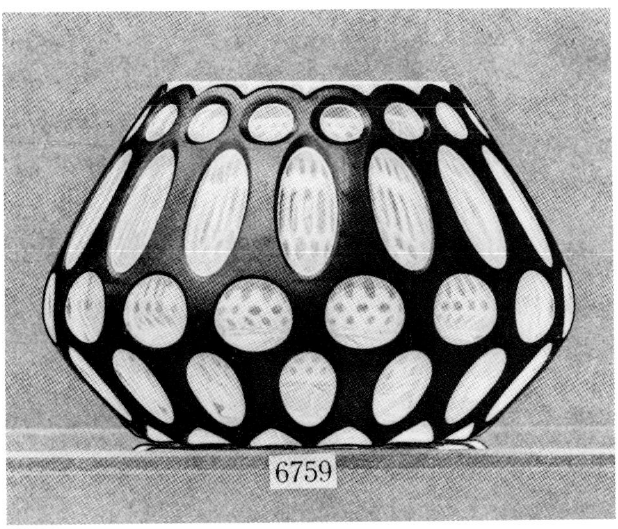

288

288
JARDINIERE
Jardinière Nr. 6759
Reproduktion aus:
Kat. Schappel, Borussia

289
POKAL
Pokal Nr. 6724
Reproduktion aus:
Kat. Schappel, Borussia

290

291

290
VASE
Vase Nr. 6717
Reproduktion aus:
Kat. Schappel, Borussia

290
VASE
Vase no. 6717
Reproduced from:
Kat. Schappel, Borussia

291
VASE
Vase Nr. 6751
Reproduktion aus:
Kat. Schappel, Borussia

291
VASE
Vase no. 6751
Reproduced from:
Kat. Schappel, Borussia

292
VASE
Carl Schappel, Haida
Crystal, casing (white and black), cut
H 26.4, Dm (foot) 9
Exhibition(s):
ÖMKI 1913/14, no. 987 (K 22). – ÖMAK 1973
Lit.:
Kat. Schappel, Borussia, no. 6717 oder 6751 (K 45 and 25)
Neuwirth 1973, no. 186, p. 325
Inv.: ÖMAK, W.I. 1320 (inventoried 04/03/14; donated by Schappel)

292
VASE
Carl Schappel, Haida
Kernkristall, Überfang (weiß und schwarz), geschliffen
H 26,4, Dg (Fuß) 9
Ausst.: ÖMKI 1913/14, Nr. 987 (K 22)
ÖMAK 1973
Lit.:
Kat. Schappel, Borussia, Nr. 6717 oder 6751 (K 45 bzw. 25)
Neuwirth 1973, Nr. 186, S. 325
Inv.: ÖMAK, W.I. 1320 (inventarisiert am 4. 3. 1914, Geschenk von Schappel)

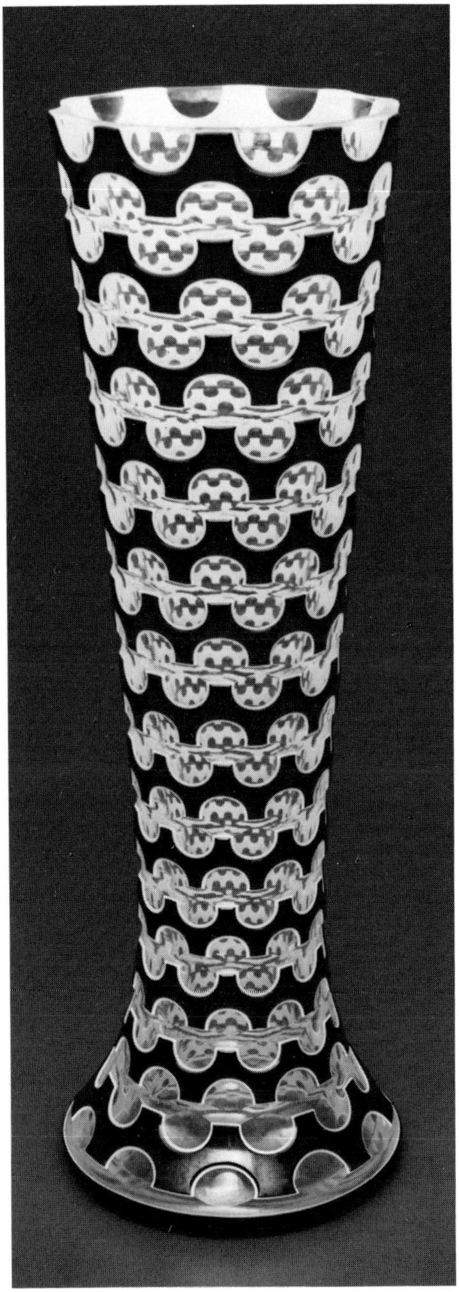

292

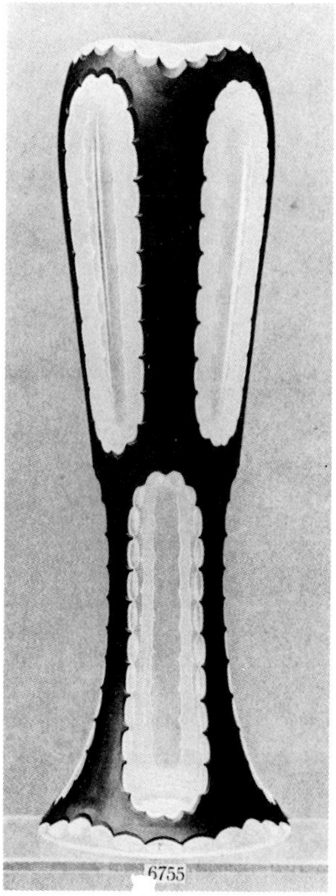

293

293
VASE
Vase Nr. 6755
Reproduktion aus:
Kat. Schappel, Borussia

293
VASE
Vase no. 6755
Reproduced from:
Kat. Schappel, Borussia

294
VASE
Carl Schappel, Haida
Borussia-Glas,
Modell Nr. 6755
Kernkristall, Überfang
(weiß und schwarz),
geschliffen (vierfache
Motivwiederholung)
H 25,8, Dg (Fuß) 8,2
Kat. Schappel, Borussia,
Nr. 6755 (K 22,50)
Inv.: ÖMAK, W.I. 1315
(inventarisiert am
4. 3. 1914, Geschenk von
Schappel)

294
VASE
Carl Schappel, Haida
Borussia glass
Model no. 6755
Crystal, casing (white
and black), cut (motif
repeated four times)
H 25.8, Dm (foot) 8.2
Kat. Schappel, Borussia,
no. 6755 (K 22,50)
Inv.: ÖMAK, W.I. 1315
(inventoried 04/03/14;
donated by Schappel)

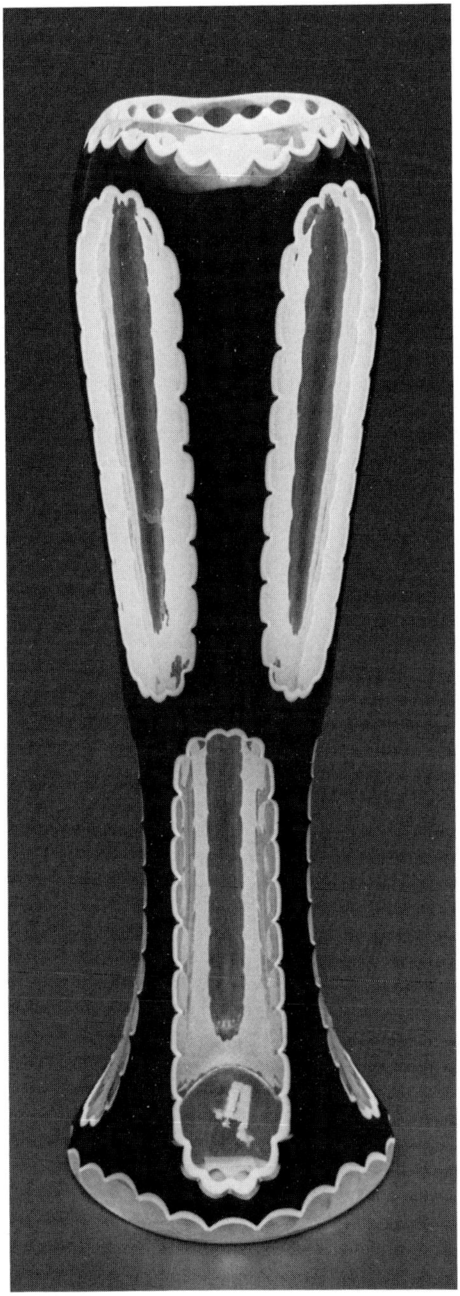

294

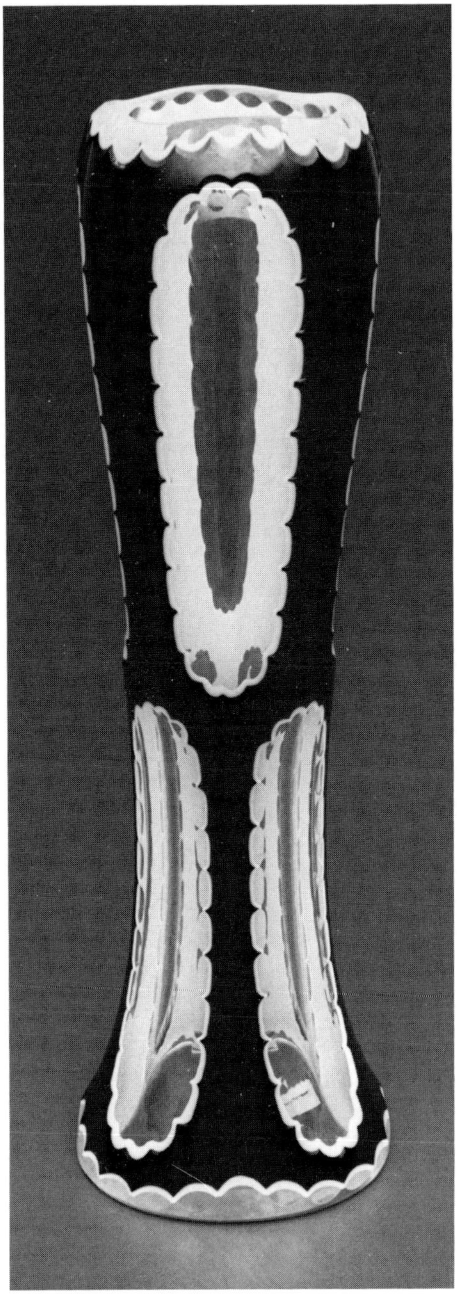

294

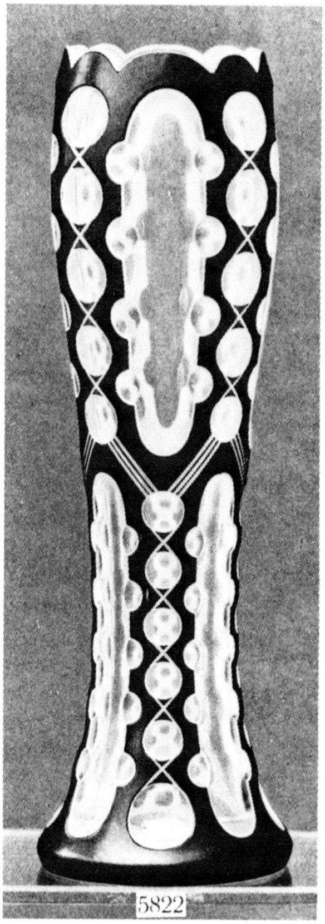

295

295
VASE
Vase Nr. 5822
Reproduktion aus:
Kat. Schappel, Borussia

295
VASE
Vase no. 5822
Reproduced from:
Kat. Schappel, Borussia

296
VASE
Carl Schappel, Haida
Borussia-Glas, Modell
Nr. 5822 (K 14,50)
Kernkristall, Überfang
(weiß und schwarz),
geschliffen (vierfache
Motivwiederholung)
H 21,1, Dg (Fuß) 6,9
Ausst.: ÖMKI 1913/14,
Nr. 989 oder 990 (K 24)
ÖMAK 1973
Lit.: Kat. Schappel,
Borussia, Nr. 5822
Neuwirth 1973, Nr. 187,
S. 326-327
Inv.: ÖMAK, W.I. 1316
(inventarisiert am
4. 3. 1914, Geschenk von
Schappel)

296
VASE
Carl Schappel, Haida
Borussia glass, model
no. 5822 (K 14.50)
Crystal, casing (white
and black), cut (motif
repeated four times)
H 21.1, Dm (foot) 6.9
Exhibition(s):
ÖMKI 1913/14, no. 989 or
990 (K 24). – ÖMAK 1973
Lit.: Kat. Schappel,
Borussia, no. 5822
Neuwirth 1973, no. 187,
p. 326-327
Inv.: ÖMAK, W.I. 1316
(inventoried 04/03/14;
donated by Schappel)

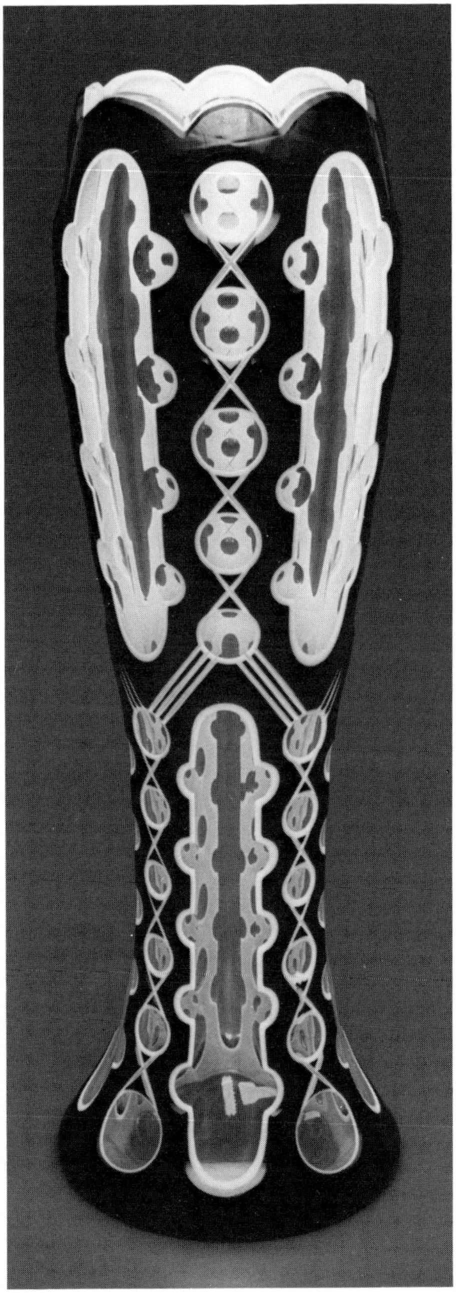

296

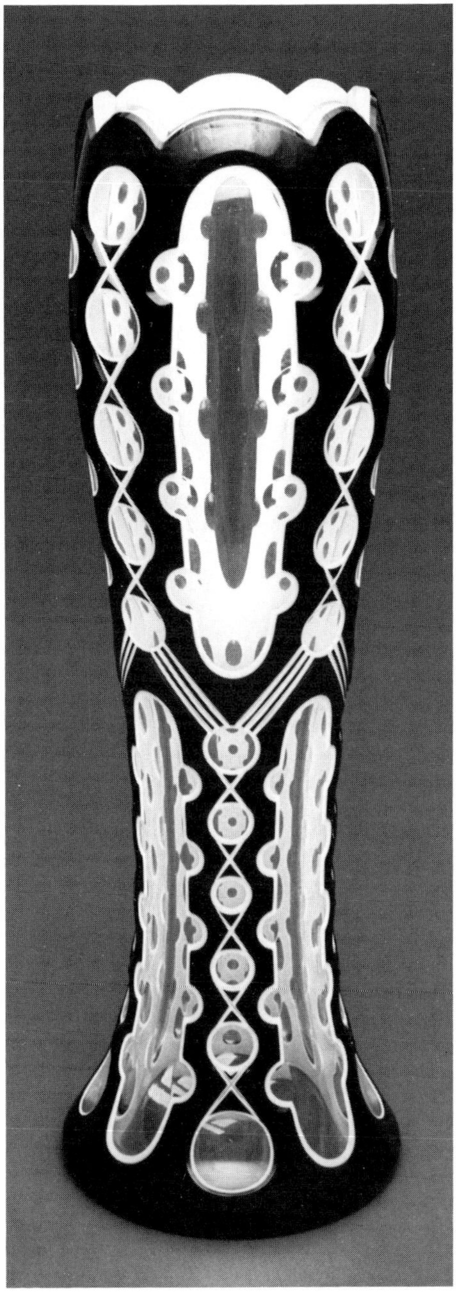

296

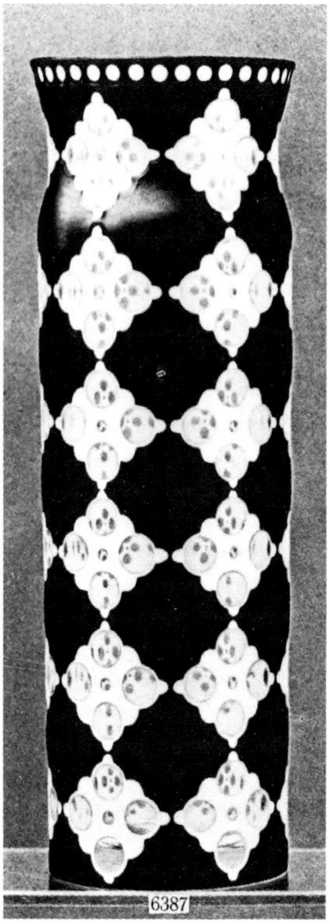

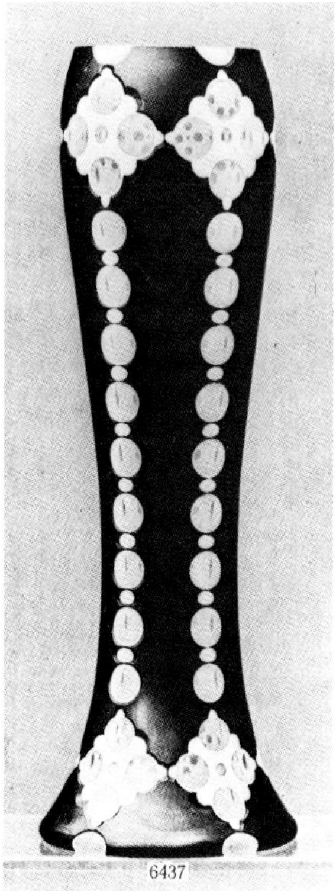

300
VASE
Carl Schappel, Haida
Borussia glass
Model no. 6753 (K 27)
Crystal, casing (white and black), cut (motif repeated 12 times)
H 22.7, Dm 10.6
Lit.:
Kat. Schappel, Borussia, no. 6753
Inv.: ÖMAK, W.I. 1324 (inventoried 04/03/14; donated by Schappel)

297

298

297
VASE
Modell Nr. 6387
Reproduktion aus:
Kat. Schappel, Borussia

297
VASE
Model no. 6387
Reproduced from:
Kat. Schappel, Borussia

298
VASE
Modell Nr. 6437
Reproduktion aus:
Kat. Schappel, Borussia

298
VASE
Model no. 6437
Reproduced from:
Kat. Schappel, Borussia

300
VASE
Carl Schappel, Haida
Borussia-Glas,
Modell Nr. 6753 (K 27)
Kernkristall, Überfang
(weiß und schwarz),
geschliffen (12fache
vertikale Gliederung)
H 22,7, Dg 10,6
Lit.:
Kat. Schappel, Borussia,
Nr. 6753
Inv.: ÖMAK, W.I. 1324
(inventarisiert am
4. 3. 1914, Geschenk von
Schappel)

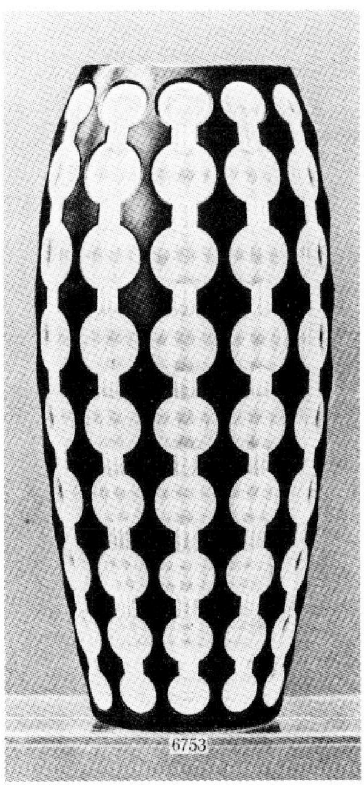

299

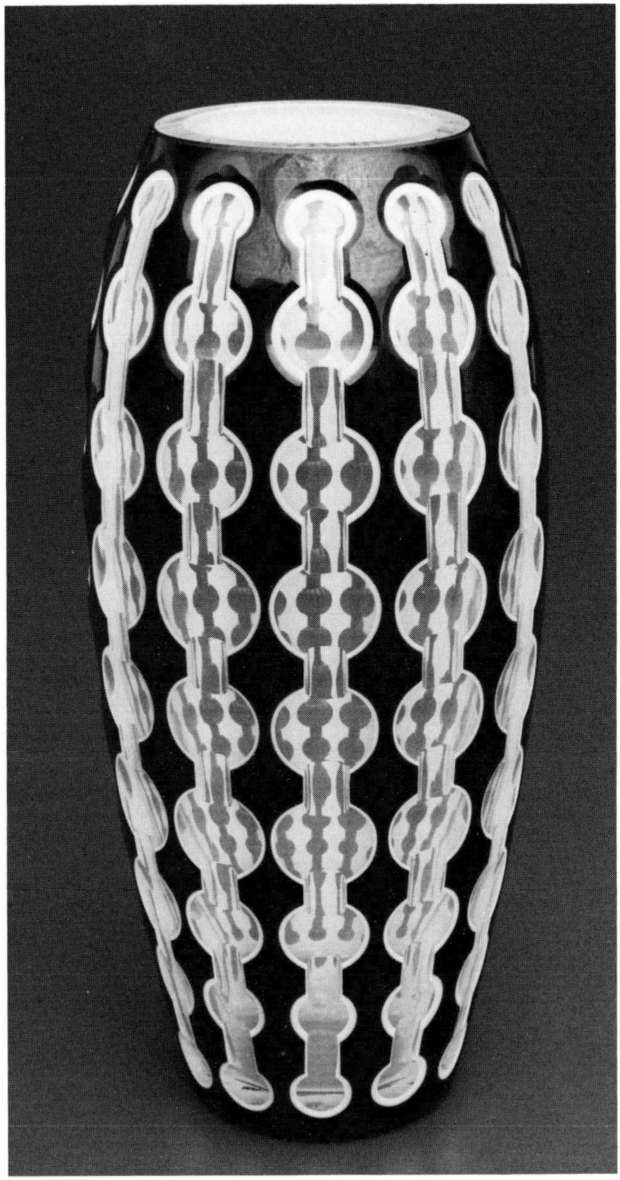

300

299
VASE
Modell Nr. 6753
Reproduktion aus:
Kat. Schappel, Borussia

299
VASE
Model no. 6753
Reproduced from:
Kat. Schappel, Borussia

301

302

301
TEILE EINER GARNITUR
Modelle Nr. 6470-6474:
Nr. 6471 (Zuckerdose),
Nr. 6472 (Zuckerstreuer),
Nr. 6474 (Sahnekännchen),
Nr. 6473 (Milchkännchen),
Nr. 6470 (Rumflakon)
Reproduktion aus:
Kat. Schappel, Borussia

301
PARTS OF A SET
Model nos. 6470-6474:
no. 6471 (sugar bowl),
no. 6472 (sugar caster),
no. 6474 (cream jug),
no. 6473 (milk jug),
no. 6470 (rum bottle)
Reproduced from:
Kat. Schappel, Borussia

302
DECKELPOKAL
Modell Nr. 6749
Reproduktion aus:
Kat. Schappel, Borussia

302
LIDDED GOBLET
Model no. 6749
Reproduced from:
Kat. Schappel, Borussia

304
LIDDED GOBLET
Carl Schappel, Haida
Borussia glass, similar
to Model no. 6723
Crystal, casing (white
and black), cut (motif
repeated 9 times)
H 23, Dm (lid) 10.8
Lit.: Kat. Schappel,
Borussia, no. 6723
Inv.: ÖMAK, Gl 3478
(inventoried 1985,
acquired from the
Vienna art trade)

304
DECKELPOKAL
Carl Schappel, Haida
Borussia-Glas, ähnlich dem Modell Nr. 6723
Kernkristall, Überfang (weiß und schwarz), geschliffen (9fache vertikale Gliederung)
H 23, Dg (Deckel) 10,8
Lit.: Kat. Schappel, Borussia, Nr. 6723
Inv.: ÖMAK, Gl 3478 (inventarisiert 1985, erworben aus dem Wiener Kunsthandel)

303

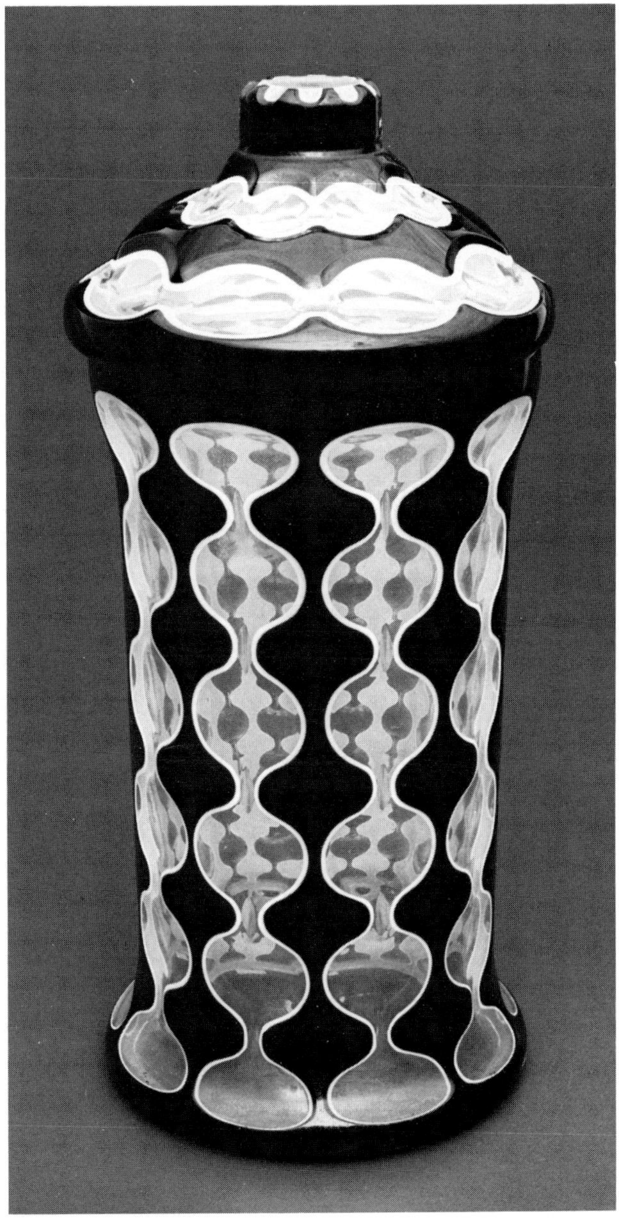

304

303
DECKELPOKAL
Modell Nr. 6723
Reproduktion aus:
Kat. Schappel, Borussia

303
LIDDED GOBLET
Model no. 6723
Reproduced from:
Kat. Schappel, Borussia

305

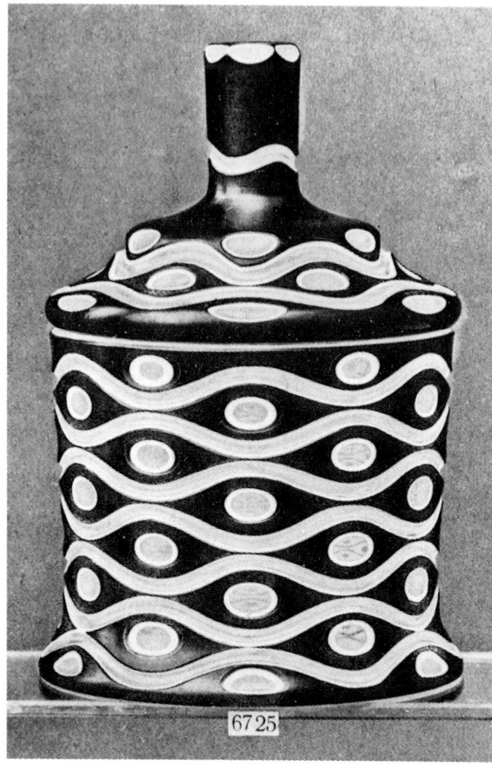

306

305
RÖMER
Modell Nr. 6204
Reproduktion aus:
Kat. Schappel, Borussia

305
RUMMER
Model no. 6204
Reproduced from:
Kat. Schappel, Borussia

307
JARDINIERE
Modell Nr. 6462
Reproduktion aus:
Kat. Schappel, Borussia

307
JARDINIERE
Model no. 6462
Reproduced from:
Kat. Schappel, Borussia

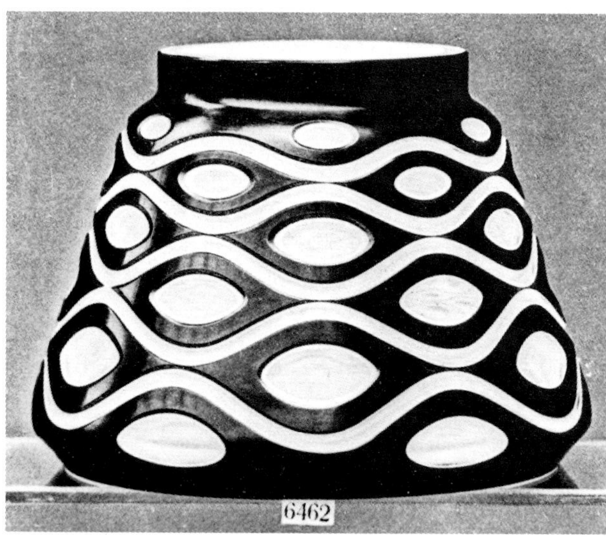

307

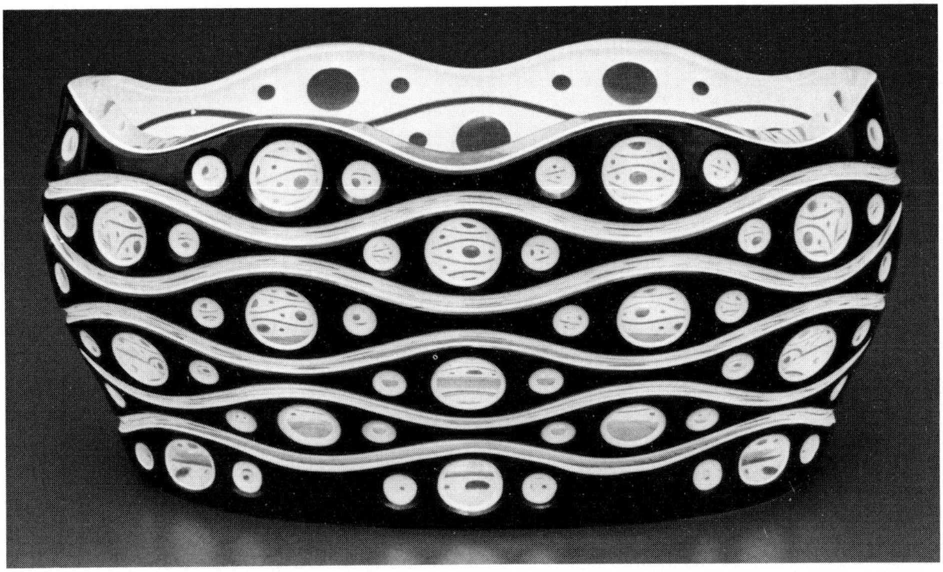

308

308
OVALE JARDINIERE
Carl Schappel, Haida
Borussia-Glas,
Modell Nr. 6746 (K 26)
Kernkristall, Überfang
(weiß und schwarz),
geschliffen (6fache
horizontale Gliederung)
H 8,9, Schulter 9 × 18,4
Lit.: Kat. Schappel,
Borussia, Nr. 6746
Eisler 1916, S. 164
Inv.: ÖMAK, W.I. 1310
(inventarisiert am
4. 3. 1914, Geschenk von
Schappel)

306
TABAKDOSE
Modell Nr. 6725
Reproduktion aus:
Kat. Schappel, Borussia

306
TOBACCO JAR
Model no. 6725
Reproduced from:
Kat. Schappel, Borussia

308
OVAL JARDINIERE
Carl Schappel, Haida
Borussia glass
Model no. 6746 (K 26)
Crystal, casing (white
and black), cut
(6 horizontal sections)
H 8.9 × 18.4 (shoulder)
Lit.: Kat. Schappel,
Borussia, no. 6746
Eisler 1916, p. 164
Inv.: ÖMAK, W.I. 1310
(inventoried 04/03/14;
donated by Schappel)

309
OVALE JARDINIERE
Modell Nr. 6746 (K 26),
Länge 18,5
Reproduktion aus:
Kat. Schappel, Borussia

309
OVAL JARDINIERE
Model no. 6746 (K 26)
L 18.5
Reproduced from:
Kat. Schappel, Borussia

309

310
WEINFLASCHE
UND WEINBECHER
Modelle Nr. 6756 und 6757
(K 40 bzw. K 8,50),
H (Weinflasche) 39,25
Reproduktion aus:
Kat. Schappel, Borussia

310
WINE BOTTLE
AND WINE BEAKER
Model nos. 6756 and 6757
(K 40 and K 8.50),
H (wine bottle) 39.25
Reproduced from:
Kat. Schappel, Borussia

310

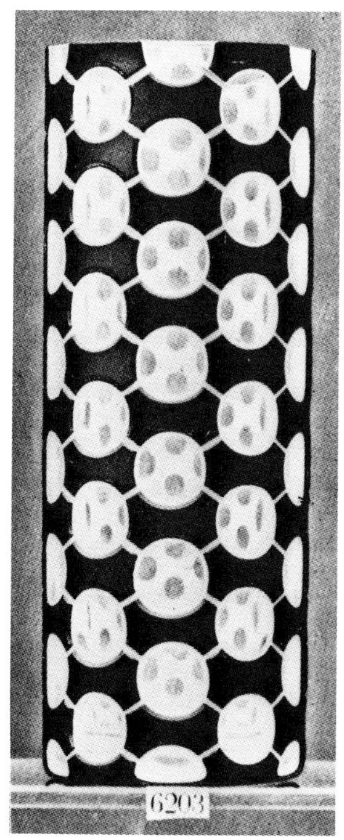

311

311
VASE
Modell Nr. 6203 (K 7,70)
Reproduktion aus:
Kat. Schappel, Borussia

311
VASE
Model no. 6203 (K 7.70)
Reproduced from:
Kat. Schappel, Borussia

312
WEINFLASCHE
Carl Schappel, Haida
Borussia-Glas,
Modell Nr. 6756 (K 40)
Kernkristall, Überfang
(weiß und schwarz),
geschliffen (10fache
Gliederung der Wandung,
Schulter und Hals sechs-
fache Motivwiederholung)
H 32,6 (Stöpsel fehlt)
Ausst.: ÖMAK 1973
Lit.: Kat. Schappel,
Borussia, Nr. 6756
Neuwirth 1973, Nr. 195,
S. 332-333
Inv.: ÖMAK, W.I. 1317
(inventarisiert am
4. 3. 1914, Geschenk von
Schappel)

312
WINE BOTTLE
Carl Schappel, Haida
Borussia glass
Model no. 6756 (K 40)
Crystal, casing (white
and black), cut (motif
repeated 10 times;
motif on shoulder and
neck repeated 6 times)
H 32.6 (stopper missing)
Exhibition(s): ÖMAK 1973
Lit.: Kat. Schappel,
Borussia, no. 6756
Neuwirth 1973, no. 195,
pp. 332-333
Inv.: ÖMAK, W.I. 1317
(inventoried 04/03/14;
donated by Schappel)

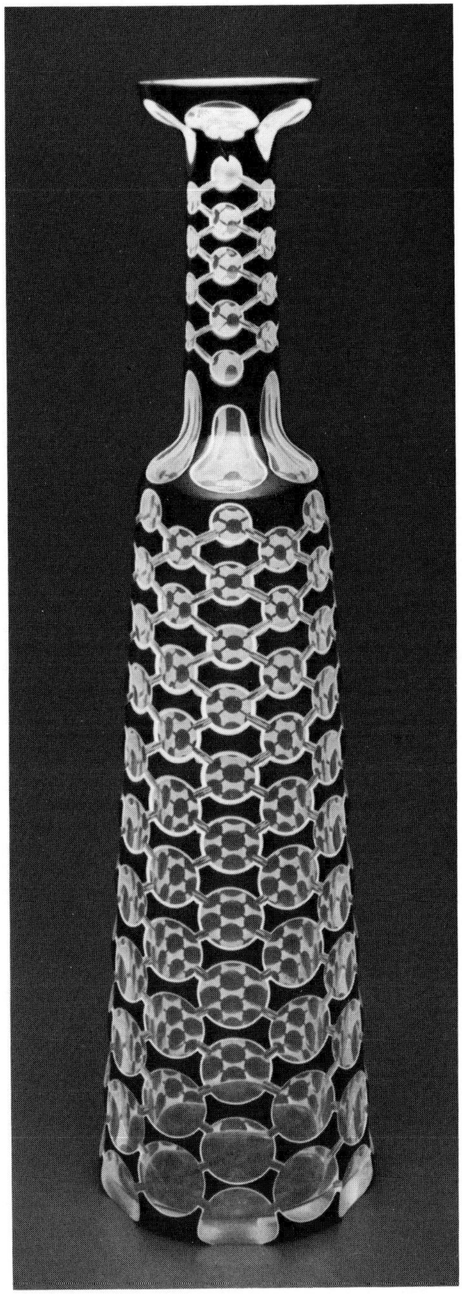

312

313

313
TABAKDOSE
Modell Nr. 6748 (K 33,50)
Reproduktion aus:
Kat. Schappel, Borussia

313
TOBACCO JAR
Model no. 6748 (K 33.50)
Reproduced from:
Kat. Schappel, Borussia

314
TABAKDOSE
Carl Schappel, Haida
Borussia-Glas,
Modell Nr. 6748 (K 33,50)
Kernkristall, Überfang
(weiß und schwarz),
geschliffen (10fache
Gliederung)
H 9,9 (Deckel fehlt),
Dg (Fuß) 12,1
Ausst.: ÖMAK 1973
Lit.: Kat. Schappel,
Borussia, Nr. 6748
Eisler 1916, S. 164
Neuwirth 1973, Nr. 197,
S. 332
Inv.: ÖMAK, W.I. 1312
(inventarisiert am
4. 3. 1914, Geschenk von
Schappel)

314
TOBACCO JAR
Carl Schappel, Haida
Borussia glass
Model no. 6748 (K 33.50)
Crystal, casing (white
and black), cut (motif
repeated 10 times)
H 9.9 (lid missing)
Dm (foot) 12.1
Exhibition(s): ÖMAK 1973
Lit.: Kat. Schappel,
Borussia, no. 6748
Eisler 1916, p. 164
Neuwirth 1973, no. 197,
p. 332
Inv.: ÖMAK, W.I. 1312
(inventoried 04/03/14;
donated by Schappel)

314

315
TABAKDOSE
Carl Schappel, Haida
Borussia-Glas,
Modell Nr. 6748 (K 33,50)
Kernkristall, Überfang
(weiß und schwarz),
geschliffen (10fache
Gliederung)
H 17,6, D Mundrand 11,6,
Du 12,3
Ausst.:
ÖMKI 1913/14, Nr. 986
ÖMAK 1973
Lit.: Kat. Schappel,
Borussia, Nr. 6748
WWMB 61, S. 380 (gleiche
Form, Schliff des Deckels
etwas anders: Rechnung
von Oertel, Haida, 1912)
Eisler 1916, S. 164
Neuwirth 1973, Nr. 197,
S. 332
Inv.: Joanneum,
AKGW, Nr. 15503
(erworben am 23. 11. 1913
um 30 Kronen vom ÖMKI)

315

315
TOBACCO JAR
Carl Schappel, Haida
Borussia glass
Model no. 6748 (K 33.50)
Crystal, casing (white and black), cut (motif repeated 10 times)
H 17.6, D (lip) 11.6, Db 12.3
Exhibition(s):
ÖMKI 1913/14, no. 986
ÖMAK 1973
Lit.: Kat. Schappel, Borussia, no. 6748
WWMB 61, p. 380 (similar shape, cutting of lid different; invoice by Oertel, Haida, 1912)
Eisler 1916, p. 164
Neuwirth 1973, no. 197, p. 332
Inv.: Joanneum, AKGW, no. 15503 (acquired 23/11/13 for 30 crowns from ÖMKI)

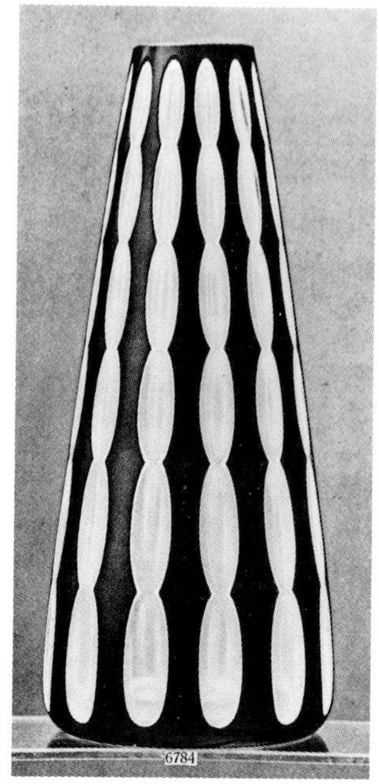

316

316
VASE
Model no. 6784 (K 30.-)
Reproduced from:
Kat. Schappel, Borussia

316
VASE
Modell Nr.6784 (K 30,-)
Reproduktion aus:
Kat. Schappel, Borussia

317
JARDINIERE
Modell Nr. 6461 (K 29,-)
Reproduktion aus:
Kat. Schappel, Borussia

317
JARDINIERE
Model no. 6461 (K 29.-)
Reproduced from:
Kat. Schappel, Borussia

317

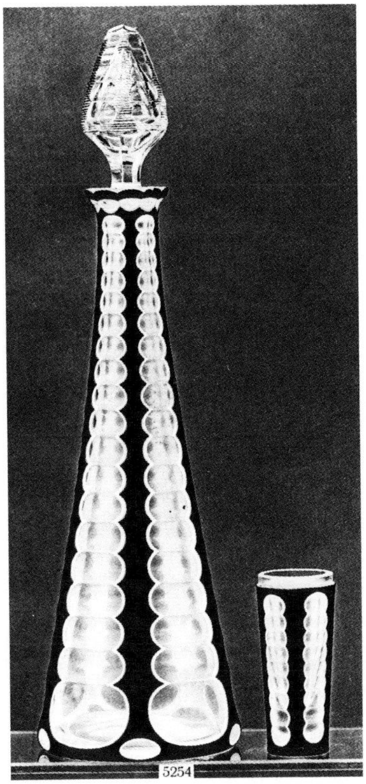

318

319

318
LIKÖRFLASCHE
UND LIKÖRBECHER
Modell Nr. 5254
(Likörflasche, K 23,-;
Likörbecher: K 4,50)
Reproduktion aus:
Kat. Schappel, Borussia

318
LIQUEUR DECANTER
AND LIQUEUR BEAKER
Model no. 5254
(Decanter: K 23.-;
Beaker: K 4.50)
Reproduced from:
Kat. Schappel, Borussia

319
TEILE EINER GARNITUR
Modelle
Nr. 6466 (Zuckerdose,
H 15,5, K 19,20),
Nr. 6467 (Zuckerstreuer,
H 14,5, K 13,20),
Nr. 6469 (Sahnekännchen,
H 11,5, K 11,50),
Nr. 6468 (Milchkännchen,
H 15, K 13,40),
Nr. 6465 (Rumflakon,
H 16,3, K 9,40)
Reproduktion aus:
Kat. Schappel, Borussia

319
PARTS OF A SET
Models
no. 6466 (sugar bowl,
H 15.5, K 19.20),
no. 6467 (sugar caster,
H 14.5, K 13.20),
no. 6469 (cream jug,
H 11.5, K 11.50),
no. 6468 (milk jug,
H 15, K 13.40),
no. 6465 (rum bottle,
H 16.3, K 9.40)
Reproduced from:
Kat. Schappel, Borussia

320
JARDINIERE
Modell Nr. 6726
(Länge 23, K 25,-)
Reproduktion aus:
Kat. Schappel, Borussia

320
JARDINIERE
Model no. 6726
(L 23, K 25.-)
Reproduced from:
Kat. Schappel, Borussia

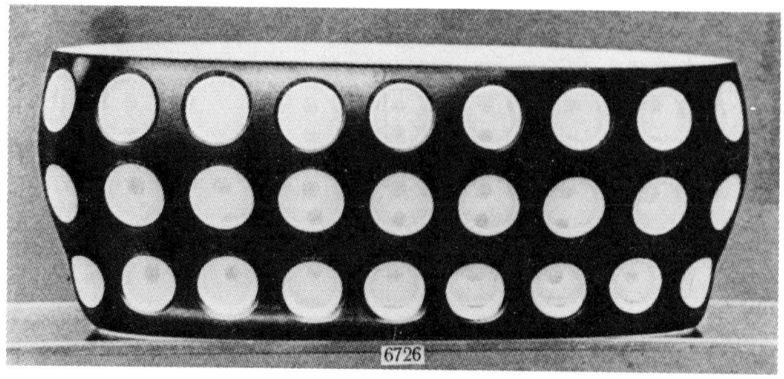

320

321

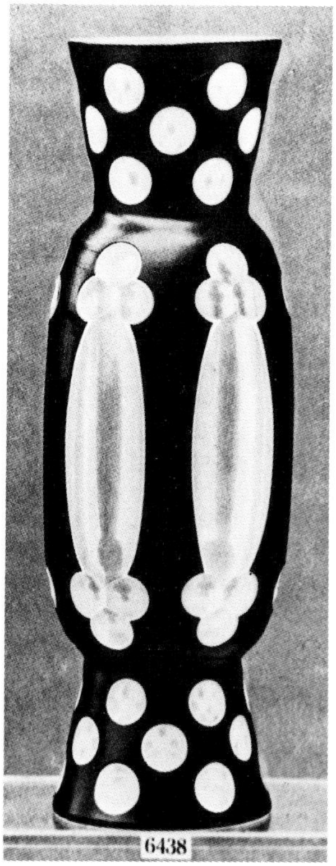

322

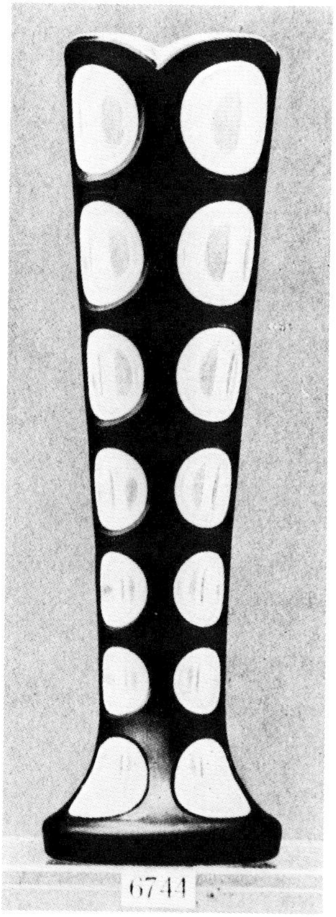

323

321
VASE
Modell Nr. 6511 (K 17,20)
Reproduktion aus:
Kat. Schappel, Borussia

322
VASE
Modell Nr. 6438 (K 17,20)
Reproduktion aus:
Kat. Schappel, Borussia

323
VASE
Modell Nr. 6744 (K 6,20)
Reproduktion aus:
Kat. Schappel, Borussia

324
VASE
Carl Schappel, Haida
Borussia-Glas,
Modell Nr. 6744 (K 6,20)
Kernkristall, Überfang
(weiß und schwarz),
geschliffen (4fache
vertikale Gliederung)
H 16,5, Dg (Fuß) 4,9
Ausst.: ÖMAK 1973
Lit.: Kat. Schappel,
Borussia, Nr. 6744
Neuwirth 1973, Nr. 192,
S. 330
Inv.: ÖMAK, W.I. 1319
(inventarisiert am
4. 3. 1914, Geschenk von
Schappel)

324
VASE
Carl Schappel, Haida
Borussia glass
Model no. 6744 (K 6.20)
Crystal, casing (white
and black), cut (motif
repeated four times)
H 16.5, Dm (foot) 4.9
Exhibition(s): ÖMAK 1973
Lit.: Kat. Schappel,
Borussia, no. 6744
Neuwirth 1973, no. 192,
p. 330
Inv.: ÖMAK, W.I. 1319
(inventoried 04/03/14;
donated by Schappel)

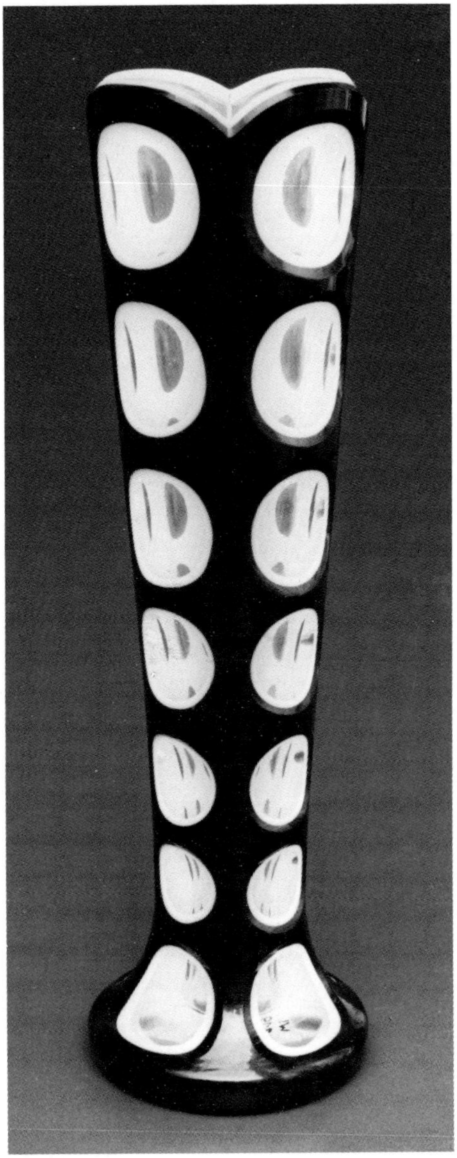

324

321
VASE
Model no. 6511 (K 17.20)
Reproduced from:
Kat. Schappel, Borussia

322
VASE
Model no. 6438 (K 17.20)
Reproduced from:
Kat. Schappel, Borussia

323
VASE
Model no. 6744 (K 6.20)
Reproduced from:
Kat. Schappel, Borussia

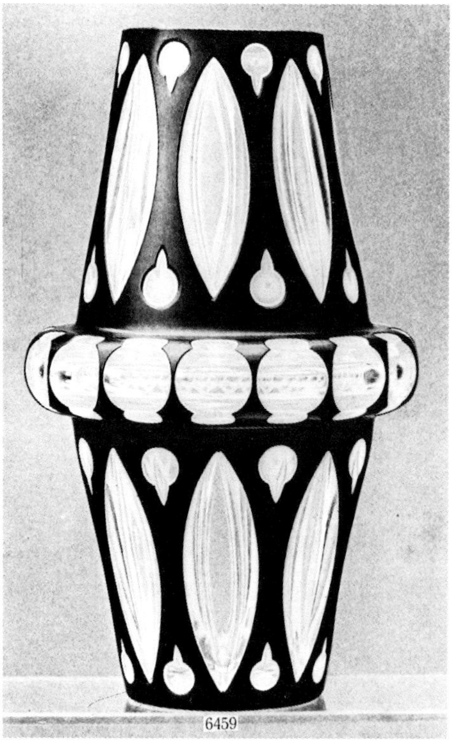

325

325
VASE
Modell Nr. 6459 (K 76,-)
Reproduktion aus:
Kat. Schappel, Borussia

325
VASE
Model no. 6459 (K 76.-)
Reproduced from:
Kat. Schappel, Borussia

326

327
VASE
Carl Schappel, Haida
Borussia-Glas,
Modell Nr. 6459 (K 76,-)
Kernkristall, Überfang
(weiß und schwarz),
geschliffen (Wulst: 16fache
Wiederholung des Motivs,
sonst 5fache Gliederung)
H 24,6, Dg 15,4, Du 7,8,
Do 8
Lit.: Kat. Schappel,
Borussia, Nr. 6459
Inv.: ÖMAK, Gl 3482
(inventarisiert 1985,
erworben aus dem Wiener
Kunsthandel)

327
VASE
Carl Schappel, Haida
Borussia-Glas,
Model no. 6459 (K 76.-)
Crystal, casing (white
and black), cut
(motif in middle repeated
16 times, otherwise five
vertical sections)
H 24.6, Dm 15.4, Db 7.8,
Dt 8
Lit.: Kat. Schappel,
Borussia, no. 6459
Inv.: ÖMAK, Gl 3482
(inventoried 1985,
acquired from the
Vienna art trade)

326
JARDINIERE
Modell Nr. 6510 (K 46,-)
Reproduktion aus:
Kat. Schappel, Borussia

326
JARDINIERE
Model no. 6510 (K 46.-)
Reproduced from:
Kat. Schappel, Borussia

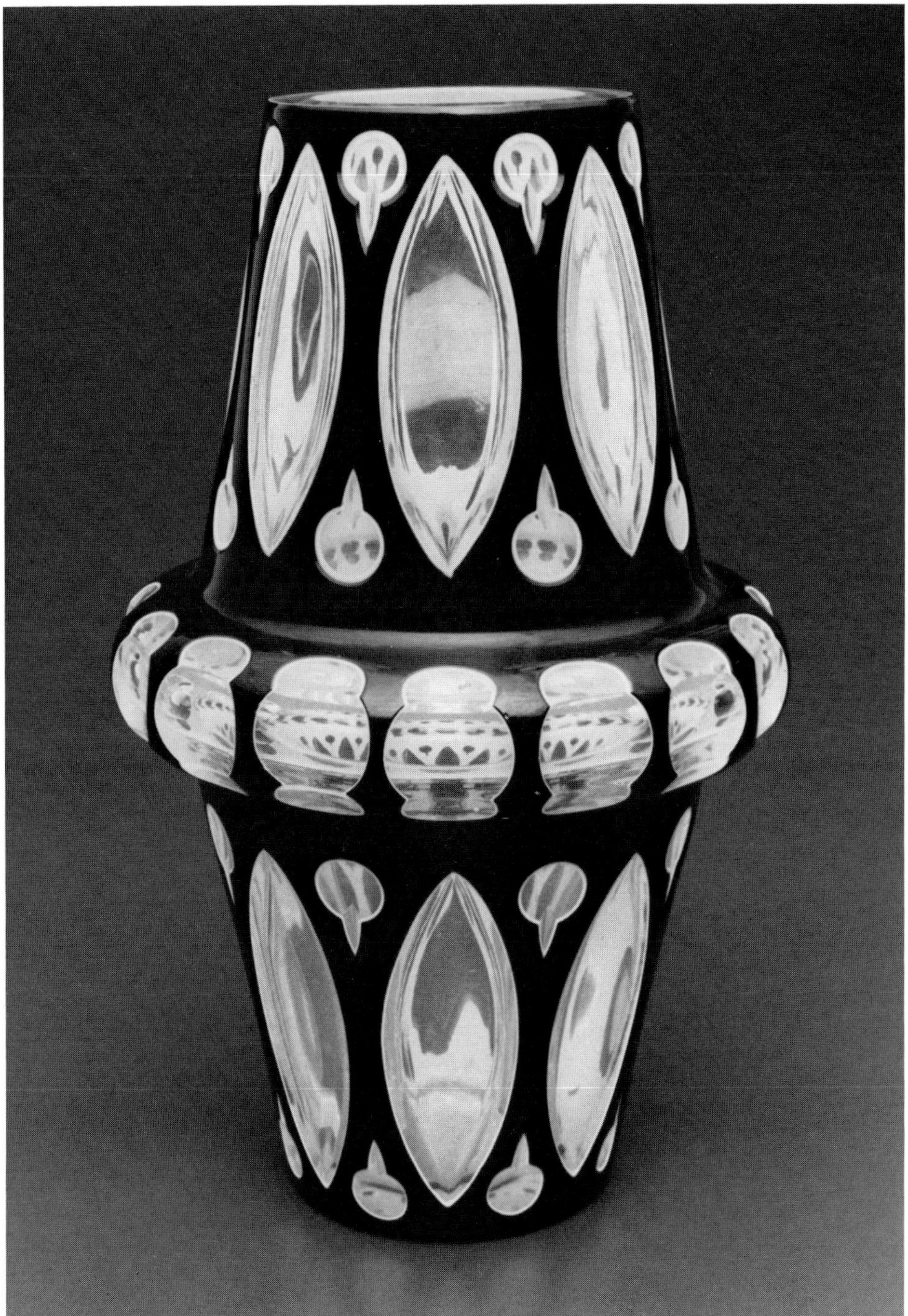

327

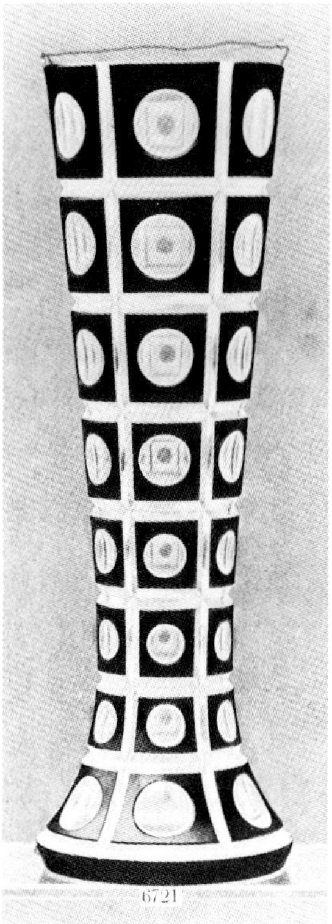

328

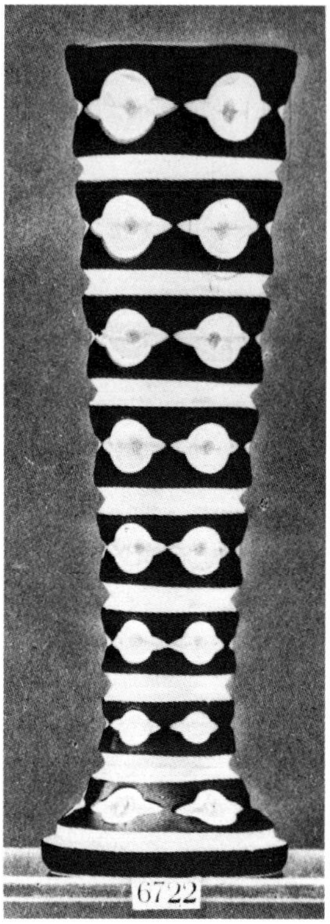

329

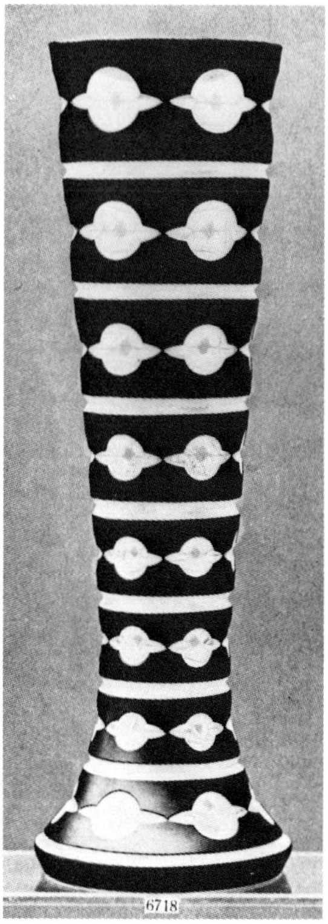

330

328
VASE
Modell Nr. 6721 (K 25,60)
Reproduktion aus:
Kat. Schappel, Borussia

328
VASE
Model no. 6721 (K 25.60)
Reproduced from:
Kat. Schappel, Borussia

329
VASE
Modell Nr. 6722 (K 7,60)
Reproduktion aus:
Kat. Schappel, Borussia

329
VASE
Model no. 6722 (K 7.60)
Reproduced from:
Kat. Schappel, Borussia

330
VASE
Modell Nr. 6718 (K 33,-)
Reproduktion aus:
Kat. Schappel, Borussia

330
VASE
Model no. 6718 (K 33.-)
Reproduced from:
Kat. Schappel, Borussia

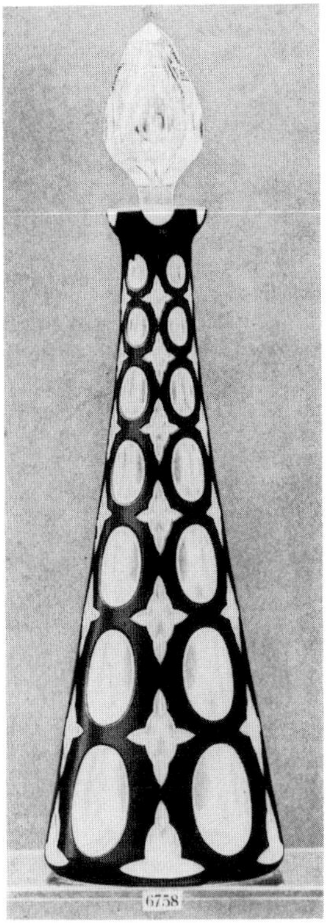

331

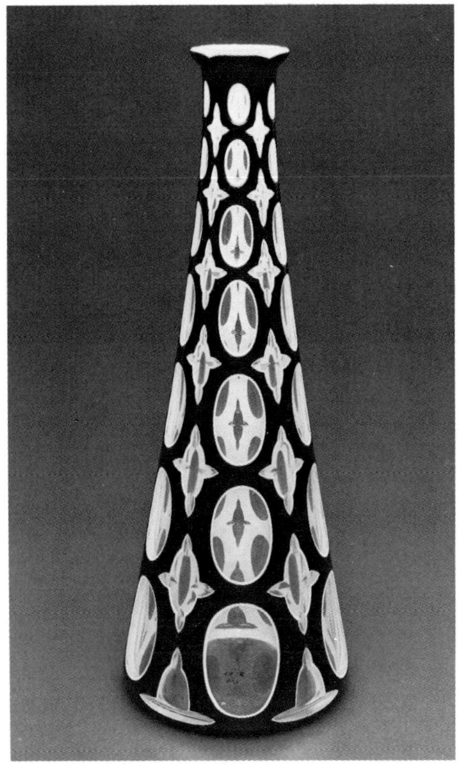

332

331
LIKÖRFLASCHE
Modell Nr. 6758 (K 28,-)
Reproduktion aus:
Kat. Schappel, Borussia

331
LIQUEUR DECANTER
Model no. 6758 (K 28.-)
Reproduced from:
Kat. Schappel, Borussia

332
LIKÖRFLASCHE
Carl Schappel, Haida
Borussia-Glas,
Modell Nr. 6758 (K 28,-)
Kernkristall, Überfang
(weiß und schwarz),
geschliffen (5fache
Gliederung), Mundrand
fünfpaßförmig
H 23,8, Dg (Fuß) 8,8
Ausst.: ÖMAK 1973
Lit.: Kat. Schappel,
Borussia, Nr. 6758
Neuwirth 1973, Nr. 194,
S. 330-331
Inv.: ÖMAK, W.I. 1318
(inventarisiert am
4. 3. 1914, Geschenk von
Schappel)

332
LIQUEUR DECANTER
Carl Schappel, Haida
Borussia glass
Model no. 6758 (K 28.-)
Crystal, casing (white
and black), cut (five
vertical sections),
lip in shape of cinquefoil
H 23.8, Dm (foot) 8.8
Exhibition(s): ÖMAK 1973
Lit.: Kat. Schappel,
Borussia, no. 6758
Neuwirth 1973, no. 194,
pp. 330-331
Inv.: ÖMAK, W.I. 1318
(inventoried 04/03/14;
donated by Schappel)

333

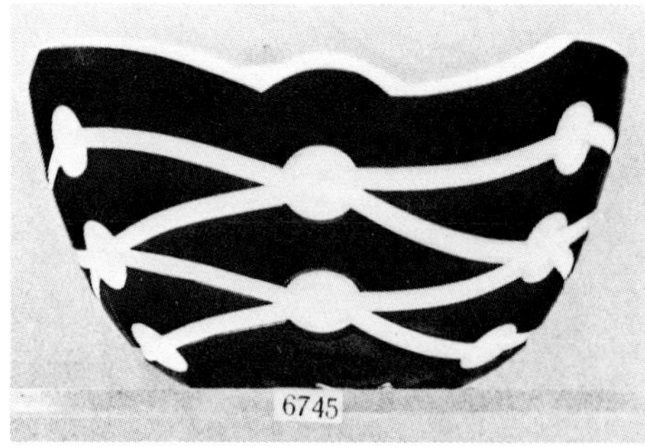

334

333
JARDINIERE
Modell Nr. 6460 (K 29,-)
Reproduktion aus:
Kat. Schappel, Borussia

334
FINGERSCHALE
Modell Nr. 6745 (K 10,-)
Reproduktion aus:
Kat. Schappel, Borussia

335
VASE
Modell Nr. 6389 (K 26,50)
Reproduktion aus:
Kat. Schappel, Borussia

336
BLUMENKUGEL
Modell Nr. 6443 (K 24,60)
Reproduktion aus:
Kat. Schappel, Borussia

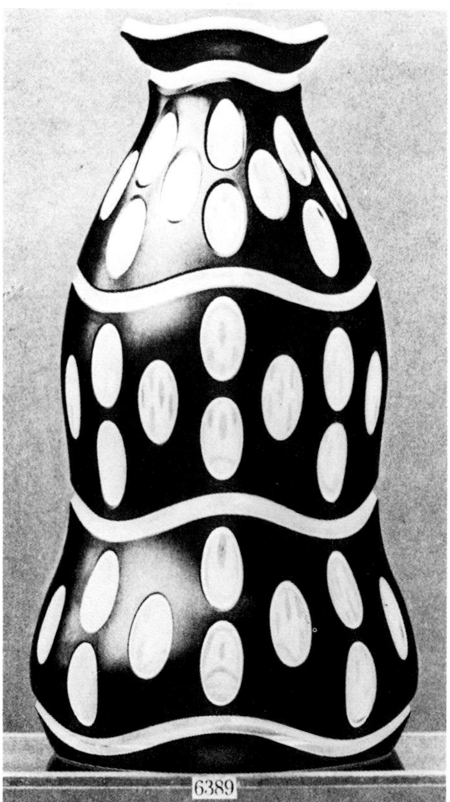

335

336

337
JARDINIERE
Carl Schappel, Haida
Borussia-Glas,
Modell Nr. 6752 (K 10,70)
Kernkristall, Überfang
(weiß und schwarz),
geschliffen (8fache
Motivwiederholung)
H 7,7, Dg 11,8
Ausst.: ÖMAK 1973
Lit.: Kat. Schappel,
Borussia, Nr. 6752
Neuwirth 1973, Nr. 191,
S. 328, 329
Inv.: ÖMAK, W.I. 1313
(inventarisiert am
4. 3. 1914, Geschenk von
Schappel)

337

337
JARDINIERE
Carl Schappel, Haida
Borussia glass
Model no. 6752 (K 10.70)
Crystal, casing (white
and black), cut (motif
repeated 8 times)
H 7.7, Dm 11.8
Exhibition(s): ÖMAK 1973
Lit.: Kat. Schappel,
Borussia, no. 6752
Neuwirth 1973, no. 191,
pp. 328, 329
Inv.: ÖMAK, W.I. 1313
(inventoried 04/03/14;
donated by Schappel)

333
JARDINIERE
Model no. 6460 (K 29.-)
Reproduced from:
Kat. Schappel, Borussia

334
FINGER BOWL
Model no. 6745 (K 10.-)
Reproduced from:
Kat. Schappel, Borussia

335
VASE
Model no. 6389 (K 26.50)
Reproduced from:
Kat. Schappel, Borussia

336
FLOWER BOWL
Model no. 6443 (K 24.60)
Reproduced from:
Kat. Schappel, Borussia

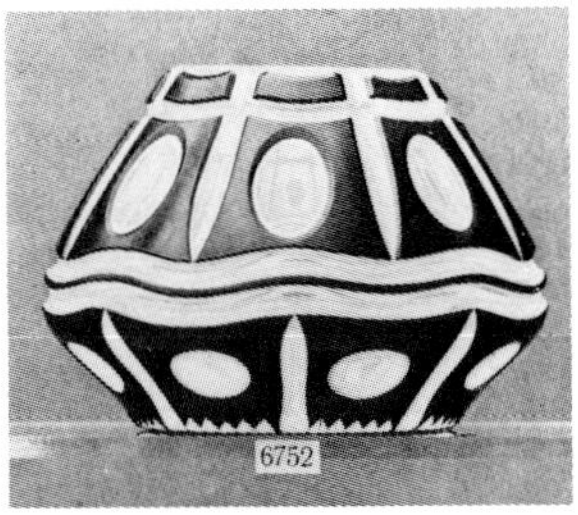

338

338
JARDINIERE
Modell Nr. 6752 (K 10,70)
Reproduktion aus:
Kat. Schappel, Borussia

338
JARDINIERE
Model no. 6752 (K 10.70)
Reproduced from:
Kat. Schappel, Borussia

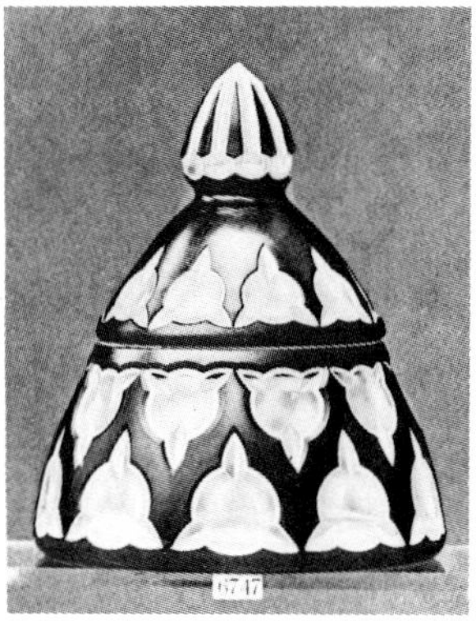

339

340

339
ZUCKERDOSE
Modell Nr. 6747 (K 17,50)
Reproduktion aus:
Kat. Schappel, Borussia

339
SUGAR BOWL
Model no. 6747 (K 17.50)
Reproduced from:
Kat. Schappel, Borussia

340
ZUCKERDOSE
Carl Schappel, Haida
Borussia-Glas,
Modell Nr. 6747 (K 17,50)
Kernkristall, Überfang
(weiß und schwarz),
geschliffen (10fache
Motivwiederholung)
Boden geschliffen
H 13,4, Dg 11,8
Ausst.: ÖMAK 1973
Lit.: Kat. Schappel,
Borussia, Nr. 6747
Eisler 1916, S. 164
Neuwirth 1973, Nr. 190,
S. 328-329
Inv.: ÖMAK, W.I. 1311
(inventarisiert am
4. 3. 1914, Geschenk von
Schappel)

340
SUGAR BOWL
Carl Schappel, Haida
Borussia glass
Model no. 6747 (K 17.50)
Crystal, casing (white
and black), cut (motif
repeated 10 times),
cut bottom
H 13.4, Dm 11.8
Exhibition(s): ÖMAK 1973
Lit.: Kat. Schappel,
Borussia, no. 6747
Eisler 1916, p. 164
Neuwirth 1973, no. 190,
pp. 328-329
Inv.: ÖMAK, W.I. 1311
(inventoried 04/03/14;
donated by Schappel)

343
KOMPOTTSCHALE
Carl Schappel, Haida
Borussia-Glas,
Modell Nr. 5255 (K 37,-)
Kernkristall, Überfang
(weiß und schwarz),
geschliffen (10fache
Motivwiederholung
Boden geschliffen
(20teilig)
H 8, Dg 17,1
Ausst.: ÖMAK 1973
Lit.: Kat. Schappel,
Borussia, Nr. 5255
Neuwirth 1973, Nr. 189,
S. 328-329
Inv.: ÖMAK, W.I. 1321
(inventarisiert am
4. 3. 1914, Geschenk von
Schappel)

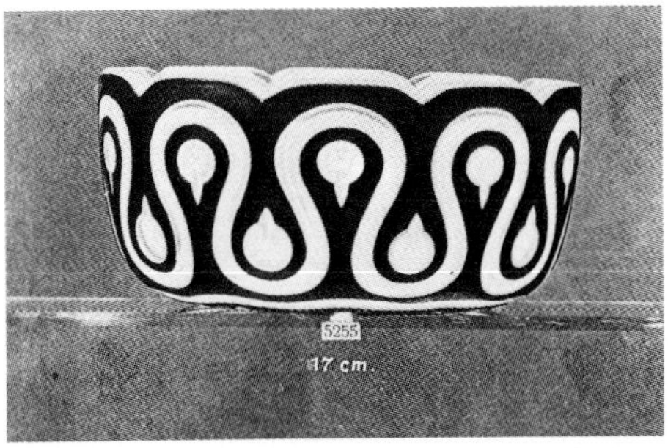

341

342

341
KOMPOTTSCHALE
Modell Nr. 5255
(Durchmesser 17, K 37,-)
Reproduktion aus:
Kat. Schappel, Borussia

341
FRUIT BOWL
Model no. 5255
(D 17, K 37.-)
Reproduced from:
Kat. Schappel, Borussia

342
KOMPOTTSCHALE
Modell Nr. 6783
(D 22,5, K 62,50)
Reproduktion aus:
Kat. Schappel, Borussia

342
FRUIT BOWL
Model no. 6783
(D 22.5, K 62.50)
Reproduced from:
Kat. Schappel, Borussia

343
FRUIT BOWL
Carl Schappel, Haida
Borussia glass
Model no. 5255 (K 37.-)
Crystal, casing (white and black), cut (motif repeated 10 times),
cut bottom
(20 sides)
H 8, Dm 17.1
Exhibition(s): ÖMAK 1973
Lit.: Kat. Schappel, Borussia, no. 5255

343

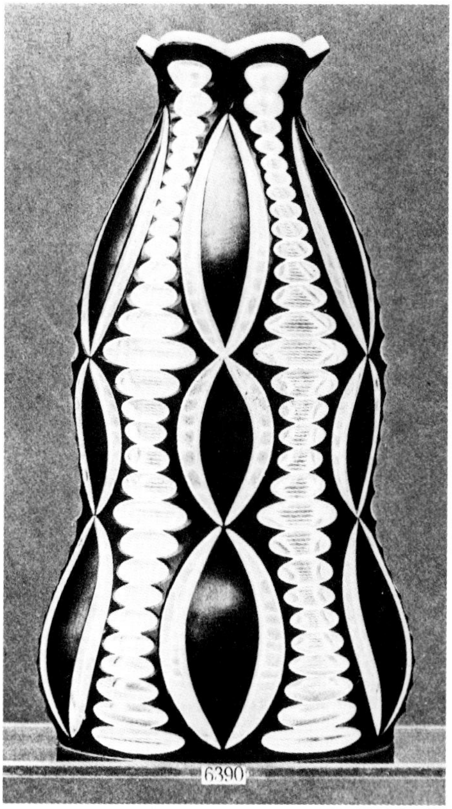

344

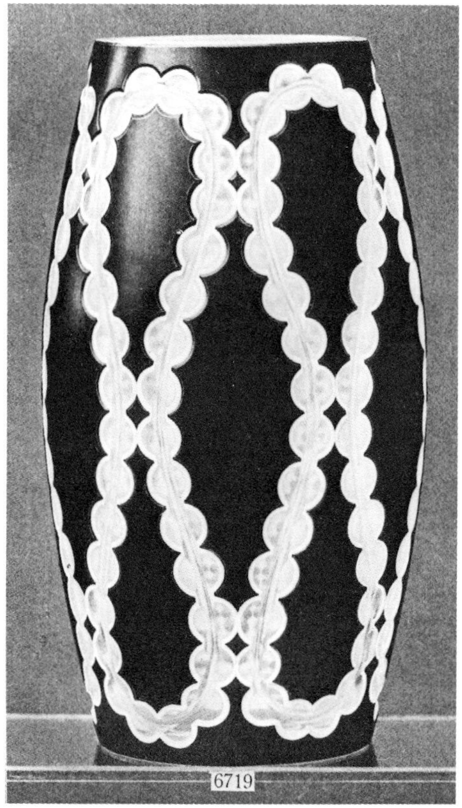

345

344
VASE
Modell Nr. 6390 (K 39,-)
Reproduktion aus:
Kat. Schappel, Borussia

345
VASE
Modell Nr. 6719 (K 36,-)
Reproduktion aus:
Kat. Schappel, Borussia

344
VASE
Model no. 6390 (K 39.-)
Reproduced from:
Kat. Schappel, Borussia

345
VASE
Model no. 6719 (K 36.-)
Reproduced from:
Kat. Schappel, Borussia

Neuwirth 1973, no. 189,
pp. 328-329
Inv.: ÖMAK, W.I. 1321
(inventoried 04/03/14;
donated by Schappel)

346

347

346
VASE
Modell Nr. 6391
(K 75,-, „Vase mit
erhabenem Walzenschliff")
Reproduktion aus:
Kat. Schappel, Borussia

346
VASE
Model no. 6391
(K 75.-, "Vase with
cutting in relief")
Reproduced from:
Kat. Schappel, Borussia

347
VASE
Modell Nr. 6385 (K 30,-)
Reproduktion aus:
Kat. Schappel, Borussia

347
VASE
Model no. 6385 (K 30.-)
Reproduced from:
Kat. Schappel, Borussia

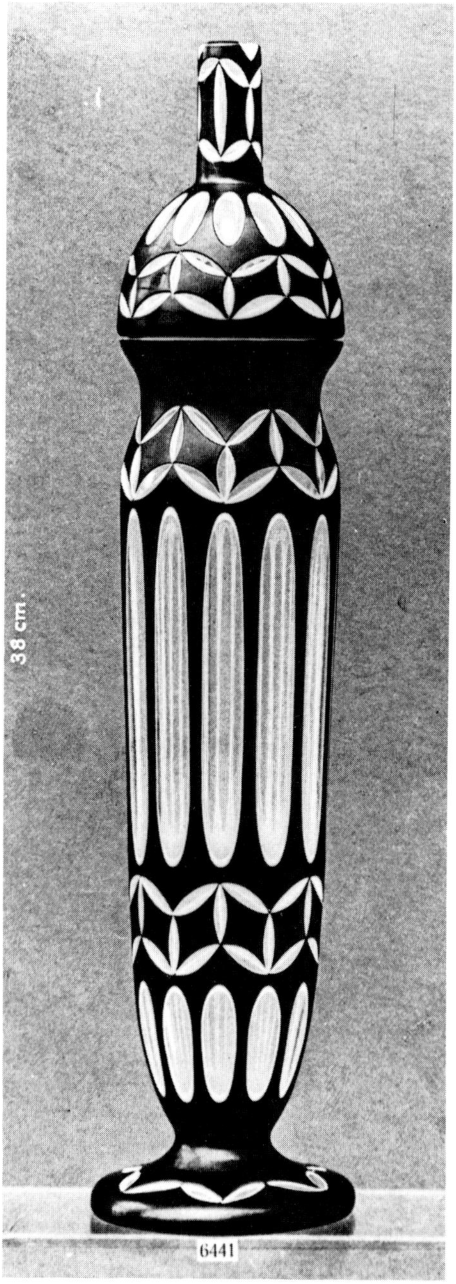

348

348
ZIERPOKAL
Modell Nr. 6441 (K 45,-)
Reproduktion aus:
Kat. Schappel, Borussia

348
DECORATIVE CUP
Model no. 6441 (K 45.-)
Reproduced from:
Kat. Schappel, Borussia

349

349
VASE
Modell Nr. 6442 (K 13,50)
Reproduktion aus:
Kat. Schappel, Borussia

349
VASE
Model no. 6442 (K 13.50)
Reproduced from:
Kat. Schappel, Borussia

350

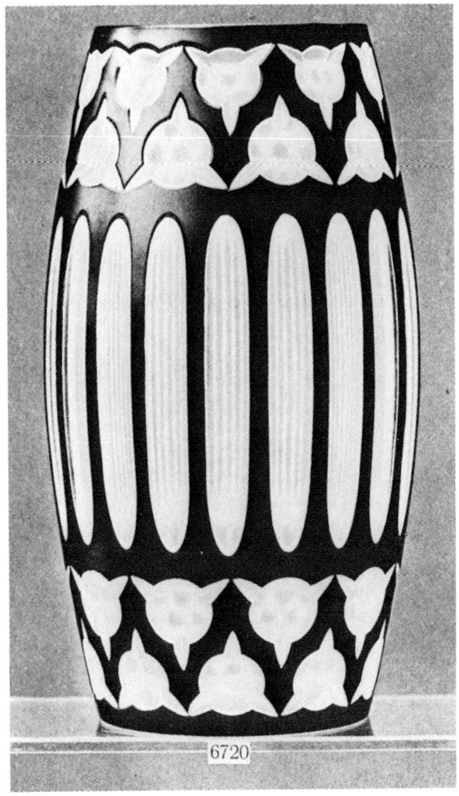

351

350
ZIERRÖMER
Modell Nr. 6464 (K 17,30)
Reproduktion aus:
Kat. Schappel, Borussia

350
DECORATIVE RUMMER
Model no. 6464 (K 17.30)
Reproduced from:
Kat. Schappel, Borussia

351
VASE
Modell Nr. 6720 (K 32,-)
Reproduktion aus:
Kat. Schappel, Borussia

351
VASE
Model no. 6720 (K 32.-)
Reproduced from:
Kat. Schappel, Borussia

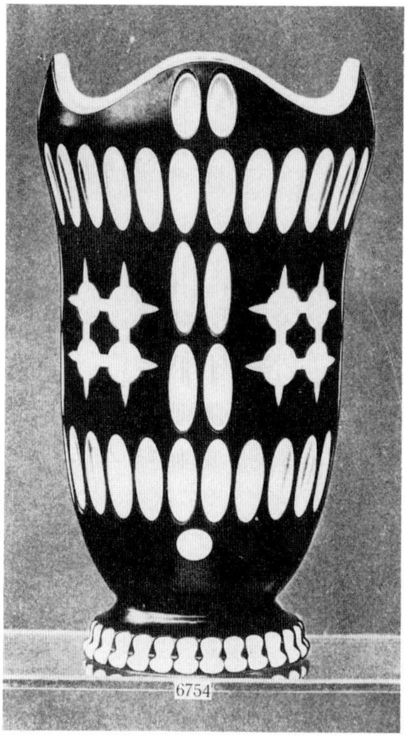

352

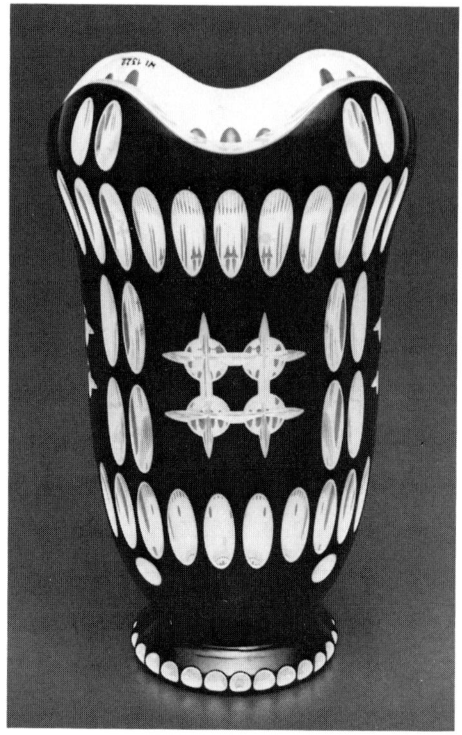

353

352
TRAUBENSPÜLER
Modell Nr. 6754 (K 27,-)
Reproduktion aus:
Kat. Schappel, Borussia

352
GRAPE BOWL
Model no. 6754 (K 27.-)
Reproduced from:
Kat. Schappel, Borussia

353
GRAPE BOWL
Carl Schappel, Haida
Borussia glass
Model no. 6754 (K 27.-)
Crystal, casing (white and black), cut (motif repeated 4 times), quatrefoil-shaped lip
H 20.5, Dt 12.1
Exhibition(s): ÖMAK 1973
Lit.: Kat. Schappel, Borussia, no. 6754
Neuwirth 1973, no. 188, pp. 326-327
Inv.: ÖMAK, W.I. 1322 (inventoried 04/03/14; donated by Schappel)

353
TRAUBENSPÜLER
Carl Schappel, Haida
Borussia-Glas,
Modell Nr. 6754 (K 27,-)
Kernkristall, Überfang (weiß und schwarz), geschliffen (vierfache Motivwiederholung), vierfach geschwungener Mundrand
H 20,5, Do 12,1
Ausst.: ÖMAK 1973
Lit.: Kat. Schappel, Borussia, Nr. 6754
Neuwirth 1973, Nr. 188, S. 326-327
Inv.: ÖMAK, W.I. 1322 (inventarisiert am 4. 3. 1914, Geschenk von Schappel)

353

354
BONBONNIERE
Modell Nr. 6785 (K 17,70)
Reproduktion aus:
Kat. Schappel, Borussia

356
VASE
Modell Nr. 6386 (K 48,-)
Reproduktion aus:
Kat. Schappel, Borussia

354

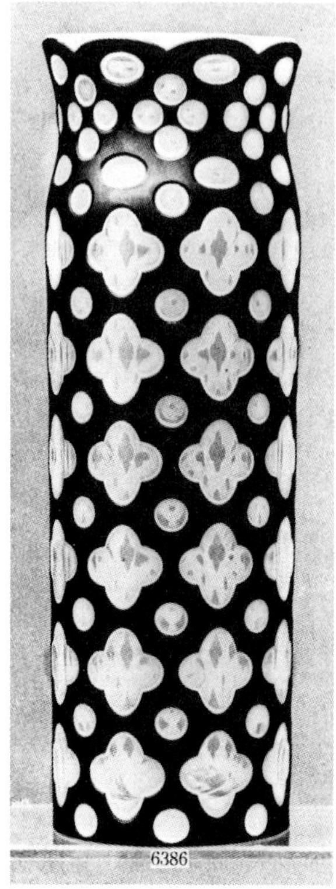

355

354
SWEET JAR
Model no. 6785 (K 17.70)
Reproduced from:
Kat. Schappel, Borussia

356
VASE
Model no. 6386 (K 48.-)
Reproduced from:
Kat. Schappel, Borussia

355
KEKSDOSE
Modell Nr. 6750 (K 53,-)
Reproduktion aus:
Kat. Schappel, Borussia

355
BISCUIT JAR
Model no. 6750 (K 53.-)
Reproduced from:
Kat. Schappel, Borussia

356

NAMENSREGISTER

INDEX OF NAMES